MEETING NEEDS IN AN AFFLUENT SOCIETY

Meeting Needs in an Affluent Society

A multi-disciplinary perspective

Edited by

ANNE CORDEN
Social Policy Research Unit

EILEEN ROBERTSON
York Health Economics Consortium

KEITH TOLLEY
Centre for Health Economics

Avebury

Aldershot · Brookfield USA · Hong Kong · Singapore · Sydney

Published by
Avebury
Ashgate Publishing Limited
Gower House
Croft Road
Aldershot
Hants GU11 3HR

Ashgate Publishing Limited
Old Post Road
Brookfield
Vermont 05036
USA

A CIP catalogue record for this book is available from the British Library
and the US Library of Congress

ISBN   1 85628 257 0

Printed and Bound in Great Britain by
Athenaeum Press Ltd., Newcastle upon Tyne.

Contents

Acknowledgements

This book originates from a selection of papers presented at the third conference of the Institute for Research in the Social Sciences (IRISS) at the University of York. A number of people contributed to the success of the conference, and to the production of this book. We are indebted to Professor Keith Hartley for his encouragement and practical support. Margaret Johnson provided much help, and special thanks go to Barbara Dodds for her invaluable work in organising and preparing the manuscript. We also acknowledge other contributors, including those who chaired conference sessions and read draft chapters: Robert Walker, Julia Twigg, Phil Stanworth, Ian Sinclair, Roy Sainsbury, Trevor Pinch, Gillian Parker, Owen O'Donnell, Mike Mulkay, Sue Mendus, Eithne McLaughlin, Rosella Levaggi, Peter Kemp, David Gowland, Maria Goddard, Tony Fowles, John Ernst, Tony Eardley, John Ditch, John Brown, Jonathan Bradshaw and Hugh Bayley.

Part One
MEETING NEED OR FEEDING GREED?

Introduction

A. Corden, E. Robertson and K. Tolley

Social scientists have a long history of examining human need. The concept of social need has a central position in understanding contemporary social policy, and provides a framework for considering the provision of welfare, the allocation of resources and developments within the welfare state. However, the subject is by no means the monopoly of social policy analysts. Philosophers, economists, sociologists and political scientists have all given consideration to a range of related issues and questions. Do ideas about need reflect absolute or relative values, and what are the distinctions between needs and wants? How far are needs social constructions that are formulated according to ideology and power? If the concept of meeting needs is valuable in policy terms how is need to be measured and whose judgements and values are important in this respect? Do other criteria such as supply, demand and priority provide more appropriate mechanisms for determining patterns of allocation than meeting needs?

Within the social science research community these questions are of continuing interest, and are constantly revisited and explored anew. They remain to the fore as topics for analysis in current policy oriented research for the 'needs' terminology has been much used in recent policy formulation. In the field of health care, for example, changes in the organisation of the National Health Service (NHS) aim 'to make the health service more responsive to the needs of patients' (DH, 1989, p. 4). In the context of social security, one of the main objectives of the reformed benefits system that

3

came into effect at the end of the 1980s was to direct resources 'more effectively to areas of greatest need' (DHSS, 1985, p. 2). Recent social work legislation, the Children Act 1989, gives to local councils a general duty to 'safeguard and promote the welfare of children who are in need' (section 17). In these and related policy areas, considerable research attention is directed towards assessing and meeting needs. The debate brings researchers together across academic disciplines in search of new approaches and greater understanding.

The 1980s have brought major challenges to those whose work is rooted in the concept of need. Despite persistence of the 'needs' terminology in policy formulation, the methods for allocating resources are increasingly those that belong to the culture of the market. Allocating anything according to market forces, from housing to defence equipment, from health care to third world aid, may result in allocations based on wants, not needs. Where is the place, in a market economy, for needs–based resource allocation?

We may also wonder what happens to ideas about meeting financial and material needs when a government claims to have effectively abolished poverty. Such was the claim made in 1989 when general improvements in living standards were said to have been the result of 'decades of economic expansion' (Moore, 1989). One of the major political tenets of the 1980s was a belief in 'trickle down' – the idea that wealth creation among the more affluent trickles down to those 'in need', for example by creation of more and better job opportunities. The real incomes of the poorest ten per cent of UK households appear, however, not to have risen at all over the past two decades (Jenkins, 1991). It is true that significant changes in the general income distribution have occurred over this period. Average real incomes have risen and increases for those at the top of the income distribution have been substantial. Certainly, the 1980s have been years in which economic development and technological advances have led to new levels of personal possession and consumption. We are reminded of some of the characteristics of 'the affluent society' identified much earlier (Galbraith, 1958). While this makes the claims of the needy in the third world perhaps even more compelling, some might consider it paradoxical that in this country so many social scientists are still engaged on policy oriented research directed towards 'meeting needs'. What arc the needs that 'an affluent society' aims to meet? Are they long recognised and well known aspects of human need, now residualised and intensified by greater inequalities in society, or have the rapid economic developments which have solved problems for some, in turn created new needs for others? Is it perhaps possible that what the research community in Britain is now addressing is no longer 'meeting need' but 'feeding greed'?

These were the questions which social scientists drawn from the Institute for Research in Social Sciences (IRISS) addressed at their third annual

4

conference. IRISS is the umbrella organisation to which all engaged in social science research at the University of York belong. The first IRISS conference was held in 1987, and was planned as a forum for researchers working on common topics. The success of the venture established the conference as a regular event, and the papers presented here derive from the third conference in the series, held at the University of York on 28–29 April, 1990.

The subject of this conference was 'Meeting need or feeding greed? – using the new affluence'. The contributors and audience were drawn from the social science teaching departments and research units at the University of York. The purpose of the conference was to draw together those working in related areas but within different disciplinary frameworks. This book is a collection of papers from the conference, many of which draw upon the authors' empirical research.

The breadth of subject matter in the following chapters indicates the range of disciplines involved, but the themes are consistent – the concept of need and its usefulness; the distinction between need and greed; financial effects of recent changes in society which create different patterns of resources and needs; how to balance the needs of different and perhaps competing groups; and the extent to which our 'more affluent' and technologically developed society meets the needs of the community, either collectively or individually. The multi–disciplinary perspective enables those working within their own disciplinary frameworks and paradigms to question and learn from different approaches.

In Part I four authors choose different conceptual frameworks from which to critically appraise the idea of meeting needs, and to respond to the challenge set by the conference organisers, the relationship between need and greed. The collection begins with a philosopher's examination of the concept of need. Megone (Chapter One) first considers briefly distinctions marking off need from two other motivational or evaluative concepts – desire and interest. He argues for a distinction between two types of need, instrumental need and categorical need, claiming that categorical needs, which are more basic, depend directly on human nature, whilst instrumental needs depend on the desires that an agent or group of agents happen to have. According to this view the force of a need claim depends on whether an instrumental or categorical need is in question, since the latter basic needs have intrinsic value, whilst the former depend for their value on the value of the end or purpose for which they are necessary.

The view adopted in this chapter thus conflicts with that put forward by Culyer (Chapter Two) in his consideration of the relationship between need and greed. For Culyer argues that all needs are contingent and instrumental, involving both the ends and means of policy. The concept of greed, however, lies in a different realm of discourse; need and greed are by no means opposite sides of the same coin. Both lie at the heart of much social science. Culyer goes on to explore the interplay between need and greed in the context of efficiency of social programmes. Emphasis is laid on the morality of the objective of meeting needs efficiently and suggestions are made about the proper role of the social scientist in policy formulation.

Leftwich (Chapter Three) also recognises the moral and economic questions relevant to the relationship between need and greed, but his chapter is more concerned with political questions. He uses notions of need and greed as shorthand terms for two contrasting sets of structural principles according to which the economic life and structure of human societies should be organised. The tension between the two is identified as a universal problem in the politics of development policy and practice. This chapter examines the issues in the Third World context. Using many examples, Leftwich shows how initial concerns to meet collective need, which were at the core of developmental interest of most newly independent post–war Third World regimes, were often abandoned in the rediscovery of pursuit of personal enrichment. The tension between need and greed is one of the major coordinates around which politics revolve, and the Third World pattern underlines the primacy of politics in development, and hence in its implications for social policy.

Williams also considers the distinction between need and greed, exploring need in the context of delivery of medical care (Chapter Four). He argues that the language of need tends to be a language of absolutes. For policy formulation, which entails judgements about relative values of different potential benefits to different potential beneficiaries, the language of 'priorities', a language of relativities, may be more helpful. To link the two requires careful analysis of the context of need statements so as to make explicit their value content. It is especially important to clarify who is, and who has the right to be, assessing a person's alleged needs, and whose values do, and should count in the event of conflict. Megone would deny Williams' claim that the language of needs is a language of absolutes, since he holds that instrumental needs do not make absolute demands, and even categorical need claims, though carrying more force, can be overridden. Clearly, the debate between the views expressed in Part I is not purely theoretical but has a direct bearing on the assessment of the force of competing need claims, and thus decisions about the call that such claims make on public or private measures. This issue of competing needs in policy formulation is very much to the fore in the final three chapters of the book.

The authors in Part Two take a rather different approach in the debate about 'meeting needs'. They are concerned with the effects of recent changes in society. Drawing on empirical research they consider some of the new resources and opportunities that have been created. While these can provide new means for meeting the needs of some people, the same societal changes can result in constraints and reduced opportunities for others, with the emergence of different kinds of needs, and sometimes social problems.

In Chapter Five Hooper et al consider the 'peace dividend' – the savings from cuts in UK defence spending. There is the possibility of spending the peace dividend to enhance economic growth, thus providing potential future resources for meeting social needs, rather than spending it directly on current welfare needs. Using existing empirical data the authors provide preliminary evidence that military expenditure constrains spending in such areas as health and education, but find no evidence that military spending has marked effect on investment and hence economic growth. Nor however, do they find strong evidence that military research and development expenditure 'crowds out' civil research and development investment. Their results suggest that the peace dividend will free resources for current expenditure on welfare, but is unlikely to have much impact on economic growth and hence the generation of additional resources to meet welfare needs in the future.

Lowe (Chapter Six) also sees potential new resources for welfare spending, this time in the field of housing. The increase in home ownership has meant rapid capital accumulation for some families, and assets accumulated through owner occupation have become available for spending. This 'new affluence' has become more equally spread within the social structure of the nation bringing new possibilities of using home equity to finance service provision and welfare choices. Lowe argues that the privatisation of welfare is connected to the growth of home ownership, drawing on examples of services for elderly people that have developed during the 1980s. He concludes that home ownership has become in the 1980s a major source of wealth, which may increasingly influence the way in which households can defend or satisfy their welfare needs.

Recent changes in society have also affected young people, and Hutton, S. considers the experince of young people making the transitions from home and school to work and independence (Chapter Seven). Since the 1960s, there have been positive changes for young people which have led to a wider range of options within family life and education. However, economic changes and the rise in unemployment among young people have brought new constraints. Accessibility of housing and changes in social security arrangements have also affected their opportunities, reducing choices for many. For some young people in the 1980s it seems that it has become harder to meet basic adult needs for personal income and accommodation in ways that enable them to achieve independence.

Chapter Eight provides an example of conflicts that can arise when government measures to create wealth apparently contribute to the growth of social problems, in turn creating additional needs. Ensor and Godfrey address the tension between results of wealth creation and social cohesion, by looking at the relationship between alcohol consumption, one of the apparent consequences of an 'affluent society' (particularly among young people), and criminal behaviour. The authors derive a basic economic model of alcohol and crime. Using regression analysis they find some evidence that increasing alcohol consumption has a significant positive effect on the level of violent crime. Their tentative conclusion that higher incomes and alcohol consumption are responsible for higher levels of crime raises interesting questions as to whether there is a social 'need' for corrective policies to restrict some of the harmful consequences of individual 'greed'.

The focus in Part Three is new technology. Economic growth of the 1980s has both resulted in, and been generated by, new technological developments. Whilst new scientific achievements may solve problems and meet needs, they also create new desires and are followed rapidly by demand for access. Policy makers then face hard decisions about investment and allocation of expensive technology. In Chapter Nine, Hutton, J. argues that economists and health related professionals have devoted much effort to the evaluation of new, often high cost, medical technologies. Evaluators have generally been sceptical of the value of the technology in comparison with other uses of the resources. Hutton suggests there is a danger of overzealous evaluation leading to reduction in the growth of health care expenditure. Many would argue that better health care would be a suitable use for the benefits of increased prosperity, rather than increased private consumption. The author discusses how far there is 'a need' for high technology medicine or whether investment in this area merely 'feeds the greed' of yet another interest group –the manufacturers and users of the technology.

The communications industry is another field in which there has been major technological development in the 1980s. Increased access to word processors and cell telephones have provided new opportunities for many people. Some people require special means in order to meet their need to communicate, for example elderly people, and people with impaired hearing or speech. While their control over communications facilities may have been extended by technological development, another possibility is that they have been further marginalised by problems in using the new equipment, or resource constraints which limit their access. Thornton (Chapter Ten) considers the benefit to elderly people of one recent innovation, the development and installation of community alarms, and asks whose needs these systems meet. The service model of provision is overshadowed by three other dominant models: alarms as commercial enterprise, as a property feature, and as aid. All these models can be found operating within a single providing agency, thus scope is limited for the interventionist model associated with social service delivery. The technology is advanced, yet community alarms can only be effective with appropriate interventionist strategies to enhance individual use. The conflict between market and service values found in current alarms provision presages the situation likely to apply with other services when the government's community care reforms take effect.

Baldwin et al (Chapter Eleven) discuss how the needs of deaf people can be met by the development of technology to improve their access to the telephone, an essential part of modern life. Their research highlights the exclusion of many deaf people from the sophisticated telephone services now available to the hearing majority, despite strongly expressed need for better access. Issues raised include where responsibility lies for improving services. Recent developments, based on philanthropic gestures and administration by a charity, do not address the claims of deaf people to have access to a basic public utility as of right. The authors discuss whether deaf people are better viewed as potential customers, currently excluded from a service, or as dependent people in need of special equipment and help with extra costs. Their view is that the private and public sectors both have responsibilities, and an integrated approach is likely to be most successful in ensuring that deaf people have the chance to use today's sophisticated telephone systems to meet their basic needs for personal autonomy and social participation.

Leese et al (Chapter Twelve) are also concerned with people who require special means to meet the need to communicate. They examine whether the needs of speech impaired people for communication aids are being met by six specialist Communication Aid Centres (CACs) set up in England and Wales during the 1980s. They discuss results from an evaluation of the CACs, focusing on views of clients who attended the centres over a one year period and the effects on their quality of life of the communication aid recommended. The authors claim that the users of the CACs were generally satisfied with the service they received, but that problems in access to the service and access to funding for purchasing the recommended aids were limiting the extent to which the centres were meeting the needs of all users.

The final part of the book provides examples of ways in which 'needs' are currently being assessed for purposes of resource allocation in three different policy arenas. Smith (Chapter Thirteen) examines the geographical implications of recent reforms in local government finance policy – replacement of local business rates and domestic rates by a national business property tax and the community charge; revision of the system of central government grants to local authorities and simplification of the 'needs assessment procedures' used to distribute central government grant to local authorities. He shows that the switch to the community charge has resulted in a higher average tax liability for people in the north of England and inner London, whilst the introduction of a revised needs measure has been of most benefit to people living in south east England. He offers a hypothetical assessment of the likely impact of the proposed council tax which will replace the community charge, and predicts that this may partially reverse the geographical effects on tax liabilities of the community charge. Smith feels the focus of research attention should now turn to a closer examination of the equity implications of the methods used for measuring spending needs, for the purpose of local public service finance.

The restructuring of the health service provides the background for the investigation by Ryder et al. (Chapter Fourteen). As the NHS moves towards new administrative frameworks, and hospitals experiment with new management structures, the location of hospital specialties will take on new significance. In an ideal world, the best configuration of hospital specialties would be determined by reference to a body of research into the effectiveness of different combinations of specialties in achieving desired outcomes for patients, coupled with data on staffing and cost implications. (We are reminded here, of Culyer's suggestions about the proper role of the social scientist, as well as Williams' arguments in Chapter Three that policy formulation entails judgements about relative values of different potential benefits to different potential beneficiaries.) In the absence of this body of research, one line of enquiry is through the opinions of clinicians. Ryder et al. describe the development of a practical tool for assessing the relative importance of specialties being in close proximity – an interspecialty links matrix. The technique has been applied in several district health authorities, as a means of assessing quality of service delivery and while the method is not based on scientifically validated results of service efficiency, it has proved a useful stimulus to debate.

In the final chapter Huby (Chapter Fifteen) explains a mechanism for allocation of financial help which assigns different kinds of need to particular priority levels. Introduced in 1988, the social fund represents the ultimate safety net provided by the welfare benefits system. A system of grants and loans, it was intended to channel resources towards those groups most in need. The underlying ethos was to achieve cost effectiveness and efficiency in conjunction with increased flexibility in responding to individual need. Huby examines first the way in which the success or failure of the social fund in targeting help depends upon definitions of greatest need, and secondly how the structure of the fund ensures that it will operate within its budget. She argues that targeting help on areas of greatest need is not synonymous with focusing resources in particular areas, and tensions are likely to remain between needs defined by administrators and needs perceived by social fund applicants. Even if these could be resolved and a socially acceptable set of basic needs derived, if all needs in question were of equal importance, the problem would remain of how to choose which of these needs to meet when resources are insufficient to cover them all.

The experience of the two previous IRISS Conferences* confirmed the advantages of bringing together social scientists from different academic disciplines to share their current ideas and research findings within a general theme. We hope that this volume provides a further example of the benefits to be gained from a cross–disciplinary approach. Taken together, these chapters contribute to the debate about the continuing usefulness of the concept of 'needs' in current policy formulation and evaluation. They highlight differences in the ways that 'needs' are conceptualised within the social sciences, as well as the broad range of research topics and methodologies from which useful contributions can be made in this debate. The chapters provide examples of ways in which ideas about 'meeting needs' are currently being translated into practical measures of assessment for resource allocation. Finally, but of equal importance, the chapters offer new insights into the extent to which the resources of society as a whole are being shared with those 'in most need'. The issues will continue to challenge social scientists – those who engage in theoretical debate as well as those who conduct policy analysis and evaluation. More will be learned by applying an array of perspectives, and sharing the fruits of such analysis.

* Publications from the two previous IRISS conferences are:

Baldwin, S., Godfrey, C. and Propper, C. (eds) (1990) *Quality of Life: Perspectives and Policies,* Routledge, London.
Hutton, J., Hutton, S., Pinch, T. and Sheill, A. (eds) (1991) *Dependency to Enterprise,* Routledge, London.

References

DH (1989), *Working for Patients, Cm. 555,* Department of Health, HMSO, London.
DHSS (1985), *Reform of Social Security: Programme for Action, Cm. 9691, Department of Health and Social Security,* HMSO, London.
Galbraith, J.K. (1958), *The Affluent Society,* Hamish Hamilton, Harmonds–worth.
Jenkins, S. (1991), 'Income inequality and living standards: changes in the 1970s and 1980s', *Fiscal Studies,* vol. 12, no. 1, pp. 1–28.
Moore, J. (1989), 'The end of the line for poverty', speech delivered by Secretary of State for Social Security, St Stephens Club, 11 May.

1 What is need?

C.B. Megone

Introduction

The chapters in the second half of this volume exhibit empirical work on the meeting of needs. Such work exemplifies the fact that different individuals in different circumstances, or even different societies, have a wide range of needs. Given limited resources there will be conflicts over how many, and which, of these needs claims should be met. The resolution of such conflicts depends in turn on the priority to be allocated to different needs and the force that may be supposed attributable to any such claims. Such a resolution requires, first, some account of the nature of needs, second, some view of whence the moral force of a needs claim is derived, and derivatively some view of the relative force of different needs claims.

In this chapter the focus is on the concept of need. The chapter thus constitutes some very preliminary spadework towards sorting out the problems outlined above. Three topics will be commented on: the relation between need and two other motivational or evaluational concepts, desire and interest; the different types of need that there are; and the force of need claims. The second of these topics takes up the bulk of the chapter. In much social science literature all needs are taken to be of one type. They are taken to be instrumental and thus always contingent on the desires that agents happen to have. However, in this chapter a distinction is defended between two types of need, instrumental and categorical. It is claimed that if there are such things as categorical (human) needs then their existence must be grounded in human nature, and that there are such needs. Relating needs to human nature raises the question of the objectivity or relativity of their status so in the final section of the chapter the objectivity of both categorical and instrumental needs is briefly discussed.

Needs, desires, and interests

A preliminary to grasping the concept of need is to compare it with nearby concepts (cf. Wiggins, 1987, p. 6 and pp. 16–17). On the face of it what each person needs and what each wants are quite separate. Intuitively an individual may need something without desiring it, or desire something without needing it. However this apparent gap might be rapidly closed by the suggestion that what each person needs is the same as what each rationally desires. Thus what is needed may not in fact be wanted, but is rationally desirable; and what is rationally desired must be needed. Such a claim may appear austere. Can it only be reasonable to desire what is needed? But this doubt may rest on an ambiguity in the notion of need, to be clarified shortly. For to the question just put a further question provides a reply: can it really be reasonable to desire something that is not in any way needed?

The temptation to respond that there are many objectives worthy of desire yet not needed may well remain. In any case, though, if need is assimilated to rational desire, rather than desire, the notion of rationality is doing considerable work. Thus it is at least plausible that what makes the desire rational is that its object is needed, in which case need is a notion quite separable from desire. (The alternative is to hold that a need is whatever is rationally desired, so that desire is basic, but this then requires grounding in an elucidation of the notion of rationality.)

A further grammatical argument has been given to distinguish need and desire (Wiggins, 1987, p. 6). This rests on the view that desire is an intentional verb, whilst need is not. The thought here is that where an agent desires to ψ, and ψ'ing is φ'ing, it is yet possible that he will not desire to φ; by contrast if an agent needs to ψ, and ψ'ing is φ'ing, then necessarily the agent needs to φ. What this difference may reflect is that there is a sense in which desire is necessarily mind dependent, whilst need is not. Desire is a mental attitude of the agent. Need, by contrast, picks out what is necessary for the agent (in the circumstances), and what is necessary for the agent may not reflect any attitude of his mind.

In the light of these latter remarks, it may be fruitful to consider the relation between needs and interests. For interests also appear to be, in this sense, mind independent. That is, a state of affairs may be in an agent's interest whatever attitude of mind he has to it (desire, aversion, belief etc.). A reductionist about need might thus try to claim that an agent's needs are reducible to his interests. At first sight it may be said that when an agent has a need that state of affairs carries with it a seriousness not implicit if some situation is merely in his interest. But again this may rest on an ambiguity in the notion of need (between categorical and instrumental need) already referred to, yet to be clarified. (This suggestion might be met by distinguishing between deeper and more shallow interests.) For, on the other hand, if a state of affairs is in an individual's interest, then is it not necessary (needed) that it come about if he is to achieve some valuable goal? Yet there are two reasons to reject any such reduction. First, there may be circumstances in an agent's interests, in the sense that they have some desirable quality, yet which he does not in any way need given the style of life that he has chosen. Second, there may, on the other hand, be interests of an agent which it is inappropriate to describe as needs, such as survival or security. Whilst survival is valuable it would be inappropriate to talk of an agent's need to survive, save in special circumstances (see on this Thomson, 1987, p. 19).

If this is so, then need seems related to desire in having motivational force, that is in giving an agent some reason to act, and it seems related to interest in having evaluative force, that is in expressing a value; nonetheless it remains separate from either of these concepts. How then is it to be elucidated?

Categorical and instrumental need

It has already been said that need picks out what is, in some cases, necessary for an agent and this idea has been a focus for some recent writers on need. Thus Wiggins and Thomson claim that need is a modal concept of a special kind – the central modal idea being that of necessity (Wiggins 1987,pp.9–26; Thomson 1987). Wiggins cites Aristotle's philosophical lexicon on 'necessary' in support of this:

> We call Necessary (a) that without which, as a joint cause, it is not possible to live, as for instance breathing and nourishment are necessary for an animal, because it is incapable of existing without them: and (b) anything without which it is not possible for good to exist or come to be ... (*Metaphysics IV*, 4, 1015^a 20ff; quoted in Wiggins, 1987, p. 25).

The idea that might be taken to underlie both formulations (a) and (b) is that where an agent is said to have a need that means that it is necessary that, if the agent is to come to be in a certain condition, other conditions now hold.

A simple example illustrating this idea would be: if I need to go to London that means it is necessary that, if I am to achieve a given end, I now go to London. If there is no necessity – that is, if the future in which I achieve that given end can be brought about in other ways, then it is no longer true to say that I have the need (to go to London).

But though such a simple idea might seem to underlie both formulations (a) and (b), Wiggins suggests that two categories of need should be distinguished, each therefore requiring its own account. One category is that of instrumental needs, plausibly related to formulation (b), and for that he suggests the following is adequate:

I need (instrumentally) to ψ if and only if
It is necessary (relative to time t and relative to the circumstances c) that if I ϕ at t_2 then I ψ at t_1. (cf. Wiggins, 1987, p. 7)

For example, if I am now in York then I need (instrumentally) to catch a train in half an hour if I am to visit London this afternoon. But there are also, on Wiggins' view, categorical needs – a category plausibly related to Aristotle's formulation (a) – and for these a different account is required.

I need (categorically) to ψ if and only if
It is necessary, things being what they actually are, that if I avoid being harmed then I ψ. (Wiggins, 1987, p.10)

For example, if I am now seriously malnourished then I need (categorically) to eat if I am to avoid being harmed through starvation.

Wiggins' purported distinction thus runs counter to the predominant social science view that all needs fall into one category (the instrumental category). A supporter of that view might try to reply to Wiggins by offering a supposedly quite general account such as the following:

I need to ψ if and only if
It is necessary, relative to the circumstances c obtaining at t that if I ϕ at t_2 then I ψ at t_1.

Within this general formula my ϕ'ing might include my avoiding harm or such things as my going to London. This generalisation might then seem to restore the simple idea that where an individual has a need there is some sort of necessary relation between that need being met and his attaining or avoiding some further state or objective. However Wiggins highlights what he takes to be a difference between the first and second formulation by saying that for the class of categorical needs alone 'need is a modal concept of a special kind and imports the linked ideas of a situation and a non–negotiable (or in–the–circumstances–non–negotiable) good, which *together* leave no real alternative but to ...' (Wiggins 1987, p. 26). This gloss suggests that where a categorical need exists then in the circumstances there is no alternative but to act in a certain way. That is, the necessity found in the elucidation of categorical need given above is supposed to be some sort of practical necessity, the necessity that something be done. But it is not at all clear that any such practical force has yet been established. For it might well be thought that the necessity referred to in the elucidation of any type of need (or in the general formula above) is merely natural necessity. That is, when an agent has a need necessity is imported in spelling out what is necessary for the agent to achieve a goal, or to be in a certain state, given the laws of nature. Such an analysis seems to apply to the simple example given earlier: if I need to go to London that may simply involve the claim that in the circumstances and given the laws of nature it is naturally necessary that I go to London to achieve my objective. In this case any practical force the need carries would seem to derive from the end towards which its fulfilment is a means. If all needs are of this sort then the necessity involved will always be merely natural. Thus whilst needs are sometimes supposed to have motivational force it is a considerable further step to claim that the need itself is the source of such practical necessity.

Indeed if the generalised formulation given above is accepted then, as already suggested, it is natural to think that when a need exists then the fulfilment of the need – the agent's ψ'ing – is a necessary condition of the agent's attaining some further objective, that it is (naturally or practically) necessary for his ϕ'ing, say. In other words it is natural to think that when I need to ψ, I need to ψ for some further goal or objective, my ϕ'ing. If I need to go to London, I need to do this in order to visit a relative. On this view need is clearly a hypothetical or instrumental term, so when a need is postulated it will always be possible to inquire for what the relevant item is needed. Several writers have insisted that the notion of need is always elliptical in this way. (The claim I need to ψ is elliptical for I need to ψ in order to ϕ, or for the sake of my ϕ'ing.) They further suggest that if need claims are thus elliptical, then the citing of a need is not a normative claim but rather has merely hypothetically imperative force (Barry, 1965, pp.47–49; Flew, 1981, p. 120; White, 1975, pp. 105–06).

Both these points bear examination. It is certainly true that need may be elliptical and instrumental in the manner outlined. This is one clear sense of the term. So, to take another example, if I claim that I need to go to Barbados, this may well be elliptical for the claim that I need to go to Barbados in order to watch the fourth test match. Here, then, my need to go to Barbados is instrumental towards the objective of watching the fourth test. But it is possible to be more precise about the notion of an instrumental need. In the light of remarks thus far, where the need to ψ is an instrumental need its value depends on the contribution of its fulfilment to a further goal or end, ϕ'ing, that is,

(A)   the fulfilment of the need, ψ'ing, is necessary for the bringing about of the further goal ϕ'ing; and

(B)   the value of the fulfilment of the need to ψ derives from its contribution to the bringing about of the agent's ϕ'ing.

Furthermore distinctions can then be made amongst the goals of instrumental needs. So,

(B1)   the value of the fulfilment of the need to ψ may be dependent upon the value of a goal ϕ'ing which is desired by the agent;

(B2)   the value of the fulfilment of the need to ψ may be dependent upon the value of a goal ϕ'ing which is desired by some group of agents; or

(B3)   the value of the fulfilment of the need to ψ may be dependent upon the value of a goal ϕ'ing which is a non–instrumental need. (This category of instrumental need might be thought a sub–class of categorical need instead.)

All instrumental needs are characterised by (A) and one of (B1), (B2) or (B3). Most of the examples so far involve (A) and (B1) – thus, for example, my need to go to Barbados derives its value from my desired objective of watching the fourth test. But an example involving (B2) might be an agent's need to do an apprenticeship which might depend for its value on an inter-subjectively desired goal, in a given society, that individuals attain a certain degree of training. Cases involving (B3) differ only from those involving (B1) in that the agent's goal is specified as a non–instrumental need, not some desired objective. An example might be an agent's need for medicine, depending for its value on the need for health.

The second point made by the writers noted was that elliptically expressed instrumental needs have only hypothetical imperative force, that is, the requirement to act on a need, or not, depends on the motivational force of the end for which the need is necessary. The characterisation of instrumental needs just given suggests this will be so. Take again, for example, my claimed need to go to Barbados. Here it may be said that the need in itself lacks any practical, or motivational force, and its motivational force depends entirely on the value of the end or purpose for which it is a means. On this view of need then, contrary to the suggestion earlier of categorical needs which practically necessitate action, need in itself has no practical force.

This discussion thus brings together the two points at issue. On the one hand there is the question of whether all needs are of a uniform type, whether there exist anything other than instrumental needs as just characterised. On the other hand is the issue of the practical force a need claim brings with it. If all needs are instrumental, then the motivational force that any need carries with it derives from the end or goal towards which it is implicitly directed.

But such force is then contingent on the value of the goal or end desired by an agent or agents. There is no question of need importing 'the linked ideas of a situation and a non–negotiable good which together leave no real alternative but to ...' (Wiggins, quoted above). In the instrumental case, the alternative in which the goal desired is not sufficiently valuable, so that there is no requirement to meet the need, seems very real. Needs which carry practical necessity, which demand, in themselves, their fulfilment must be categorical needs.

However, as already indicated, some writers hold that there are no such categorical needs but rather that all need statements are elliptical and instrumental. If this is so the motivational force of a need always derives from its end or goal, so the importance of a need depends on the importance of that further objective. Thus, for the instrumentalist, formulating a hierarchy of needs rests on the formulation of a hierarchy of ends or goals, if that is possible.

But writers such as Wiggins and Thomson (Wiggins, 1987, pp. 8–9; Thomson, 1987, pp. 8–9), whilst admitting that there is a very significant category of instrumental or hypothetical needs, have held that in addition there is a category of absolute or categorical needs. A categorical need does not elliptically express some further goal, does not therefore depend for its existence on the existence of such a goal, and thus if it has motivational force it is itself the source of that force. If there are such needs, then in their case the necessity involved in a need might well be the practical necessity Wiggins claims to be implicit. Thus these needs would, in themselves, provide powerful reasons for action.

Categorical needs

In defending his case, Wiggins cites Anscombe and Feinberg as predecessors (Wiggins, 1987, pp. 8–9; Anscombe, 1981, p. 31; Feinberg, 1973, p. 110), and presents the following argument. In the case of an elliptical need, as where S needs £200, it can be asked what S needs £200 for. If S claims to need it for a suit then, after the necessity of £200 as a means has been fully explored, such a need claim can always be met with the response that S does not need £200 because he does not need a suit. This seems right: an instrumental need can always be queried by querying the value of the end or objective for which it is needed. However Wiggins then claims that if S tries to defend his need for a suit by citing another goal for which it is needed, he misses the point. The only appropriate response is for S to show 'that *he cannot get on without that suit,* that *his life will be blighted without it*' (Wiggins, 1987, p. 9. In Wiggins' view this shows that S must reply by citing a non–instrumental, categorical need, such that he needs £200 to avoid being harmed. On this view instrumental needs are elliptical and place no limits on the purpose specified in the non–elliptical version, whilst categorical needs are not elliptical, because the term need here itself logically fixes the purpose – namely the need to avoid harm. In the categorical sense of need, 'what a person needs he cannot do without' (Thomson, 1987, p. 16). Such needs then have their special practical force because of 'the [practical] necessity for the avoidance of harm to human beings' (Wiggins, 1987, p. 9).

It should be noted that this argument provides an implicit account of categorical need that distinguishes such needs from instrumental needs in two separate ways. According to the account, where the need to ψ is a categorical need:

(C1) the fulfilment of the need to ψ is not necessary as an instrumental means to the bringing about of a further goal, φ'ing; (the need's existence does not depend on the existence of such a further goal φ'ing); so

(C2) the value of fulfilling the need to ψ, derives from the need itself and not from some further goal for which the fulfilment of the need to ψ is a necessary means. That is, the categorical need to ψ has an internal goal, ψ'ing, and the value of ψ'ing itself gives a reason to fulfil the need to ψ; and

(C3) the value of fulfilling a categorical need to ψ is overriding.

So far as (C1) and (C2) are concerned Wiggins in fact claims that a categorical need is non–elliptical yet still an instrumental means to a purpose (that is, his claims differ slightly from (C1) and (C2)). His claim, as seen above, is that the purpose in a categorical need, the avoidance of harm, is logically fixed by the term need, and that the value of avoiding harm to humans is not in question. However it is open to doubt as will be seen below whether a need claim whose purpose is analytic is non–elliptical. The ellipse is simply analytic. More importantly it will be argued below that (C1) and (C2) are a better characterisation of categorical needs on the grounds that categorical needs are not at all instrumental. As given here (C1) and (C2) are illustrated by the example above. If the individual's need for a suit is to be a categorical need then the internal goal, his having a suit must not be an instrumental means to a further goal, and so must itself provide a reason for fulfilling the need. That is, there must not be recourse to some separate goal, such as his attending an interview, for which its fulfilment is a necessary means and which imparts value to his having a suit.

The third feature (C3) is indicated by Thomson's words 'what a person needs he cannot do without' and implicit in Wiggins' claim that where a categorical need is in question the situation and a non–negotiable good 'together leave no real alternative but to ...' (Wiggins, 1987, p. 26 – also cf. p. 9). Furthermore the term categorical might well be associated with the

19

philosopher Immanuel Kant's conception of a categorical imperative where such imperatives provided overriding reason for action (Kant transl. Paton, 1964). Thus the use of the term categorical itself suggests such overriding force. (In fact Wiggins gives an account of the practical force of a categorical need, in terms of the claim made upon society by a statement of such a need, in terms therefore of the political force of such a claim. This is in turn spelt out in terms of an individual's rights. So in the end Wiggins may not be committed to (C3) as capturing the moral force of categorical needs, despite the implications of the comments cited.)

Features (C1), (C2) and (C3) are plausible characteristics of a categorical need, and at least implicit in the writings of Wiggins and Thomson who defend the existence of such needs. It remains to be seen both whether all these features are required to distinguish categorical needs from instrumental needs and whether all these features are defensible.

Categorical needs and human nature

What then is to be made of Wiggins' argument? First, it is a little rapid. Of course S could reply, when challenged that he did not need a suit, that he needed it to go to a wedding. Such a reply would have some adequacy. But Wiggins' point is that such a reply would not be adequate if the criticism is that S does not really need to have a suit, that, after all, he does not really need to go to a wedding. In other words if S is criticised in this way he can only reply by citing his real or fundamental needs which, if not met, will leave him really harmed. But then, second, are such fundamental, or real, needs categorical, not elliptical and thus not instrumental?

In the first place they are not clearly distinguished by having as their purpose the avoidance of harm to the agent. For in so far as the agent is, in some sense, harmed if any of his goals are not met, all needs have as their purpose the avoidance of harm. Rather these fundamental needs must be distinguished by having as their purpose the avoidance of serious harm to the agent. But then are such fundamental needs really not elliptical, and thus hypothetical? Serious harms most obviously pertain to the agent's survival. So why is a fundamental need to ψ not elliptical for the need to ψ in order to survive? (Since survival depends on a variety of factors, such fundamental needs might be elliptical for needs for warmth, or food, or water, or health, or security.) And if so, why would the practical force of such a need not derive from the value of the agent's surviving, so that the need is once more hypothetical?

Wiggins reply to this, already seen, is that in the case of such fundamental needs the need to ψ is not elliptical because the need logically entails its purpose (the avoidance of harm). But Barry, who takes all needs to be hypothetical, attributes their supposed categorical nature to a subtlety in the concept of need. Thus, according to him, when A needs to ψ, where A is a person, 'the concept is no less derivative [than usual], but the ends to which it may refer are limited. Any "objectivity" or justificatory independence of need (e.g. in connection with "basic human needs") stems from this limitation in ends. At the core is physical health ...' (Barry, 1965, p. 49). Thus Barry agrees with Wiggins that in the case of basic or fundamental human needs, needs can appear categorical, and that this is because the ends to which the concept may apply are limited, but insists that the concept is none the less hypothetical. For Barry, even though a basic human need may logically be limited in its ends, as Wiggins insists, it is still hypothetical.

Some progress in this dispute may be made if Anscombe's example of a categorical need, not involving humans, is considered. Anscombe states: 'To say [of an organism] that it needs that environment is not to say, e.g., that you want it to have that environment, but that it won't flourish unless it has it' (Anscombe, 1981, p. 31). In other words the fact that the organism needs that environment is not conditional on any aim I, or a group of individuals, may have, nor conditional on any aim the organism may have. (In other words such a need claim does not exhibit feature (B1) or (B2) nor, as it turns out, does it exhibit feature (B3).) It is simply a fact about the organism that necessarily, without this environment, it will not flourish, or as Wiggins would prefer to put it, it will suffer harm. In this sense the needs of the organism are categorical. It is good for that organism, because of the kind of thing it is, to have an environment of that sort, and there is thereby a reason for the thing to have an environment of that sort. The need of the organism directly and intrinsically provides a reason for it to have such an environment, not hypothetically on some further aim. (Of course whether we (humans) see that as a practically necessitating reason depends on our attitude to organisms of that kind, nonetheless its needs inform us directly of what it has reason to have.)

In this case the categorical needs of the organism can be known because of the nature of the organism, because of the kind of thing that the organism is. An organism is picked out as a member of a kind by reference to a set of characteristic activities that good organisms of that kind perform. Without reference to that set of characteristic activities members of one kind cannot be distinguished from members of another kind. Thus the nature of an organism is given by reference to a good member of the kind. But a good member of the kind will only behave in its characteristic way in the appropriate environment. Thus a good member of the kind needs the appropriate environment. So an organism needs the appropriate environment to be a good member of its kind, to be the thing that it is. (Clearly there is a very close relation here between what a thing is and what a good member of its kind is.) Thus what environment an organism needs is given by the nature it has. And it is good for it to have the environment it needs in order for it to be a good member of its kind, in order for it to be what it is (cf. Megone, 1988).

Take, for example, an acorn. An acorn can be conceived as a set of dispositions: there are a range of different things that an acorn will become in different circumstances. But amongst those dispositions there is a subset which is realised in the case of a good acorn, an acorn which becomes a fully developed oak tree. It is by reference to the realisation of those dispositions within the subset that acorns (or the species oak) can be distinguished from other species, that it can be specified what acorns are. Thus that subset of dispositions constitutes the nature of an acorn, what an acorn (or oak) is. To be a good oak tree, to realise that subset of dispositions constituting its nature, the acorn needs the appropriate environment, appropriate soil, light, humidity, and so on, as horticulturalists know. So what an acorn needs is determined by the nature it has (cf. Megone, 1988).

These ideas can now be applied to the human case. Human beings are also members of a natural kind. Thus, certainly at a basic level, a human being has a nature, which is the nature of its kind. It is picked out as a member of the kind by reference to a set of characteristic activities that good creatures of that kind perform. Thus its nature is given by reference to a good member of the kind. At this basic level, a good human being is picked out in physical terms. A good human being develops from birth to a physically healthy adult, reproduces the kind, and maintains the physical capacity to ensure the development of the progeny. As in other cases the characteristic activities here are part of a larger cycle in which the kind itself cyclically persists. In order to perform these activities which a good member of the kind performs, the human being has certain needs. It needs appropriate quantities of food, water, warmth, shelter, security and probably (given the kind of thing a human being is) certain psychological requisites such as love. In the absence of these a human being is not able to be a good member of its kind, and thus, as before, not able to be what it is.

It is now possible to return to the debate between Wiggins and Barry. It follows from the kind of thing that a human being is, from its nature, that there are certain things a human being needs. It needs these things in order to be what it is. In the absence of them it will fail to be a good member of the kind it belongs to (and to that extent fail to be what it is). In just this sense, therefore, it is good for a human being to have these things, in the sense that without them it will not be what it is (or a good member of its kind).

Thus the point about the basic or fundamental needs which Wiggins takes to be categorical is that these needs exist in virtue of the nature of human beings. Each human being has a nature, in effect a potential to develop (fully) as a human being, and its basic needs are what it requires in order to realise what it is, to become (fully) a human being. On this account a fourth feature can now be added to the characterisation of categorical needs:

(C4)   A categorical (human) need to ψ, is such that ψ'ing, the fulfilment of the need, is constitutive of the thing (a human being) developing as the kind of thing that it is (as a human being).

Focussing now on human needs, how does this feature relate to the features (C1), (C2) and (C3) in the conception of categorical needs outlined earlier?

Take (C1) and (C2) first. Since the fulfilment of a categorical human need to ψ is constitutive of a human being developing as a human being, it is not an instrumental means to the attainment of some further end. Consequently the value of fulfilling such a need, if there is any, must derive from the need itself, not from any further goal. Take the categorical need for food. A human being categorically needs food, in virtue of its nature, so as to develop as a human being not (at least in so far as it is a categorical need) as an instrumental need towards some further goal. Consequently the value of the categorical need for food derives from the need itself, or from what the fulfilment of the need constitutes (namely a human being developing as a human being).

It follows from this that such categorical needs, resting on human nature, can be distinguished from instrumental needs as characterised above. They lack both feature (A) and any of features (B1), (B2) or (B3). They lack feature (A) since the fulfilment of this sort of need is not necessary for the bringing about of some further goal. Furthermore they do not derive their value from any end or purpose an agent or group of agents happen to desire, so ruling out features (B1) and (B2). This reflects the fact that they depend upon human nature. Nor, finally, can they share in feature (B3). Lacking any further goal, they cannot derive their value even from a further categorical need. (But, as noted earlier, needs with feature B3 might be seen as a subset of categorical needs.)

There is then a clear sense in which these needs are categorical and quite distinct from instrumental needs. How though does (C4) relate to (C3), the claim at times implied by Wiggins that the value of fulfilling a categorical need is overriding? It has already been established that the value of fulfilling a categorical need derives from the need itself, in some sense, so it is not dependent on some independently valued or valuable goal. The question is thus whether the intrinsic value of a categorical need itself is overriding.

On the account of categorical needs given here, their fulfilment concerns the development of a human being as a human being. At the limit, therefore, their fulfilment concerns the existence of a human being, since failure to develop properly (failure of health, nutrition, shelter) ultimately leads to non-existence. Thus Thomson's phrase quoted earlier can now be filled out 'what a person needs he cannot do without' (Thomson, 1987, p. 16) ... if he is to

23

develop (properly) as a human being, at the limit, if he is to survive. (He cannot do without these needs in so far as he is a human being.) Thus the value of fulfilling such a need, inherent in the need itself, rests on the value of each human being developing as a human being or, ultimately, existing at all. It rests on the intrinsic value each human being has. In Wiggins' terms this captures the very fundamental sense of harm, in relation to this intrinsic value, if a human being's categorical needs are not met. At times Thomson, though, seems to confuse matters (Thomson, 1987, p. 27) by assuming that categorical needs derive their practical force from the fact that death, whose avoidance is logically entailed as their purpose on his view, is so bad. But their practical force does not derive from such an evaluative claim. The needs associated with human nature derive their force from the fact that if they are not met the human in question will not develop properly (or fully) as a human being (and only in that sense would death be derivatively bad), and this rests on the intrinsic value of each human being.

It is clear then that the value of fulfilling categorical needs is more fundamental than that of fulfilling instrumental needs since it pertains to the intrinsic value of each human and since instrumental needs presuppose an individual's development as a human being. But do categorical needs, when present, 'leave no real alternative but' to act in a certain way as Wiggins claims? Although it does not normally arise, it can still be seen that it is possible to raise the question of the value of a human being developing fully as a human being or even, in some circumstances, of a human surviving at all. Thus while these needs derive their value from each human being's value, it can still be asked whether S needs food, say, by asking whether, in the circumstances, S's full development or even S's survival matters. If this is so then even basic categorical needs may not always have overriding force, and feature (C3) may not be a characteristic of all categorical needs.

Categorical need summarised

The position with regard to categorical needs can now be summarised. If (C4) is taken as the fundamental characterisation then a categorical human need is one whose fulfilment is constitutive of a human being developing fully as a human being. As such, categorical needs are tied to human nature, to what it is to be a human being. On this characterisation categorical needs are clearly distinct from instrumental needs since their fulfilment is not a means to some further end and the value of their fulfilment does not therefore derive from that end. Thus Wiggins' claim that categorical need claims are not elliptical because such needs are a special kind of instrumental need in which the purpose or goal is logically fixed is subtly wrong in two ways, even though he is correct in rejecting Barry's view that all needs are

24

hypothetical in their practical force. First categorical need claims are elliptical: a categorical need to ψ is a need to ψ in order to properly develop as a human being. However the relation between the need as means and the end here is not instrumental. Rather the fulfilment of a categorical need is a constitutive means to the end in question. And for that reason categorical needs are not hypothetical. To recognise the force of categorical needs it is not necessary to accept the value of some further independent goal. On the contrary, to recognise the force of such needs is to recognise the value of a human being (just as to recognise the value of a human being is to recognise the force of such needs).

On the other hand Barry may be misled into claiming that all needs are instrumental and hypothetical precisely because he rightly holds, against Wiggins that all need claims are elliptical in expression. For it does not follow from the fact that both categorical and instrumental need claims can be elliptical in expression that all needs are instrumental and hypothetical. Consider the categorical need for food and the instrumental need to go to Barbados. The categorical need for food is elliptical for the categorical need to have food in order to develop as a human being, whilst the instrumental need to go to Barbados is elliptical for the instrumental need to go to Barbados in order to watch a test match. But this superficial similarity disguises a crucial distinction. The fulfilment of the categorical need to have food is a constitutive means to developing as a human being; feeding is developing as a human being. To recognise or query the value of the need is not to recognise or query the value of some further goal. Thus the need is not, in this sense hypothetical. By contrast the fulfilment of the instrumental need to go to Barbados is simply an instrumental means to watching a test match. Watching a test match is quite separable from going to Barbados. So here recognising or querying the value of the need does depend on recognising or querying the value of the goal. Such needs are, in this sense, hypothetical. (For the distinction between constitutive and instrumental means cf. Ackrill, 1974).

This distinction is also lost in the generalised conception of need attempted earlier:

I need to ψ if and only if
It is necessary, relative to the circumstances C obtaining at t, that if
I ϕ at t_2 then I ψ at t_1.

Such an account does indeed cover both types of need. However it buries the key difference just noted. Where the need to ψ is categorical then ψ'ing is a necessary constitutive means to developing fully as a human being. Where the need to ψ is instrumental, ψ'ing is a necessary instrumental means to some further goal, ϕ'ing.

The Wiggins/Thomson view is therefore vindicated (against Barry and others) on one general point. There are two types of need, instrumental needs and needs which are categorical in the sense just given. However it is important to distinguish them in the way just indicated, where a categorical need is one whose fulfilment is constitutive (given human nature) of development as a human being, not merely a need with a fixed instrumental purpose of the avoidance of harm to humans. On a second point, these needs are of a different order in their practical force, yet it is not clear that categorical needs have the categorical force that Wiggins at times suggests (feature (C3)), that the existence of a categorical need leaves no real alternative but to act in a certain way. The requirement to meet a categorical need derives its force, on the view developed above, from the value of each human being. It is certainly unusual to question the value of a human being developing as a human being, or even of his persisting at all. But as has been suggested, there may be circumstances in which this issue arises and if so the requirement to meet a categorical need may not be overriding in all circumstances.

This latter point reflects a distinction between the ways in which a requirement to act may be hypothetical. The requirement may be hypothetical if its acceptance depends on the acceptance of some further end towards which it contributes, or it may be hypothetical if there are circumstances in which it does not override all other considerations. Categorical needs as characterised here are hypothetical in the second sense, but not the first. Wiggins' conception of categorical need appears to run the two ideas together.

The distinction drawn between categorical and instrumental needs is of considerable practical importance in resolving conflicts amongst need claims. The distinction indicates that the claims of categorical needs carry greater practical weight than those of instrumental needs. For whilst the requirement to meet a categorical need is not overriding in all circumstances, it will in general outweigh that of needs which derive their value from some further goal. This is because categorical needs reflect directly the value of each human being whilst instrumental needs reflect the value of goals a human being may have. In one clear sense meeting such categorical needs is more important than meeting instrumental needs because the meeting of categorical needs is a condition of the meeting of an agent's (or agents') goals. (The only exception might be instrumental needs having feature (B3) which, as already noted, might in fact be thought of as a subset of categorical needs.) To be a human being able to pursue goals it is necessary to be developing properly as a human being, that is to have categorical needs met. So far as instrumental needs themselves are concerned, as has been observed conflicts between them must be resolved by reference to the value of the goals towards which their fulfilment is a means.

It is also worth noting that this account of the requirement to meet either sort of need shows clearly that accepting the force of such claims does not involve adherence to some further principle such as a principle of equality. The requirement to meet a need, whether instrumental or categorical, is not an offshoot of the requirement to treat persons equally. (There are, in any case, notorious problems with specifying a plausible principle of equality.) Rather the requirement that a need be met depends on the condition of the individual *per se,* not the individual's condition relative to others, save in so far as any need claim must be weighed against other claims on action (cf. Wiggins, 1987, pp. 27–31).

Mind dependence, objectivity and relativity of needs

The distinction between categorical and instrumental needs can be pursued a little further by noting the way in which the two types of need show up in terms of mind dependence and objectivity. To make these distinctions three different types of mind independence can be distinguished. A state of affairs is mind independent if

(i)   its existence is not dependent on the desires, aims or preferences (i.e. certain mental states) of particular agents;

(ii) its existence is not dependent on there being any minds at all;

(iii) its existence does not depend on properties of particular mental conceptions of the world.

This third type of mind independence relates to one notion of objectivity where a state of affairs is subjective if it figures only in a particular subjective conception of the world and more objective the closer the conceptions of the world it figures in are to the absolute conception.

Sense (ii) of mind independence is least interesting here. Trivially both categorical and instrumental human needs are mind dependent in this sense since humans have minds so if there were no minds there would be no humans so no human needs. However even in a fictional world in which humans existed with their minds destroyed they could not have any instrumental needs (at least involving feature (B1) or (B2)) since they could not desire goals. In such a world, though, they might have some categorical needs reflecting their needs as animals – for food and shelter, say. To this extent categorical needs are, in sense (ii), less mind dependent.

In the first sense, the two types of need can be clearly distinguished. Instrumental needs (at least those involving (B1) and (B2) which are certainly instrumental) clearly depend for their existence on the desires of particular agents, so are mind dependent in this sense. Categorical needs exist in virtue of human nature and thus are in this sense mind independent.

27

The third sense of mind dependence is most difficult to assess in this connection. Instrumental needs might seem mind independent to the extent that the desires or aims that subjects have might be supposed independent at least of a particular mental conception of the world, and so the needs contingent on these desires would be similarly independent. On the other hand a subject's desires and so his instrumental needs, might reflect his values and these in turn be supposed part of a particular subjective conception of the world. If so, instrumental needs would be mind dependent and in this sense subjective. Categorical needs, by contrast, depend for their existence on human nature, so will be more or less mind dependent to the extent that a conception of human nature reflects a particular subjective conception of the world. Aspects of human nature, so distinct categorical needs, may vary in this regard, in that some features of human nature may be embedded in more objective conceptions of the world, whilst others belong to more particular subjective views of the world.

This latter point is connected to Wiggins' discussion of the relativity of categorical needs. There is one clear sense in which categorical needs bear a relativity to circumstance. This concerns the substantive needs an agent has. Whilst an African and an Eskimo may both categorically need shelter, the actual structures which they need as constituting shelter may vary with different circumstances. This point will hold equally for instrumental needs. However Wiggins claims there is a less trivial sense in which categorical needs impart a relativity to circumstance. For him categorical needs are what an agent needs to avoid being harmed (Wiggins, 1987, p. 10) and he observes that what counts as harm is to some extent relative to culture. Harm is judged according to a norm of flourishing 'some however minimal level of flourishing that is actually attainable here', and this he later suggests is an historically conditioned matter, citing Smith's notion of necessities as 'whatever the custom of the country renders it indecent for creditable people even of the lowest rank to be without' (Wiggins, 1987, pp. 11; 13; 26).

In present terms, categorical needs reflect human nature, so will be relative to culture to the extent that human nature is a culturally subjective conception. If different cultures have different conceptions of what it is to be human, and relatedly what it is to develop properly as a human, then the categorical needs that exist in those cultures will differ. In the terms of mind independence above, categorical needs will be culturally relative if a conception of human nature is merely part of an inter–subjective (cultural) conception of the world, not of a more objective conception. As noted above, it may well be that some aspects of human nature, and thus some categorical needs, are embedded in more objective conceptions of the world than others. If so, some categorical needs will be more fundamental than others.

These last points can be illustrated by reference to the need to have a television. Since television is a modern invention it could not be held that its possession was always a requirement of full human development, so that it was always a categorical human need (unless the bleak view were taken that for much of history proper human development was impossible). Furthermore it is implausible that in certain peasant societies even now having a television could be seen as a requirement of proper development. In these societies television remains an instrumental need. However it might be held that the ready general availability of certain inventions such as television alters a society's conception of what is, in that society, a proper human development, to the extent that in such a case television becomes a categorical need. Part of the implausibility about this example, and perhaps the whole line of argument, is that some living in such a modern society might argue that they develop properly without television. There is also something unattractive about the view that some human beings require more for their proper development than do others. But if the line of argument were accepted then there would be some vagueness as to whether the need for television (for example) was or was not categorical.

By the same token, then, the needs that count as instrumental will be affected by the extent to which a conception of human nature is supposed subjective. Beyond that no developed claim about the relativity to culture of instrumental needs is possible. What instrumental needs exist will depend on the goals that agents, or groups of agents, hold. Thus such needs will only be relative in this sense to the extent that the value attaching to different goals, and so the value attaching to associated instrumental needs, is culturally determined.

In sum, no clear cut claim is possible to the effect that categorical needs are, whilst instrumental needs are not, mind independent, objective, or non-relative. Instead the difference between the two types of need shows up in the different ways in which they are mind independent, objective, or relativised.

Note

As those who have read it will realise this chapter is heavily indebted to David Wiggins' characteristically subtle and thought provoking paper 'The claims of need' (Wiggins, 1987). Thanks are also due to David Charles, and to members of the Political Theory group at York.

References

Ackrill, J.L. (1974), 'Aristotle on Eudaimonia', *Proceedings of the British Academy*, vol. 60, pp. 339–59.

Anscombe, G.E.M. (1981), *Ethics, Religion and Politics,* Blackwell, Oxford.
Barry, B. (1965), *Political Argument,* Routledge and Kegan Paul, London.
Feinberg, J. (1973), *Social Philosophy,* Prentice Hall, New Jersey.
Flew, A. (1981), *The Politics of Procrustes,* Temple Smith, London.
Kant, I., trans. Paton, H.J.   (1964), *Groundwork of the Metaphysics of Morals,* Harper and Row, New York.
Megone, C. (1988), 'Aristotle on essentialism and natural kinds: physics, II:1', *Revue de Philosophie Ancienne,* vol. 6, no. 2, pp. 185–212.
Thomson, G. (1987), *Needs,* Routledge and Kegan Paul, London.
White, A. (1975), *Modal Thinking,* Blackwell, Oxford.
Wiggins, D. (1987), *Needs, Values, Truth,* Blackwell, Oxford.

2 Need, greed and Mark Twain's cat

A.J. Culyer

The juxtaposition of 'greed' and 'need' suggests a false antithesis, as though feeding one implied not being able to meet the other, or perhaps a moral assessment that the feeding of the one must be inherently less worthy than the meeting of the other. In academic circles the latter distinction has, in some instances, come dangerously near to being accepted as the distinguishing hallmark of a social science discipline, even its very definition. I have in mind Richard Titmuss's famous notion of 'commitment' (Titmuss, 1968) or his even more famous attempt to lay the moral foundations of social policy in Titmuss (1970). It takes, however, small reflection to realise that the apparent conflict between need and greed is far from self–evident. What moral status, for example, would one ascribe to the meeting of the needs of the greedy? Or what if one is greedy for more for others? Or is it really true, even if the greed of some means that the needs of others are left unmet, that the resultant distribution of resources is bound to be a maldistribution? Or, if it *is* so judged, is it the case that the maldistribution is sufficiently serious to justify the pains involved in putting it right?

It seems to me that questions of this sort cannot be resolved without adding some prepositions. We need to ask: greed *for what*; and, possibly, greed *of whom for what*; and need *for what;* and need *of whom for what*? In answering such questions it seems at least possible (indeed likely) that the apparent tension between 'need' and 'greed' will evaporate, becoming on closer examination a species of unhelpful rhetoric whose object is to do down

31

the social priorities of one set of protagonists while simultaneously casting those of another in the most favourable light possible. The unhelpfulness lies particularly in the way that this kind of rhetoric actually suppresses key elements of social choice, confusing, rather than clarifying through analysis, the tradeoffs that have to be made and the philosophical frameworks in which they can be made.

A popular conviction amongst social scientists is that the welfare state in Britain is facing a serious threat, that the social services are seriously underfunded and that distributive concerns occupy a low priority in the thinking of our current political masters (mistresses). There is a danger that the 'commitment' school of social policy analysis sees this current culture as one to which the only possible response is a call to arms. There are several possible battle areas: in direct party political activity; in the battle between the grand ideologies for the intellectual high ground; in the moral battle for the hearts and minds of ordinary people whose basic traditional decency is being corrupted by the new Samuel Smilesianism of the age; in the production of research results that demonstrate through logic and empiricism the social evils of rampant radical libertarianism.

The danger is that the analytical and empirical strengths of the social sciences will become banished to the backseat and, even worse, get a contaminated reputation by virtue of association with a particular form of anti–Conservative commitment. The techniques of academic social scientists then come to be seen as *theirs* and not *the others'*, while at the same time they jettison what is their only strength and justification for being social scientists. See how corrupting it is – which academics, for example, might seriously entertain the speculation that the universities are overfunded or that their own teaching and research practices might be more open to external scrutiny? Is it not an insidious form of self–censorship that makes them not ask the questions this way round, or even avoid such dangerous terrain altogether, lest the answers prove embarrassing or provide dangerous hostages to fortune? Yet putting the questions the other way about surely does not change the method of analysis, nor should it change the conclusions. The answer to the question whether the universities are underfunded should not yield a substantively different answer. Either way of putting the question invites, perhaps, bias and the possibly unconscious pretence that what is truthfully only greed is a need. So perhaps it is better to ask how one might set about telling whether universities were under– or overfunded, what the principles are that should determine expenditure in this field, and how one might set about making practical assessments of the reality in the light of those principles.

Whether the aim is to be a good social scientist or a good moral philosopher, a first requirement is to separate and distance the rational self from the passions such thoughts provoke. Sharing ideas with others from different backgrounds offers one opportunity to attempt this. It is often only as one writes or talks that the mind begins to engage with issues in a way that is impossible through mere silent meditation or talk with likeminded members of a safe coterie sharing the same values – safe, that is, from the threat that the consensus may be shattered, or cherished values might be shown to be merely the product of lazy (or at least cosy) thought. Social scientists must not be like Mark Twain's cat who sat on the hot stove lid. She wouldn't sit on a hot stove lid again – but then she wouldn't sit again on a cold one either. Analysis, which must be social scientists' forte, depends on making careful distinctions; like the difference between hot and cold stove lids and the suitability of one (and only one) for sitting. Passion is too undifferentiating in its effects and is thus destructive of analysis. It is therefore also destructive of social science. The more social scientists seek to appear to be on the side of the angels, the more their birthright is sold for a mess of pottage.

The quest for greater *efficiency* is also evidently a major political flavour of the age. This too provokes a hostility that is usually misplaced. Again we need some propositions: efficiency at doing what, for whom? It can scarcely be objected that efficiency in the pursuit of a moral objective is objectionable. So, again, as with need and greed, it all depends on what one is talking about. If the objective is appalling, then efficiency in its pursuit may be likewise appalling. But if the objective is good, then being inefficient at being good must imply that one is doing less good than one could or should do. In this case it is inefficiency, not efficiency, that is objectionable. Efficiency, of course, is associated with male sexist overtones – it is 'hard' and 'dry' rather than 'soft' and 'wet' and is again under threat from some current strands in our culture. Again we have got to be careful not to let emotional reactions prejudice or destroy our genuine and sustainable pretensions as social scientists.

For better or worse, then, I propose to challenge what may seem to some to be irrefragable taboos.

Need

Here is a useful slogan:

Only the end can justify the means.

You will recognize at once that the slogan is consequentialist, though not necessarily utilitarian. I find theories of need cast in consequentialist terms more attractive – and conjecture them to be more widely appealing to others – than deontological theories derived, say, from ideas about the nature of the duty each of us has towards our neighbours. This seems particularly so when

33

such ideas come from an authoritarian source such as God (whom not all will recognize as an authority), and also when such ideas tend towards absolutism, so that needs have an absolute priority over other claims on resources. It seems to be extremely difficult in a deontological context to discuss important theoretical and practical matters such as the extent to which needs may be graduated in terms of their urgency of being met, or how responsible decision makers are to choose morally, for example in a Third World context, when the resources available are simply insufficient to meet all the needs that are asserted to exist.

The opening assertion does not imply that every or even any means can be justified by *some* end. There are some means that no end could possibly justify. There are some ends that justify no means. Nor indeed does it imply that there is only one end or that, if there is more than one, they cannot be in mutual conflict. It may therefore be that a means which is conducive towards one end may not be conducive to another and is thus ruled out. What, however, the slogan does uncompromisingly assert is that if a means is to be justified at all it can be justified only in terms of the ends sought.

This leads immediately to a contingent and instrumental interpretation of need. In considering the allocation or redistribution of resources, then resources are needed *for* the more ultimate purposes of policy. There may be more than one means available that passes this test (viz. that it serves a relevant purpose) in which case the entities said to be needed will not be uniquely determined and further criteria for choice may be required – of which one may be that of efficiency. One asks whether one acceptable means is more efficient than some other no less acceptable means. For example, if the end is the avoidance of starvation, and the need is for food, we have some choice as to what sorts of food may be most appropriate and, in this sense, therefore most needed. Or if the end is the avoidance of the kinds of circumstance out of which starvation may result, then an appropriate means may be to ensure that individuals in the relevant population are endowed with adequate 'entitlements', to use Sen's term in Sen (1981). Though precisely which entitlements are the most appropriate would be subject to further choice according to circumstance. For example, entitlements might be those that ensure that each has sufficient tradeable wealth to enable sufficient food to be purchased, or those that ensure that each has sufficient self-dependency via own-grown food, or those that ensure sufficient price stability to guarantee the adequacy of the purchasing power of non-food forms of wealth.

It is possible, of course, to talk about the need for particular ends. For example, if one were to take 'better community health' as a possible moral end for whose realisation particular resources (such as food and housing, and even health care) may be needed, one could also push the level of discourse back (or up) a stage by talking about the need for better health (warranted,

34

perhaps, if individuals are to flourish as full human beings, and hence still instrumental). In this way, one is likely to be driven to some ultimate good, not itself instrumental for anything. However, when one deals with needs in social policy, one is normally (I conjecture invariably) dealing at the level of resources, and at this level one is well within the stages at which instrumentality and consequentialism are dominant factors.

In this approach to need, it seems that the social scientist's contribution is twofold. The first consists in discussing with policy makers what the objectives or ends are and whether the ends initially specified are really those they care about; in suggesting some that may have been overlooked; in finding out whether the ends are mutually inconsistent; in determining what degree of explicitness about ends is desirable (and possible); in eliciting the kind of priority attaching to each end; in working out ways in which 'success' in achieving the ends is to be assessed, and so on. The policy making customers of social scientific advice are not necessarily government ministers or opposition shadows; they may be select committees, professional or industrial pressure groups, senior managers in national public or private agencies, or local authorities of various kinds, including managers and decision takers at relatively lowly levels.

The role of social scientists in this phase of policy analysis (at whatever level it may be) is to elicit the policy values of policy makers by trying to make explicit what is often only implicit and to clarify the policy issues at stake. It is not to insist upon their (viz. social scientists') own values. In general there is no reason to suppose that the policy value judgements of social scientists are better than those of policy makers. Indeed there is one good reason for supposing that the policy value judgements of policy makers are better than those of social scientists – namely that they are being made by people who have been assigned the task of making them by some legitimate social and political process. If policy makers are not, in this procedural sense, legitimate, then it may not be proper for social scientists to work with them at all. Moreover, even if the policy makers are there through some legitimate process, a social scientist who does not share their (legitimate) policy values does not have to work with them. In any event, however, social science researchers have clearly not themselves been granted such a status of political legitimacy (unless, of course, they happen also to be legitimate policy makers themselves).

An objection to this might be that not all policy research is directly provided for policy making research customers, and in such cases there is little else to be done than for the researcher to supply her own policy values and then proceed with more detailed analysis. That is clearly so. What is required of the researcher in such cases is, first, that she be frank and open about the value judgements being made and, secondly, that no claim should be made or implied that society (as, for example, represented by policy makers) ought to share such judgements. When one offers, say, a philosophical discussion of the ethics of policy, one is, in effect, offering a hypothesis about what may be 'socially' acceptable, whose test is whether or not the values, and the analysis built upon them, are actually accepted by 'society'. That seems appropriately humble. The alternative is to be a missionary in the space of values and, as suggested before, to risk prejudicing social science itself, which is particularly dangerous if the missionary activity might be clearly perceived as scholarship trapped out in party politician's garb.

The second contribution of social scientists is as expert assessors of alternate means. The task here is to identify what is needed (and by whom) if the ends elicited by the preceding procedures are to be realized. This includes analysis of the 'in principle' consistency of alternative policy instruments with the objectives sought, and various empirical assessments of the practical (cost) effectiveness of the instruments. It is inherent in this instrumental view of need that the ends sought are not so much 'needed' as desired (perhaps on moral grounds), and that they can be traded off against other policy objectives. The need is for the means (rather than the end) and – since I find it hard to conceive of a need for an ineffective means – the need also has to be only for effective means.

Greed

Greed is the insatiable appetite for more, usually for more wealth or food. Perhaps it is natural to think of greed as being a desire for more for oneself. But is it not possible to speak of a greed (viz. an insatiable desire for more) for others? Was not St. Francis greedy in this sense? I suppose it is also natural to think of greed as being a desire for things unnecessary, or surplus to requirements (whatever these may be and however they may be determined).

Economists are accustomed to the proposition that more is desired. Indeed the whole edifice of their subject is erected upon this very foundation, which is the tail of the coin having scarcity on its head. Economists are also accustomed to dealing with the idea of externality: for example that one may want more for others as well as, or even instead of, for oneself. They even draw indifference curves for such cases!

We have, however, to be wary of assigning moral status to greed – even a noble one of the sort described – on the same grounds as I have just adduced in connection with the selection of policy objectives: namely that there is nothing in the disciplinary backgrounds of social scientists that entitles them to take on the role of moral evaluators of the worthiness or unworthiness of the desires of others. That role may legitimately belong to

36

some, but it does not belong to those who play the role of social scientists.

However, the notion of greed does have an important role to play in the kind of activity I described earlier as clearly lying within their competence: the eliciting of objectives from policy makers and the assessment of alternative means. In particular, the idea of greed as a characteristic of *maximising* behaviour is extremely insightful in discussions of the expected outcomes of alternative means. For example, maximising behaviour by insurance agencies in a competitive environment can be shown to imply premium setting by experience rating, which is in turn highly likely to offend against a wide variety of equity objectives, especially in insurance against unemployment or ill-health. Moreover, it is frequently possible to make quantitative estimates of the size of behavioural responses to various institutional frameworks which may be crucial determinants in the eventual choice of policy instruments and the design of systems of finance. Almost all of economists' understanding of the workings of capitalism is based upon one or another form of maximising (the maximand is not invariably profit) as is the most widely used approach to individual behaviour (viz. utility theory), and so is the usual approach to value laden questions in welfare economics in which a social welfare function is posited and which is to be maximised.

The postulate of greed thus lies at the heart of much of *positive* social science (especially in economics): the basis on which we explain what has happened, what is, and predict what may be expected to happen. That it is not usual to describe economics as the science of greed – quite apt though this may in truth be – may be attributed to the false hares the term is likely to set running and, in particular, the fear that an analysis which has serious pretentions as a positive exercise would be seen as passing itself off as a set of moral judgements.

But greed – in the sense of an insatiable appetite for more – also, as indicated above, underlies *normative* social science, especially, again, economics. And this brings me to my next topic: efficiency.

Efficiency

The 'injection' of the 'hard' notion of efficiency into the 'soft' notion of social policy seems offensive. I want to argue, on the contrary, that it is necessary if there is to be any morally acceptable social policy. Let us begin with some clear definitions:

> Technical efficiency means not using more resources than are necessary to achieve a particular objective.

> Cost effectiveness means not incurring a greater cost than is necessary to achieve a particular objective (or, symmetrically, maximising outcome in terms of the fullness with which an objective is achieved for a given cost).

> Full efficiency means selecting the ideal balance of achievement across a variety of objectives in a variety of programmes, each of which is fully cost effective.

These definitions are evidently clearly related to the ends–means approach described earlier and are, hence, inextricably interwoven into the business of specifying and meeting needs.

The first, technical efficiency, enjoins us not to waste resources in the most obvious sense of 'waste'. This is necessarily a moral pursuit if the objective served is itself a moral objective, for to use more resources than are necessary to achieve an end means that either more of that same moral end could be achieved by some suitable redeployment of resources or that more of some other moral ends could be achieved than is being achieved. The limitation of this notion of efficiency in policy analysis is that there is usually more than one technically efficient way of delivering a policy objective. For example, it may be possible to alter the balance of institutional and community care, or that of doctors and nurses, or that of subsidies to home owners and home renters, in appropriate ways such as to leave the outcome sought unchanged.

The question then becomes one of cost effectiveness: which of the various technically efficient resource combinations is the least cost combination? This really highlights the moral issue, for cost is the best of the forgone desired alternative outcomes. Using resources in one way denies their use in another. The least cost way of using them to achieve a given objective ensures that the value of what is forgone is minimised. The conclusion seems inescapable: failure to be efficient in the second sense must be immoral to the extent that it fails to maximise the degree to which other moral ends are achieved. Needs are left unmet that ought to be met, and could have been, out of the general quantity of resources at the policy maker's disposal.

Failure to achieve full efficiency must likewise be judged a moral failure for, even if whatever is achieved is achieved with technical efficiency and, of the various technically efficient means available only those that are cost effective are used, then, unless we also ensure that the rate and scale of each activity are balanced correctly, it must follow that some needs are being met that, at the margin, are less urgent – or at least have a lower priority – than some which are not being met.

Needs should therefore be met efficiently for, if the meeting of needs is morally right, then failure to meet them as fully as is feasible must be morally wrong. As I said before, it is not for social scientists to determine the moral ends of social policy. But, once these have been identified (and in this process I have tried to explain that social scientists still have an important role), the evaluation of the means and the inferred identification of the need for resources must embody the moral worth – whatever it may be – of the objectives. Hence the exercise of what may superficially appear to be 'mere' technical skills is inescapably a moral pursuit. It is neither more nor less moral than the objectives are themselves.

The social scientist as moral philosopher

I guess that many will agree that our world is very much lacking in efficiency as I have described it. It seems – though this may smack of a utilitarianism that I do not want to commit myself to – that a small minority of the world's population is able to (and chooses to) meet relatively trivial needs while the bulk of the human race lacks the means to satisfy the most elementary needs and, in particular, those that are fundamental to mere existence, let alone anything else that, culture for culture, might be needed for real life as a human being. I have put in the qualifying phrase because I am not as confident as Rawls (1972) that it is possible to identify a culture–free concept of justice. You may prefer to see this distributional issue as one that transcends the utilitarian view of redistribution (I do myself). But at least I hope to have convinced you that efficiency, even in distributional concerns, is an essential component of any policy having pretensions to morality.

I do not pretend to be a moral philosopher, having neither relevant skills nor any pretension to having those skills. Indeed there is much to be said for leaving moral philosophy to the professionals. However, there are many questions of a moral kind with which social scientists cannot avoid becoming embroiled. As I have tried to show, while social scientists have no legitimacy to settle such questions on behalf of society, they can often shed light on them to the benefit of those who wrestle with such matters as a practical part of their own legitimate professional life.

I conjecture that it is ambivalence about their own morality that causes some social scientists to take on the missionary role that I have argued they should deny themselves. I also conjecture that it is the perceived personal morality of other social scientists that is often the immediate spur to academic debate. In both cases, if they succumb, they are succumbing to a lamentable inability to behave as professionals, in which behaviour both their personal moral adequacy and that of their academic enemies ought to be an irrelevance. This is just as well, as there are lots of ways in which I know myself (to take someone whom I know reasonably well) to be a moral both in having failed to figure out what I ought to be doing and, even when I have figured that out in some particular, failing through sins of omission and commission to live up to it.

Here, as a case in point, is an incomplete list of my personal moral failures. I do not know what is one's moral duty, mine or anyone else's, (to use the word 'duty' already assumes too much) in response to the maldistribution (granted for the sake of argument that it is a maldistribution) of the world's, or my country's resources. (But I do think I know my duty as regards any maldistribution of, say, my health authority's or my family's resources, even if I do not always act in the way in which my duty requires.) I do not know, starting from where we are, how far I may morally sacrifice the meeting of my children's needs for the sake of other people's children's needs, particularly if I do not know them personally, and they are far away, and there is the possibility that the others would feel no general duty towards my own children. I do not know what weight, if any, to attach to the fact (if it turned out to be a fact) that others, were our respective fortunes to be reversed, may be willing to sacrifice little for me or my children. I do not know what weight to put upon the merit or deserts of the needy. Are they needy because they were dissolute, or 'less eligible', or voted for the wrong government, or failed to mount the successful revolution that would have destroyed the political system that locally helped create their plight, replacing it with another that would have relieved it? I do not know what weight to place upon the difficult–to–predict second round consequences of redistributions which may be undesired. I do not know whether I am being unconscionably greedy to live by the rules of the capitalist society I inhabit, which affords me simultaneously the opportunity to be both richer than I choose to be and the opportunity to give more of that greater wealth away than I am prepared to give of that lesser wealth I actually have. Should not (moral) I maximise my wealth (in moral ways of course) in order to give more away to those in need? Should not you too? But I enjoy other things too much to maximise my wealth, even in moral ways, and I select priorities for the use of that wealth in which the really needy do not, in all conscience, figure particularly prominently. And so do you!

I have put these questions as matters of personal morality but each, of course, has a collective and policy correspondent. For example, to what extent should the State enforce personal morality or act on our moral behalves in matters of judging need and the desired redistribution?. I have also made it pretty clear that I suffer from both personal moral confusion and personal moral turpitude.

Fortunately, I do not think that these incompetences in me as a moral philosopher/moral person are an impediment to the exercise of my professional role in policy analysis. The reason will be clear. It is not the business of social scientists when giving (or selling) help to policy makers to *make* these kinds of moral judgement, but rather to help the policy makers to make them better, that is, more consistently with what they truly aspire to – meeting needs efficiently and fairly, where the needs are those of people whose personal morality (like that of social scientists) will be rather average and whose greed is whatever it is. In that task, the role of the social scientist is not to be on the side of the angels or to be approved (by, of course, the right people). Their appropriate morality is a professional morality which consists, chiefly, in humility – by offering no more (but this is already quite a lot) to the process of policy making than they are professionally competent to offer: the elucidation of ends, the analysis of means, and the unpacking within explicit systems of thought of difficult and polysemic ideas, like 'need'.

References

Rawls, J. (1972), *A Theory of Justice*, Clarendon Press, Oxford.
Sen, A.K. (1981), *Food and Famines: an Essay on Entitlement and Deprivation*, Oxford University Press, London.
Titmuss, R.M. (1968), *Commitment to Welfare*, Allen and Unwin, London.
Titmuss, R.M. (1970), *The Gift Relationship: from Human Blood to Social Policy*, Allen and Unwin, London.

3 Let some get rich first? A perspective from the Third World

A. Leftwich

Adam Smith, Adam Smith
Listen what I charge you with!
Didn't you say
In the class that day
That selfishness was bound to pay?
Of all the doctrines that was the pith,
Wasn't it, wasn't it, wasn't it, Smith?
(Leacock, 1936)

Introduction

The tension between the two apparently polar notions of 'need' and 'greed', is a universal problem in the politics of development policy and practice, world–wide. Moral and economic questions of the kind that Culyer has addressed in the previous chapter are of course involved. But so are political ones, and this chapter will be more concerned with these. For present purposes the notions of 'need' and 'greed' are shorthand terms for two contrasting sets of structural principles according to which the economic life and structure of human societies should be organised. This tension therefore constitutes one of the major coordinates around which much modern politics in the West has revolved from the 19th century, and is now, also, a critical political issue in the developing world. In examining these issues in the Third World context, I will argue that the inevitable arbiter between 'need' or 'greed' is politics, and always will be.

I take the terms 'need' and 'greed' each to signal the core ideas of two distinct networks of related issues. In terms of its socio–economic and political implications, the defining characteristic of 'greed' is the relentless and selfish pursuit of self–interested gain by individuals or groups, *irrespective, unmindful or even at the cost of others or of the collectivity* (whatever it may be – family, village, department, firm or nation state). This may occur in the search for more and more of some resource, whether it be material (such as money, land, colonies) or non–material (such as status, prestige, respect or affection – all of which may of course have very material consequences). In terms of socio–economic policy considerations, the focus is on the individual, group, organization or nation to the exclusion of others. 'Greed', as the more or less unconstrained pursuit of self–interest is, of course, seldom defended in its own terms but is usually given a wider social justification. As I shall illustrate later, this is usually that it is a powerful engine for economic growth and capital accumulation. For in Britain, as in Third World development circles, there are those who have argued that greed promotes growth and its benefits will 'trickle down', so that in the long run it is good for all.

The idea of 'need' on the other hand, signals an alternative social vision and is a notion which evokes much stronger distributive and redistributive echoes. And while it is also concerned with individuals or units, it has a stronger communitarian concern and implies a sharper sense of collective or social responsibility, whether between individuals or countries. It implies that individuals or communities, are *entitled* to have, or have access to, certain resources which they do not need to win, earn, deserve, justify or fight for and that there is a public obligation to make sure that those who do not have them (the poor, the less fortunate, the infirm, the elderly, etc.) are somehow provided with them. This idea applies to individuals or groups (or even regions) within societies, but also between them, as for instance in some of the moral arguments for and against overseas aid (Riddell, 1987). Moreover, the concept of 'need' is quite closely bound up with the concept of 'rights', extended from its conventional political domain into the field of social and economic welfare.

The 'needs' approach also has its own economic justification. For instance, the 'basic human needs' development strategy of the 1970s was in part justified by the claim that meeting basic human needs would, in the medium and long run, *also* enhance productivity and thus be good for economic growth. As such it has been said to be 'twice blessed' (Streeten and Burki, 1978, p. 414).

These labels of greed and need thus symbolise a wider set of dichotomous

43

policy choices in the politics of all human societies and their development. They include, for instance, the tensions between: growth and equity, enterprise and planning, individualism and collectivism, freedom and structure, rights and responsibilities, democracy and development, markets and states. And at the heart of all these lies the even more fundamental question of all politics: how may we *simultaneously* promote both the collective welfare of all and the individual fulfilment and potential of each? This issue everywhere affects all interpersonal, intergroup, interclass and international relations. Thus the question of 'meeting need or feeding greed' in the context of British social policy is part of a set of universal problems in the moral, economic and political life of all human societies. How can we best live and prosper together in communities? What should our responsibilities and obligations to each other and ourselves be? Is growth possible without gross inequalities occurring? Moreover, these are problems which are never resolved simply by appeal to the court of technical economic calculations; they are always and everywhere matters that are decided by politics. The rest of the chapter will explore these questions in the shifting sequences of development policy and practice in the Third World.

Meeting need: suppressing greed

At the core of the developmental rhetoric and intent of most newly independent Third World regimes in the post–war era there was an overwhelming concern to meet collective need and often to suppress what was seen as individual greed. Two brief examples will illustrate the point.

On the eve of Indian independence, Jawaharlal Nehru declared that his government's aim was '... the ending of poverty and ignorance and disease and inequality of opportunity' so that (in Gandhi's words) it would be possible to '... wipe every tear from every eye' (Moraes, 1957, p. 2). Twenty years later, a similar theme shaped the ideas and policies of Julius Nyerere in Tanzania. Commenting on the Arusha Declaration (which was to guide the government), he said that its purposes were, inter alia, equality, a 'rejection of wealth for its own sake', the pursuit of national autonomy before economic growth and the equal right of everyone to 'a decent life before any individual has a surplus above his needs' (Nyerere, 1968, pp. 314–326).

Whether they were explicitly Marxist Leninist regimes (as for instance in China, Angola and Cuba), nominally democratic socialist regimes (as in India and, at times, Jamaica) or even the more common hybrid regimes involving elements of populism, foreign and local varieties of socialism and radical nationalism (as in Algeria, Ghana, Tanzania, Indonesia and Egypt), most new governments in the Third World expressed similar objectives. It is uncommon to find encouragement of 'enterprise', 'initiative', 'entrepreneurism' and 'incentives', or public policy geared to stimulate the development and growth of an aggressive private sector as the main engine of development. Indeed, such ideas were often thought to be immoral and contrary to the spirit of the new post–independence age that was dawning.

It may have been naive of the new elites to believe that the Third World state could build a new Jerusalem in the tropics on the principle of meeting need by suppressing greed. But when they looked to the experience of the West over the previous century, and despite the obvious achievements that could be seen there, they saw no reason to emulate what they took to be the direct consequences of the pursuit of greed. They pointed to the grim human and social costs and conflicts of the industrial revolution, the clash of competitive economic and imperial nationalisms (whose effects they knew only too well), the horrors of the Great War, the Crash of 1929, the ensuing despair and depression of the 1930s, the rise of facism and the further devastation of the second world war. Rightly or wrongly, this was at least how the small indigenous elites interpreted the Western capitalist inheritance (Nehru, 1939), with what they saw as the principle of greed enshrined at its centre.

Thus a policy of national development explicitly aimed at meeting human need inevitably meant a major role for the state, whether it more or less eliminated the market (as in China), curtailed it (as in India) or guided it very firmly (as in South Korea). Typically, therefore, the new states sought to plan their way to prosperity and the meeting of national and community need. This task could not and certainly would not be left to the market, for the engine of growth and development should not and probably could not be fuelled by the self–interested pursuit of individual greed and private accumulation.

Development strategies of course varied greatly (contrast Jamaica with Ethiopia, Zaire with Bangladesh or Sierra Leone with the Philippines). But all placed considerable emphasis on social investment (education, health, literacy etc.) as well as on directly or immediately productive investment. The state, with foreign assistance, was to be mainly responsible for this, given (especially in Africa) the very low levels of domestic capital accumulation. The private sector, both local and foreign – despite some notable exceptions such as Kenya, Philippines, Thailand and Ivory Coast – was viewed with suspicion by the new regimes and tended to be sharply constrained. In short, the pursuit of national development and welfare undertaken by the state involved not only the official eclipse of the principle of greed by that of need, but also generally involved the intended hegemony of planning over enterprise, structure over freedom, constraint over licence, state over market and, not infrequently, development over democracy, in an attempt to achieve both growth and equity through crash programmes of industrialization.

In pursuit of the publicly directed search for development, many methods were tried. Collectivization of land or land reform was tried with very mixed results. The former was often resisted by the peasants (except where peasant based revolutions as in China and Vietnam had occurred), and the latter was commonly fought, evaded or compromised by the power of landed interests (as in Pakistan). Nationalization of the few major industries was standard practice – often mainly mining, like bauxite in Jamaica or copper in Zambia, or the main components of the textile industry in India – as well as the public takeover of banks and insurance companies as in South Korea. Everywhere this involved an immense growth in the size, scope and role of the state in the social and economic affairs of these societies and public sector employment swelled. In sub–Saharan Africa an average of 54 per cent of non–agricultural workers were on the state's payroll; in Asia it was 36 per cent and in Latin America it was 27 per cent (Bienen and Waterbury, 1989).

Results

Results across the Third World were of course uneven. But, overall, between 1950 and 1970, there was a remarkable record of growth in average per capita income in the Third World, at 3.4 per cent per annum (Morawetz, 1977, p. 67). This was hardly surprising given the low levels at which most of these countries started and the world boom conditions of the early part of that period. Some countries, particularly the Newly Industrialising Countries (the NICs), such as Korea, Taiwan, Singapore and Hong Kong – and even Brazil and Mexico – did especially well, and, in the case of Korea and Taiwan, even through the difficult 1970s. There were also important advances made in education and primary health care in many Third World countries, even some of the poorest. According to one recent survey, an 'educational miracle' occurred in the Third World between 1950 and 1989 during which the advances made were greater than those made in the developed countries at comparable periods in their history (Patel, 1985). Likewise, in primary health care, some Third World countries have made major strides. For instance, infant mortality (per 1000 live births) has dropped on average by a third in the low income countries in twenty years from 150 in 1965 to 106 in 1985, and by almost a half in middle income economies from 109 to 65 – the comparative figures for the UK were 20 and nine (World Bank, 1988a, p. 286). Despite these achievements, most analysts would agree that the developmental record in meeting even basic human needs on a universal basis has not been good and that since 1970 it has been particularly bad, especially in sub–Saharan Africa. Since the end of the 1970s in Africa there has been almost a decade of falling per capita incomes and per capita food production. Export volumes (of mainly traditional raw agricultural materials) have declined in the 1970s and 1980s. As in Latin America and parts of Asia, debt in Africa grew massively in the 1970s and 1980s: it increased nineteen–fold between 1970 and 1988, and the debt service burden of the continent is now formally the highest in the world, standing at the equivalent of 47 per cent of 1988 export earnings. Primary school enrolment rates have declined since 1980 and there is now evidence of increased infant mortality in some parts of the continent since the early 1980s, reflecting public expenditure cuts in social services by governments facing intractable financial difficulties. Urban unemployment has mounted (World Bank, 1989). And although the data is patchy, the inequalities between rich and poor in most regions of the Third World are gross and in some areas have increased. Crucially, it appears that only where initial distribution or redistribution of assets and incomes was moderately even (for instance following systematic land reform, as in East Asia), have the benefits of growth been widely distributed. But for the bulk of mainly rural Third World people – some 70 per cent – this has not been so, and where there has been growth its benefits have been increasingly unevenly distributed (Morawetz, 1977, pp. 68–70).

In political terms, there have been democratic success stories, but they have been the exception and the crisis has been expressed in many ways. These have included the inability to maintain inherited representative democratic institutions or devise new ones; the establishment of authoritarian one–party regimes and the ruthless suppression of opposition and trade union movements; the emergence and re–emergence of military regimes circulating in a vacuum of underdevelopment and poverty; escalating corruption and state incapacity; often appalling human rights records and a massive refugee problem (nearly half the world's refugees are in Africa), and a host of ethnic conflicts and sub–national secessionist wars from Sri Lanka to the Sudan. None of this, it is argued, can be good for development.

In short, as the early spurt of economic growth faltered and as crises erupted, Third World regimes have found themselves unable to provide or sustain the social services they had promised or initiated, let alone extend them. The capacity of these states to meet even the basic needs of all their people has atrophied and been called into question. India is a good case, for it is a country with considerable potential having diverse natural resources, a large domestic market, a relatively stable political structure, much scientific and entrepreneurial talent, sound industrial infrastructure, accumulating savings and a useful inflow of foreign exchange from remittances abroad. Yet after 40 years of independence easily 40 per cent of the population still lives below the poverty line; more than half does not have access to safe drinking water; one third of primary school age children are not in school and adult illiteracy is widespread, especially among women, (Bardhan, 1984).

There are many explanations for the plight of Third World societies. Historically, the character and legacy of the imperial era did not give them an auspicious start. For instance, there were less than ten graduates in the Belgian Congo – now Zaire – at independence in 1960; and colonial research and development in food crops in most areas had been minimal. Industrial development, too, had generally been negligible. After the boom years of the 1950s and 1960s, uncertain or fluctuating terms of trade for their primary commodities made planning difficult, and dependence on often a single crop or commodity made them vulnerable. Tariff walls made entry to American and European markets difficult. If that was not enough, external political hostility and destabilization (for instance, by South Africa in Mozambique and Angola) exacerbated already tense internal political relationships. The oil crises, world recession, mounting interest rates through the 1980s and burgeoning debt crisis added to the enormity of their national development tasks.

Thus external factors have been there, but what has become equally clear is that internal political factors have been as important. What is loosely termed as 'state failure' or 'political failure', in contradistinction to the economists' notion of 'market failure', is merely a shorthand way of describing the inability or incapacity of many Third World states to deliver or manage either sustained growth or equity and hence their failure to be able to meet even basic human needs.

The idea of 'state' (or 'political') failure refers mainly to the inadequate 'reach' of the state through an under–resourced and over–stretched public administration, the politicization of this bureaucracy and its demoralization and corruption. Moreover, Third World states have rarely achieved relative 'autonomy' from civil society and have been 'captured' by coalitions of powerful interests. And the ferocity of the regional, sectional and clientelistic pulls on the state and its personnel have acted to steer resources, favours, projects, policies and jobs in their direction with the consequential loss of coherent direction by the state and its development planners. In short, the *politics* of the development process is critically to blame for many shortcomings and is bound to determine the outcome of any future policies.

It is important, however, to note that some Third World states have been successful. They have produced both growth and the satisfaction of basic material needs, seldom equalled by the action of markets, though often at the cost of civil liberties and political freedoms. Such states are best known as 'developmental states', having the capacity to define, pursue and achieve developmental goals to a degree not shared by most contemporary Third World states. Examples of these are of course the post–Meiji state after 1868 which transformed Japan into an industrial capitalist society within barely a generation, and other contemporary states of South Korea and Taiwan in East Asia. But generally, successful 'developmental states' (on both the 'right' and 'left') have been the exception. Elsewhere, where once the state had been seen as the *solution* to the problem of meeting need, now it is being seen as part of the problem standing in the way of this objective.

In sum, the project aimed at meeting widespread social need through planned public action by the state seems to have foundered on the rock of political failure. Excluded from large areas of economic life by restrictions on the market, and finding enlarged opportunities for advantage within the institutions of the state, greed simply transposed itself from the private domain to the public one. As President Mobutu of Zaire said in 1977:

> To sum it up, everything is for sale, everything is bought in our country. And in this traffic, holding any slice of public power constitutes a veritable exchange instrument, convertible into illicit acquisition of money or other goods, or the evasion of all sorts of obligations. Worse, even the use by an individual of his most legitimate right is subjected to an invisible tax, openly pocketed by individuals. Thus an audience with an official, enrolling children in school, obtaining school certificates, access to medical care, a seat on a plane, an import licence, a diploma, among other things, are all subject to this tax which is invisible, yet known to the whole world. Accordingly, our society risks losing its political character, to become one vast marketplace, ruled by the basest laws of traffic and exploitation (Young, 1978, p. 172).

Enrichissez–vous: the rediscovery of greed

A common response by governments on left and right to these developmental crises has been to abandon (or substantially reduce) planning and official concerns with meeting needs. Instead, they have sought to reverse policy to encourage and provide incentives for individual effort and private economic activity. 'Greed' and the pursuit of personal *enrichment* has been rediscovered and inserted at the core of the new strategy. This certainly happened in the last decade in the Third World although the justification has been that need will be better served in the long run by first satisfying greed.

Coined first by Guizot in the 1840s, the phrase 'enrichissez–vous' – enrich yourselves – has cropped up since in many surprising contexts. Launching a 'get rich' campaign in the USSR in the 1920s, Bukharin used the direct Russian translation of 'enrich yourselves' in support of extending the New Economic Policy (encouraging market forces after the austerity of 'War Communism') amongst the peasants as a means of boosting collapsing agricultural production (Nove, 1976, p. 128). The same theme emerged in China after the death of Mao and the fall of the 'Gang of Four' in the late 1970s. In support of 'modernization', slogans appeared announcing that 'To get rich is glorious'. Newspapers recommended 'Have no fear of becoming prosperous', in stark contrast to the tone of previous slogans such as 'Down with capitalist roaders'. Deng Xiaoping said it was now appropriate '... to make some people rich first so as to lead all the people to wealth' (Schell, 1985, pp. 4–15; Gittings, 1989, p. 109). Mr. Deng could have found no better theoretical mentor than F.A. Hayek who long ago argued along these lines (Hayek, 1960, pp. 44–45).

In the Third World in the 1980s and now in Eastern Europe in the 1990s, at an astonishing pace, policies built round this old and apparently simple idea have begun to be put in place. From Mexico to Mauritius and from the Soviet Union to Sierra Leone, this restructuring of the moral and political economies of both private and public sectors is intended to transform the structure and ethos of much that has been taken for granted for the last 30 years or more.

The immediate origins, pressures and impulses for these reforms have of course not always been the same. Some are external. For instance, the explicit forms of leverage through World Bank, International Monetary Fund and Western donor 'policy dialogues' have become much more forceful, globally, but especially in the poor and hence politically weakened African states in the 1980s. World Bank lending for structural adjustment in support of such policies now amounts to 25 per cent of its total (World Bank, 1988b, p. 1). While external pressures of this kind should not be underestimated, internal pressures have been important, too, arising from both failed economic policies and political repression. In Eastern Europe, most obviously, sometimes massive popular political protests have swept away the existing communist regimes, initiating profound changes. Elsewhere, for instance in Ghana and more recently in Ethiopia, military coups or the outcome of civil wars have ushered in new regimes dedicated to these kinds of policies, as have post–electoral political changes in much of Latin and Central America. Whether external or internal, or a combination of both, these forces have always been more effective where the allegedly 'needs driven' developmental policy, directed and managed by the state, has patently failed to deliver the goods.

The forms and particulars of the reforms are also not all the same, but they all flow in the same general direction. Their stated intent and rationale, of course, is to reverse the decline in growth rates that has occurred, to promote exports, to stimulate agricultural production (especially in Africa) and to reduce debt. It is not really a question of how 'affluence' is to be used, but how it is to be created. The agency for bringing about the *conditions* for this 'policy reform' will again necessarily, but only initially, be the state. But the real agents of economic change and growth are to be the newly 'liberated' farmers and entrepreneurs. They are supposed to respond to the new opportunities and incentives created in the space evacuated by the state and by the elimination of regulation, control and constraint. The theory and rhetoric associated with this will be familiar to anyone familiar with Britain in the 1980s, as Sir Geoffrey Howe, echoing Bukharin and Mr. Deng, explained to the Conservative Party conference in 1982: 'You cannot create a rich society without allowing some individuals to become rich as well'.

Known as perestroika (literally 'restructuring') in Moscow and as 'structural adjustment' in the World Bank in Washington, these complex processes all seek to restore the individual energy of more or less unconstrained 'greed' to the heart of the development process. This involves cutting back the role of the state; privatizing industries and services; limiting public expenditure on subsidies and welfare services; slimming down obese bureaucracies; deepening and widening the arena in which free enterprise and competitive market forces are allowed to operate; liberalising trade and investment policy and, crucially, instilling the values of enterprise, initiative and fending for oneself in order to promote productivity in all spheres, from the growing of paw–paws to the provision of higher education.

Reversing some of the fundamental post–independence priorities discussed earlier, we now see the intended hegemony of growth over equity, of enterprise over planning, of initiative over regulation, of individualism over collectivism, of 'freedom' over structure and of markets over states. There is little talk now of 'redistribution with growth', of 'basic human needs' or of targeting aid to the 'poorest of the poor' as was the vogue in the 1970s. Most recently, Western governments and international agencies such as the World Bank have begun to call directly for *political* change in developing countries, as a condition of aid, though they do not always call it that. They prefer the more technical term of 'good governance' and argue that this too is a condition of development. What they mean by this varies, but in general they now assert that aid will increasingly become more conditional on improvements in human rights records, respect for the rule of law and both 'accountability' and 'transparency' in government (Conable, 1991). Some refer explicitly to democratic government, by which they mean liberal and pluralist democracy (Hurd, 1990). And already, from Nepal to Nicaragua there is evidence that political change of this kind is beginning to take place alongside the economic reforms.

Prospects

Will this shift in policy meet needs better than the previous approach? It is too early for clear evidence to have emerged, but what there is suggests the following.

First, in some countries where these kinds of reforms of 'structural adjustment' programmes have been taking place, growth rates have often improved impressively. For instance, the 'contract responsibility system' in Chinese agriculture, involving in some areas an almost de facto return to private land usage (though not ownership) and a much freer market for the sale of produce, generated a sudden spurt in output between 1980–86, especially of grain production. With farmers receiving better prices for their produce, rural private incomes almost trebled and rural fairs and markets returned to the countryside (Perkins, 1988). In Ghana, often held up as the model example of structural adjustment in Africa, per capita growth has been positive and steady since the mid–1980s, substantial price liberalization has occurred and export performance has improved, the government borrowing requirement has been reduced, inflation has eased considerably and visitors report that basic consumer items are back in the shops and that the informal urban food markets (run by women) are once again thriving (World Bank, 1988a).

But, second, there have also been 'failures' or, rather, less positive performances, for instance in Mexico, Jamaica, Zambia and in the Philippines where structural adjustment programmes have simply not worked (World Bank, 1988b) or not been allowed to work by political forces within the societies or regimes.

Third, and of most importance for the present argument, the social costs of reform and adjustment have been high and have generally hit both the rural and urban poor the hardest: they are the losers (Demery and Addison, 1987). Even the World Bank agrees (World Bank, 1988b, p. 30). Though the evidence is patchy, it suggests that structural adjustment has adversely affected employment, incomes, transport, food prices, nutrition, health care, education, social services and, crucially, children (UNICEF, 1990). In Mexico, for instance, 1.5 million jobs were lost in the formal economy between 1981 and 1983 (Bienen and Waterbury, 1989). In China, efforts have been made to curtail the principle of the 'iron rice bowl' (jobs for life), especially in the industrial sector, and rural unemployment as well as regional and personal income inequalities have increased (Economist, 1987). In Ghana, cuts in health and education spending have eroded public service provision dramatically since 1981. Minimum wage levels in 1986 were lower than in 1982 and purchased far less than they did as food prices have risen, and the urban and rural poor have taken especially heavy knocks (Green, 1986; 1988). In Sierra Leone, following an intense 1986 structural adjustment programme, food prices rose by 400 per cent; the Freetown (capital city) Consumer Price Index increased from 1516.2 at the end of 1986 (1978 = 100) to 4743.2 four months later; diet of the poor suffered; rural transport costs rose, affecting both the rural poor and farmers; and the cost of drugs and textbooks rocketed, for example, aspirin up 500 per cent, chloroquin up 1000 per cent (Longhurst, et al., 1988). Comparable evidence is abundant in Latin America. In short, need – especially of the poor – has not (yet) been met by the new policies.

Conclusions

There are some important points to make here by way of conclusion. First, while 'need' and 'greed' may seem like exclusive principles of organization in the moral and political economy of societies, they are in practice only the extreme poles of a political and policy continuum between which one might be able to plot the position of different societies at different times. In Cuba, for instance, there has been a continuous tension between 'moral' and 'material' incentives in development policy and practice. And in China this has been expressed as a vacillation between policies based on the principle of 'politics in command' or 'economics in command', which in turn reflected the political struggle between factions within the regime.

Second, what is clear then is that for the first phases of their independent or post–revolution histories, most Third World societies would have to be placed nearer to the 'needs' end of the continuum. But now, as a result of both external pressures and internal forces, their development policy is in the course of turning full circle and it is hard to see how regimes like the Cuban and North Korean ones can hold out for much longer against this trend. Initially, 'needs driven' priorities helped to shape a major role for the state in managing the economy and curtailed the pursuit of private greed. But, against a background of generalised policy failure, depleted state revenues, crippling debt and a changed global political environment, 'greed' is back in fashion as a spur to growth. We will see this accelerate during the 1990s and state attention to the public meeting of need will decline.

Third, all the examples in this brief survey of the Third World pattern should underline the primacy of politics in development and hence in its implications for social policy, too. For it is politics that explains both the original approach and the current changes. For instance, it has been the politics and state capacity of successful developmental regimes (as in Japan and Korea) that explains their effective management of planned growth and hence their increasing ability to meet social need. Equally, it has been in the corrupt, patrimonial and clientelistic politics of, say, Zaire or the Philippines under the Marcos regime, that their failures and gaping inequalities need to be located. Similarly, the early successes of Algeria, Cuba and China in promoting growth and meeting primary need are likewise explicable with reference to the character of their post–revolutionary state capacities and politics. The outcome of current attempts at reform in each will in turn depend on their politics. For when people change the way they use

53

resources, they change their relations with each other and there will be winners and losers; and that is always political. Moreover, the current attempts at the imposition of institutional reform and structural adjustment policies around the world, designed to loosen the grip of the state, will paradoxically require strong and efficient states, enjoying some degree of autonomy from the pressures within civil society. Hence, the alleged 'success' of adjustment in Ghana thus seems directly the result of a tough and authoritarian military regime which came to power through a coup. On the other hand, the failure to carry through liberalisation in India may be explained politically with reference to the dominant coalition of economic and political interests which has prevented the Indian state from undertaking significant economic reform in any direction (Bardhan, 1984; Kohli, 1989).

Fourth, it is too early to know whether the new policies based on the spur of greed will generate sustained growth, but the daily evidence of disasters, famines, poverty, inequality and despair should remind us of the urgent need for it. However, what is certain is that if sustained growth does occur, then its benefits will only be used to meet need as a result of political and state action. Once again, the character, role and capacity of the state and its administrative apparatus will be crucial as will the politics of the internal and external coalitions of interest that will shape state policy. But if, in the course of economic and political 'adjustment', nothing is or can be done to even out the costs and benefits of change, then the losers in this transition will not remain idle. In the open political circumstances that may then exist, dissatisfaction and despair may combine explosively. Economic and political reform may thus unleash highly unstable variables into the politics of these societies and may, in turn, blow the reform strategy into oblivion.

For all these reasons it may thus be premature to believe that these far-reaching global shifts signify the final triumphal evidence of the supremacy of liberal (and in some places not so liberal) capitalism or, even, the 'end of history' (Fukuyama, 1989). Indeed, the social costs and political consequences of developmental strategies based on 'greed' may well outweigh the failures of those based on 'need'. If so, we may in due course see a reversion to the latter, undertaken this time by new regimes, hardened and educated by the experience of what has gone before.

References

Bardhan, P. (1984), *The Political Economy of Development in India*, Basil Blackwell, Oxford.
Bienen, H. and Waterbury, J. (1989), 'The political economy of privatization in developing countries', *World Development*, vol. 17, no. 5, pp. 617–632.

Conable, B. (1991), 'Africa's development and destiny', Address to 27th Heads of State Session of the Organisation of African Unity.

Demery, L. and Addison, A. (1987), *The Alleviation of Poverty Under Structural Adjustment*, The World Bank, Washington.

Economist (1987), 12 December.

Fukuyama, F. (1989), 'The end of history?, *National Interest*, Summer.

Gittings, J. (1989), *China Changes Face: The Road from Revolution 1949– 1989*, Oxford University Press, Oxford.

Green, R.H. (1986), *Sub–Saharan Africa: poverty of development, development of poverty*, IDS Discussion Paper, Institute of Development Studies, Brighton.

Green, R.H. (1988), 'Progress, problematics and limitations of the success story', *IDS Bulletin*, vol. 19, no. 1, p. 7–16.

Hayek, F.A. (1960), *The Constitution of Liberty*, Routledge, London.

Hurd, D. (1990), 'Promoting good government', *Crossbow*, Autumn.

Kohli, A. (1989), 'The politics of economic liberalisation in India', *World Development*, vol. 17, no. 3, pp. 305–328.

Leacock, S. (1936), *Helements of Hickonomics*, Dodd, Mead and Company, New York.

Longhurst, R., Kamara, S. and Mensurah, J., (1988), 'Structural Adjustment and vulnerable groups in Sierra Leone', *IDS Bulletin*, vol. 19, no. 1, pp. 25–30.

Moraes, D. (1957), *Jawaharlal Nehru*, Macmillan, London.

Morawetz, D. (1977), *Twenty–Five Years of Economic Development*, The World Bank, Washington.

Nehru, J. (1939), *Glimpses of World History*, Lindsay Drummond, London.

Nove, A. (1976), *An Economic History of the USSR*, Penguin, Harmondsworth.

Nyerere, J.K. (1968), *Freedom and Socialism*, Oxford University Press, Dar Es Salaam.

Patel, S.J. (1985), 'Educational "miracle" in the Third World, 1950–1981', *Economic and Political Weekly*, vol. xx, no. 31, pp. 1312–1317.

Perkins, D.H. (1988), 'Reforming China's economic system', *Journal of Economic Literature XXVI*, pp. 611–613.

Riddell, R. (1987), *Foreign Aid Reconsidered*, James Currey, London.

Schell, O. 1985), *To Get Rich Is Glorious*, Robin Clark, London.

Streeton, P. and Burki, S.J. (1978), 'Basic needs: some issues', *World Development*, vol. 6, no. 3, pp. 411–421.

UNICEF (1990), *The State of the World's Children*, Oxford University Press, Oxford.

World Bank (1988a), *World Development Report*, The World Bank, Washington.

World Bank (1988b), *Adjustment Lending, An Evaluation of Ten Years of Experience*, The World Bank, Washington.

World Bank (1989), *Sub-Saharan Africa: From Crisis to Sustainable Growth*, The World Bank, Washington.

Young, C. (1978), 'Zaire: the unending crisis', *Foreign Affairs*, vol.57, no.1, pp. 165–179.

4   Priorities – not needs!

A. Williams

As the famous episode in Oliver Twist dramatically emphasizes, the distinction between 'meeting need' and 'feeding greed' is a matter of judgement and viewpoint, not a matter of fact. It is, therefore, essential to think carefully about how we recognize 'need' when we see it, how it differs from wants, desires or demands, and what makes us decide that some needs should be met, whilst others are left unmet. And is the very existence of 'unmet need' a condemnation of 'the system', or merely an inevitable consequence of giving priority to some 'needs' over other 'needs'? This short exegesis draws heavily on much of my earlier writings on this subject, (see especially Williams, 1974) not a word of which I feel I have any reason to retract or amend in the light of the subsequent 15 years of continued confusion over what still seems to me eminently clear!

Let me start with a distinguished Medical Adviser in the Department of Health, Graham Matthew, writing in 1971:

> The 'need' for medical care must be distinguished from the 'demand' for care and from the use of services or 'utilization'. A need for medical care exists when an individual has an illness or disability for which there is an effective and acceptable treatment or cure. It can be defined either in terms of the type of illness or disability causing the need or of the treatment or facilities for treatment required to meet it. A demand for care exists when an individual

considers that he has a need and wishes to receive care. Utilization occurs when an individual actually receives care. Need is not necessarily expressed as demand, and demand is not necessarily followed by utilization, while, on the other hand, there can be demand and utilization without real underlying need for the particular service used (p. 28).

The meaning of need in this context is clearly to do with *an individual's capacity to benefit from* whatever it is they are said to 'need'. The implications are that people cannot really 'need' things that will do them no good, but people may nevertheless 'demand' and 'utilize' such things.

Going even further back (to 1965), a political scientist had made the following observations:

When we see statements to the effect that human beings need so many calories per day (and that states should make every effort to see that everyone gets this number) or that university teachers need books (which should therefore be allowed by the Inland Revenue as a claim for expenses) we may at first suppose that here is a justification for policies which ... appeals ... to an 'objective' or 'scientific' procedure by which 'needs' are established.

Whenever someone says 'X is needed' it always makes sense ... to ask what purpose it is needed for. Once an end is given it is indeed an 'objective' or 'scientific' matter to find out what conditions are necessary to bring it about .... The end in my first example might be mere survival, or good health, or the satisfaction of hunger; and differences in the 'needs' found by different studies might no doubt be attributed to differences in the end postulated.

When I say that 'need' is not by itself a justificatory principle, I mean that no statement to the effect that X is necessary in order to produce Y provides a reason for doing X. Before it can provide such a reason Y must be shown to be (or taken to be) a desirable end to pursue .... A *conclusive* reason would require showing that the cost of X (i.e. other desirable things which could be done instead of X) does not make it less advantageous than some alternative course of action (Barry, 1965, pp. 47–48).

Once again, the term 'need' appears to be related to the beneficial effects of having the things 'needed' (calories, books). But we seem to be more selective in our use of the term 'need' than this for 'too many books' or 'too many calories' would be castigated as 'feeding greed', even though the extra books or the extra calories might still be beneficial to the 'greedy' individual. So we clearly 'need' some additional criterion (that is, it would be beneficial to have one!).

To progress further we need to pose the question *'who is to assess A's needs?'* (where 'A' is a person) though I would prefer to abandon the parlance of needology and pose the question differently, namely *'who is to judge what is good for A?'*

To make inroads into this difficult territory we could do worse than follow the schema suggested by Spek in 1972, in which three parties are distinguished: Society (S), Medical Experts (M), and the Individual (I). (The 'experts' could, of course, be from whatever professional group is relevant to the problem under discussion, for example tax inspectors, or dieticians). In the health care setting each party is asked two questions:

(1)   Is the individual sick?
(2)   Is the individual in need of public care?

Indicating positive answers by S, M or I, and negative ones by $\overline{S}$, $\overline{M}$ or $\overline{I}$, we have eight (2x2x2) possible combinations of answers to the first question, and the same number for the second. But among the possible answers, a much smaller subset are of immediate interest, and it is upon these that Spek concentrates, adding an additional (factual) question, 'does the individual demand public care?' This leads him to the characterisation of the situation shown in Figure 4.1. Spek comments on this taxonomy as follows:

> Case 1 represents justified demand, with society and medical experts in agreement. Cases 2, 3 and 11 represent latent need with society and medical experts in agreement. Cases 5, 6, 7, 9, 12 and 13 represent latent need with society and medical experts in disagreement. Cases 10 and 14 represent unjustified demand with society and medical experts in agreement. Cases 4 and 7 represent demand with society and medical experts in disagreement.

> ... the answers to the first and second questions depend on knowledge and valuation, but they offer quite different educational and informational problems: this in turn will affect the ease with which the latent need in the different cases can be converted to demand, as well as unjustified demand suppressed. Latent need may also be defined as need together with absence of demand for public care. It is partly known through population studies and from individuals who, having contacted the system of public care, refuse to wait. This is not the place to discuss the problems which arise when society and medical experts are in disagreement on the latent need. If Case 4 is regarded as justified active demand, then it represents the thorny problem of how to have the doctors furnish the right care. If Case 7 is regarded as unjustified demand, it represents the thorny problem of 'over-use'. (Ibid, pp. 265–67)

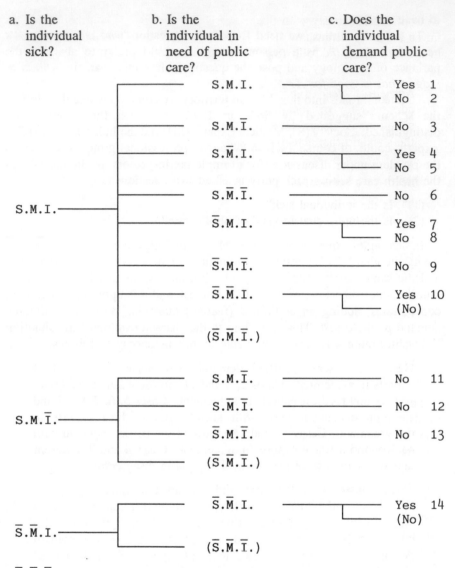

a. Is the individual sick?	b. Is the individual in need of public care?	c. Does the individual demand public care?	
	S.M.I.	Yes	1
		No	2
	S.M.Ī.	No	3
	S.M̄.I.	Yes	4
		No	5
	S.M̄.Ī.	No	6
S.M.I.	S̄.M.I.	Yes	7
		No	8
	S̄.M.Ī.	No	9
	S̄.M̄.I.	Yes	10
		(No)	
	(S̄.M̄.Ī.)		
	S.M.Ī.	No	11
	S.M̄.Ī.	No	12
S.M.Ī.	S̄.M.Ī.	No	13
	(S̄.M̄.Ī.)		
	S̄.M̄.I.	Yes	14
S̄.M̄.I.		(No)	
	(S̄.M̄.Ī.)		
(S̄.M̄.Ī.)			

Note: The four cases S.M̄.I., S.M̄.Ī., S̄.M.I. and S̄.M.Ī. are disregarded in spite of their great interest. They must not be forgotten in a more detailed analysis. In addition we do not discuss differences in agreement among representatives of society and among medical experts.

Figure 4.1   Need and demand for medical care (Spek, 1972, p. 266)

Contemporaneously with Spek, and each unaware of the other's work as far as I can see, Bradshaw (1972) was also developing a taxonomy of need, in his case using the following discriminators:

Normative need (i.e. 'that which the expert or professional, administrator or social scientist defines as need in any given situation. A "desirable" standard is laid down and is compared with the standard that actually exists').

Felt need (i.e. 'Here need is equated with want. When assessing need for a service, the population is asked whether they feel they need it').

Expressed need (i.e. 'Expressed need or demand is felt need turned into action .... Expressed need is commonly used in the health services where waiting lists are taken as a measure of unmet need. Waiting lists are generally accepted as a poor definition of "real need" – especially for pre–symptomatic cases').

Comparative need (i.e. 'obtained by study of the characteristics of the population in receipt of a service. If there are people with similar characteristics not in receipt of a service, then they are in need').

The first thing to note is that the judgements of 'society' play no role in Bradshaw's taxonomy, only those of the individual and the experts. It will also be seen that Bradshaw's 'normative need' is equivalent to Spek's medical experts answering 'Yes' to both questions (a) and (b) (Spek's Cases 1, 2, 3, 7, 8, 9, 11 and 13). Bradshaw's 'felt need' is equivalent to Spek's individual answering 'Yes' to those two questions (Spek's Cases 1, 2, 4, 5, 7, 8, 10 and 14). Bradshaw's 'expressed need' is equivalent to Spek's question (c) being answered affirmatively (Spek's Cases 1, 4, 7, 10 and 14). Bradshaw's 'comparative need' seems to be approximately equivalent to Spek's 'latent need' (Cases 2, 3 and 11; but with 9 added since 'society's' adverse judgement is no longer relevant), where the individual does not demand the service even though the medical experts think he is sick and needs public care.

Against this background we could go back to the beginning and rework the quotation from Graham Matthew, using as the key a definition of need as requiring that the medical expert believes both that the individual is sick and that the individual would benefit from medical care. It might then read (omitting the word 'need' throughout):

The medical experts' judgement as to whether or not a person is sick and capable of benefiting from medical care must be

61

distinguished from that person's use of services or 'utilisation'. A person is judged by medical experts to be capable of benefiting from medical care when that individual has an illness or disability for which they believe there is an effective and acceptable treatment or care. This phenomenon can be expressed either in terms of the type of illness or disability to which the treatment or care is directed, or in terms of the treatment or facilities for treatment themselves. An individual presents himself for treatment when he considers that he is sick and may be capable of benefiting from medical care, and wishes to avail himself of that possibility. Utilisation occurs when an individual actually receives care. An individual who would be judged by medical experts to be sick and capable of benefiting from medical care will not necessarily present himself and request treatment, and such requests are not necessarily complied with. On the other hand, there exist cases where individuals request treatment and get it even when medical experts (or society?) judge them not to be sick or not capable of benefiting from the particular service used.

So far so good, but we are still taking 'need' to be an 'on–off' concept. And even some of the discussions of 'priorities' and 'hierarchies of wants' fail to carry us much further. They frequently imply (and sometimes even assert) that some 'needs' take absolute priority over others (that is, there is a lexicographic ordering ... until one 'need' is completely satisfied you do not turn to the next). There are still important vestiges of this in the 'shroud waving' approach to medical priorities, in which it is implicitly being asserted that keeping people alive is an absolute priority requiring resources to be devoted to that end no matter what the cost in terms of other objectives.

So what is missing in all this is the notion of 'trade–offs', an ugly and unappealing phrase which, on etymological grounds, undoubtedly fully deserves its lack of prominence in debates about social policy. But for all its ugliness, it does capture the essence of what is missing in the world of needology, namely that we are in the business of making judgements about the relative values of different potential benefits to different potential beneficiaries, and we are not helped in that difficult intellectual and political task by thought stopping terms like 'need' which invite 'on–off' thinking rather than 'more or less' thinking.

If we are to make progress we 'need' (that is, we would benefit from) a clearer formulation of the policy problem. This has to entail judgements by somebody as to what actions are (on balance) more beneficial than others, remembering that in a world of finite resources every action has costs in terms of benefits foregone by others. If our objective is to maximise benefits, then they have to be described, quantified and valued in a comparable manner. If policy is to become less opaque, and hence more accountable, these processes need to become more explicit, indicating whose values have been used and what weights have been attached to benefits accruing to different people. It is this kind of thinking that has led me to pursue the Quality Adjusted Life Year (or QALY) as a composite measure of health benefit in outcome terms, for it seems to me that it satisfies all these criteria. Unless an activity yields QALYs to somebody, no one can be said to 'need' it. But yielding QALYs is only a necessary condition for the activity to be undertaken, it is not a sufficient condition. The second hurdle to be cleared is that the activity does more good (in QALY terms) than any other use of the resource required by that activity (Williams, 1987). This is the world of priorities, which encompasses, and transcends, the world of 'needs'.

'Meeting need or feeding greed?'. A plague on both your houses! Priority setting is the name of the game.

References

Barry, B. (1965), *Political Argument*, Routledge and Kegan Paul, London.

Bradshaw, J. (1972), 'A taxonomy of need' in McLachlan, G. (ed.), *Problems and Progress in Medical Care* (Seventh Series), Nuffield Provincial Hospitals Trust, Oxford University Press, London.

Matthew, G.K. (1971), 'Measuring need and evaluating services', in McLachlan, G. (ed.), *Portfolio for Health*, Nuffield Provincial Hospitals Trust, Oxford University Press, London.

Spek, J.E. (1972), 'On the economic analysis of health and medical care in a Swedish health district', in Hauser, M.M. (ed.), *The Economics of Medical Care*, Allen and Unwin, London.

Williams, A. (1974), 'Need as a demand concept (with special reference to health)', in Culyer, A.J. (ed.), *Economic Policies and Social Goals*, Martin Robertson, London.

Williams, A. (1987), 'The importance of quality of life in policy decisions', in Walker, S.R. and Rosser, R.M. (eds), *Quality of Life: Assessment and Application*, MTP Press Limited, Lancaster.

Part Two
NEW RESOURCES

5 Meeting needs: Defence and welfare

N. Hooper, K. Hartley and J. Singleton

Introduction

This chapter considers whether there is evidence of a trade–off between defence and welfare spending in the UK economy. In particular, emphasis is given to the dynamic trade–off through defence crowding out investment, so reducing growth, with possible adverse effects on future welfare spending.

Meeting society's needs involves difficult choices. The 1989–90 events in Eastern Europe and the USSR and the 1990 Conventional Forces in Europe (CFE) Treaty have created pressures for cuts in UK defence spending (the peace dividend), so enabling society to meet other needs. Critics of defence spending point to the prospects of using savings for improving welfare services. They argue that the acquisition of costly new defence equipment such as Trident (over £9 billion) and the Tornado (over £11 billion) were at the expense of new hospitals and waiting lists with effects on patient care, as well as schools and universities with adverse effects on the creation of human capital. The issue of whether defence has prevented welfare spending or reduced growth is important in the debate over the social choices involved in the use of any peace dividend. If society has foregone growth to ensure security, then society might not choose to spend a peace dividend directly on welfare but rather to raise the growth rate and hence its future potential for welfare and other spending (Kirby and Hooper, 1991).

There are four parts to the chapter. The first reviews the literature on trade–off and the mechanisms by which it may occur. Then empirical evidence is presented relating to the existence of a direct trade–off for the UK, followed by evidence of indirect effects through military research and development expenditure. The final part offers some conclusions.

The concept of a defence–welfare trade–off

Economists have devoted considerable effort to examining the relationship between military spending and economic performance since studies by Benoit (1973; 1978) unexpectedly indicated a positive (beneficial) relationship for developing countries. Benoit interpreted his results as suggesting that military expenditure involved high technology products and processes which had beneficial spin–off effects throughout the economy. Other studies point to additional beneficial effects through jobs, exports and import savings (for example Chester, 1978; Hartley and McLean, 1978). The immediate effect of increased defence spending is likely to be greater output and higher employment. However, it is claimed that in the long run there are adverse effects on the balance of payments, technical progress and ultimately on economic growth (for example Chalmers, 1985; Russett, 1970; Smith and Smith, 1983).

In developed countries military expenditure is also seen as pre–empting resources, crowding out welfare spending, reducing savings and investment and thus growth. Conversely, military expenditure may have beneficial effects through technological spin–off, particularly of materials and production methods, which lead to improved productivity and higher growth. A further strand of literature, not pursued in this analysis, sees military expenditure as necessary to sustain demand as capitalist economies face demand deficiencies through underconsumption (referred to as the underconsumption or Marxist approach, as for example in Smith, 1977).

Both sides of the debate are supported by empirical evidence for both developed and developing countries. A study of the theoretical relationship between military spending and growth in developing countries concluded that '... on *a priori* considerations one cannot give any answer to the question whether disarmament will have positive or negative consequences on economic growth. There are positive and negative effects, which will be different from country to country and from case to case' (De Haan, 1987, pp. 95–96). A review of econometric evidence reached a similar conclusion: 'The recent econometric evidence points to the conclusion that these positive effects, if they exist, are small relative to the negative effects, and that, overall, military spending has a weak but adverse impact on economic growth in developing countries' (Grobar and Porter, 1989, p. 318). Adams and Gold (1987) reviewed the arguments and evidence for the USA and concluded that

68

'the economic impact of military spending is only marginally different from that of other forms of federal spending. It is not uniquely inflationary, has an unclear relationship to productivity and technological development, and does not create significantly different numbers of jobs' (p. 266). The general level of debate is perhaps best indicated by Greenwood (1987): 'If the quest for universal propositions about the defence–growth relationship is to continue, let it be purged of prejudice; in particular please could the indisputable fact that high levels of military spending have been associated with high, medium, low (and no) growth be given the critical scrutiny which it merits?' (p. 102).

Against this background of mixed (and confusing) evidence of a relationship between military expenditure and economic growth, this chapter considers the more limited question of a trade–off between defence and welfare in the UK. The issue can be simply put: is there any evidence that spending on defence reduces spending on welfare?

To an economist, all spending can be seen as taking place at the expense of alternative uses of the spending power – the concept of opportunity cost. Why should special attention be focused on defence and welfare? Critics of defence spending see it as unnecessary and wasteful, while welfare is seen as desirable and useful. Others argue that security is basic to society and is indeed the most basic element of welfare. In reality both are important, and the debate is more realistically one of the relative levels of each. Can security be assured using less resources, and can more welfare be achieved from the resources available? There is also a question as to whether society would choose to devote any resources freed from defence to the collection of items currently grouped into a statistical category called welfare, or to some other purpose – perhaps consumption or investment, or leisure, or unproductive savings, or simply distributed to the poorer members of society to use as they wish. This issue is becoming increasingly relevant at a time when many expect changes in the world political and military situation (a reduced threat) to make significant reductions in defence spending possible without sacrificing security.

Society might be expected to devote newly released resources to welfare if there was evidence that defence had previously been crowding out or preventing spending on welfare. If, however, defence spending had been crowding out consumption or reducing growth the decisions about the use of a peace dividend might be very different. The next part looks for empirical evidence that any crowding out effect may have occurred in the UK since 1960.

Military expenditure, growth and welfare

Two possible crowding out mechanisms are considered here. Firstly, the direct relationships between military expenditure and other categories of expenditure are assessed using correlation analysis. Secondly, the methods used in previous studies (for example, Smith, 1977; Smith and Smith, 1983; Chalmers, 1985) are used to consider the effect of military spending on investment and hence growth and future welfare spending. These studies used regression equations to estimate the relationship between military expenditure and other economic performance variables. Here, more up–to–date data are used, and different versions of the equations are assessed.

Various authors have suggested different variables as potentially contributing to the explanation of the relationship between military spending and investment. The variables used in this analysis are:

M = military expenditure as a percentage of gross domestic product (GDP)

Expenditure which may be crowded out by military spending:

I = gross fixed capital formation as a percentage of GDP

NHS = national health service spending as a percentage of GDP

Ed = government education expenditure as a percentage of GDP

Other explanatory variables:

Cons = private consumption as a percentage of GDP

Gr = growth – year on year percentage change in GDP

P = inflation – year on year percentage change in retail prices index (RPI)

GDPpc = GDP per head in 1985 prices

Govt = a government dummy variable (1 for Conservative, 0 for Labour)

PrI = private investment as a percentage of GDP

U = number unemployed as a percentage of labour force

W = government welfare expenditure: non–defence government current expenditure, (excluding transfer payments such as social security) as a percentage of GDP

Def R&D = expenditure on defence research and
development, as a percentage of GDP
Def Oth = defence expenditure other than research and
development as a percentage of GDP
Civ R&D = government civil research and development
expenditure as a percentage of GDP

Trend: annual trend (1960 = 1)
Lags: Def R&D(1), for example, is 1960 defence research
and development with other data for 1961

The data relate to the period 1960–87, except for equations incorporating research and development for which the earliest year is 1961. As it is the relative size of military expenditure and other variables which is being examined the variables are expressed as shares of gross domestic product (GDP) in percentage form. Growth rates and prices are annual percentage changes, and unemployment is a percentage share of the labour force. The use of shares and percentage changes also helps to reduce distortions due to price changes. However, care is necessary to ensure that explanatory variables expressed as shares do not account for all of GDP by definition, for example by including only one component of GDP in each equation.

Growth is included in the equations as an alternative to crowding out as a source of resources for defence spending – a higher growth rate would enable more to be spent in absolute terms on both defence and welfare. If governments are assumed to seek a certain level of defence spending, then the share of GDP taken by military expenditure may be expected to fall, and the trade–off between defence and other spending to weaken as growth rates rise. The level of military expenditure may reflect the level of prosperity in the country, with the opportunity to pursue an international role, and hence a desire for higher military expenditure, increasing with prosperity. GDP *per capita* is included as an indicator of prosperity, with the expectation of a positive relationship with military spending. The tendency to pursue strategic power may also reflect the views of the government in power (Hartley and McLean, 1978), indicated by the government dummy (1 = Conservative administrations, 0 = Labour). Inflation and unemployment are used as macro indicators of expectations and variations in capacity utilisation.

The association between military spending and other categories of consumption can be assessed more directly by the correlation coefficients presented in Table 5.1. Military share of GDP is negatively associated with the investment, NHS, education and welfare variables but positively correlated with consumption. The possibility thus exists that defence spending crowds out other items of government expenditure and investment. Consumption also has negative correlations with investment, health, education and welfare variables, again raising the possibility of crowding out, but this time by consumption rather than military spending.

Table 5.1

Correlation coefficients showing associations between military and other expenditure*

	M	I	PrI	NHS	Ed	W	Cons
M	–						
I	−0.36	–					
PrI	−0.68	−0.20	–				
NHS	−0.67	−0.17	0.81	–			
Ed	−0.81	0.39	0.44	0.73	–		
W	−0.70	−0.11	0.78	0.98	0.77	–	
Cons	0.83	−0.13	−0.67	−0.82	−0.78	−0.83	–

* Data are UK time series 1960 to 1987

The correlations between investment and all the consumption variables (M, NHS, Ed, W, Cons) are weak, and all but education are negative. When private investment is substituted for total investment a stronger association is found. The coefficients for NHS and welfare are both positive (these two variables are strongly associated with each other, as might be expected from the fact that health spending forms a large part of the total welfare measure). Military and private consumption are also correlated with private investment, but this time with a negative relationship, raising the possibility of crowding out.

Previous studies have used a variety of regression equations to consider the effect of military spending on investment and hence on the growth rate. This analysis focuses on an empirical reassessment of these approaches without discussing the conceptual framework which lies behind them. Equation 1 in Table 5.2 explains military expenditure in terms of the variables used in Smith (1977). The investment share of GDP is explained in terms of military share, growth (resource availability), unemployment (cyclical constraint) and GDP *per capita* (strategic power objectives). The equation was proposed by Smith to test for the presence of a systematic pattern between nations in the transfer of resources between military expenditure and other categories of final demand (Smith, 1977, p. 71). For time–series analysis of an individual country the equation needs to be modified. Both growth and unemployment indicate the availability of resources in the economy. In addition, there is an intuitive sense of error in including both growth and level of GDP in the equation. Dropping the insignificant term for growth and introducing a political variable (the government dummy) results in equation 2 in Table 5.2.

This equation has a better fit (higher R^2) and slightly improved Durbin Watson statistic. All the terms are now significant, although military share is only significant at the ten per cent level. Again, the coefficient is negative, suggesting crowding out may occur.

Table 5.2
The impact of military and other variables on investment
(using UK time series data, 1960–87)

Equation	Variables									Statistical tests		
	Const	M	NHS	Ed	Gr	U	GDP	GDPpc	Govt	R^2	Adj R^2	DW
(1)	+	−			−	−*		+*		0.82	0.79	1.04
(2)	+	−				−*			−*	0.86	0.84	1.29
(3)	+		+*			−*		+*	−*	0.88	0.86	1.13
(4)	+			+*		−*	+*		−*	0.93	0.92	2.11

* significant at five per cent level
The entry is each cell shows the sign and statistical significance of each explanatory variable in equations which have I as their dependent variable. The R^2 test is a measure of how much the variation in investment is explained by the variables in the equation. Adjusting for degrees of freedom gives adjusted R^2 (adj.R^2). The Durbin Watson test (DW) shows whether there is any association between the independent variables. A value of 2 indicates independence.

An indication of whether military spending has a unique impact on investment can be obtained by replacing the term for military spending with NHS or education (equations 3 and 4 respectively). These equations have better explanatory power (higher R^2) than the equation with military share (equation 2) and all terms significant at the five per cent level. Interestingly, whereas the coefficient for military share is negative, those for both NHS and education are positive. All other terms have the same sign. These results suggest that military spending may reduce investment and hence growth, leading to fewer resources being available for all categories of consumption in the future.

The relationship between military expenditure and welfare may be less direct than the above assessment suggests. The literature suggests that military expenditure is qualitatively different from other forms of expenditure, in particular through the high research and development content of defence spending.

Military research and development and growth

In recent years the debate about the economic impact of defence expenditure has increasingly focused on the consequences of military research and development (R&D). Much of the discussion has been conducted at the level of intuitive reasoning, and most commentators, regardless of their political presuppositions, have concluded that defence research and development 'crowds out' civil research and development and reduces the competitiveness of the UK economy. Kaldor, Sharp and Walker argued that civil research into high technology areas has been hampered by the 'absorption of a large proportion of the pool of skilled manpower by military R&D' (p. 31). Their concerns were echoed in the report on military research and development by the Council for Science and Society (CSS, 1986), which called for a thorough examination of the opportunity cost of defence research and development. The government admitted in its statement on the 1987 defence estimates that there was a danger that 'necessary defence R&D may crowd out valuable investment in the civil sector' (Statement on the Defence Estimates I, 1987, p. 48). The report from the 1989 Advisory Committee On Science and Technology on UK military research and development warned of the 'pre-emption of civil resources' and suggested that 'too large a part of industry's innovative management and financial capacity (has been) concentrated upon military technologies which have not provided companies with a competitive advantage ... in civil areas' (ACOST, 1989, p. 16).

Given the problems involved in obtaining accurate data on certain aspects of research and development, it is not altogether surprising that these hypotheses have not been subjected to satisfactory empirical testing. The most readily available international data on defence research and development expenditure at the aggregate level are provided by the Stockholm International Peace Research Institute (SIPRI). It is much more difficult to find reliable data on research and development spending at the industrial and firm levels, as Walker has shown in his study of statistical sources for the UK defence electronics sector (Walker, 1988). Data on the employment of research and development workers in defence research and development are not available, making it difficult to test the hypothesis that scientific labour is crowded out of civilian research. Although the government produces annual statistics on the public sector's civil research and development expenditure it is a major drawback that data on civil research and development financed by British industry are available only for every third

74

Table 5.3

The impact of research and development expenditure and other variables on investment (using U.K. time series data, 1961–87)

Military research and development

Equation	Constant	W	DefR&D	Gr	P	U	Def Oth	GDP	GDPpc	Gcvt	T	R^2	$AdjR^2$	DW
(5)	+	*–	*–	+	*+	*–			*+			0.88	0.86	1.47
(6)	+		*–	+		*–		*+		*–		0.87	0.85	1.08
(7)	+	*–	*+ Lag=1 –*	–			*–				*+	0.91	0.88	1.40
(8)	+	*–	*– Lag=6 –*	–			*–				*+	0.94	0.92	1.42
(9)	+	*–	*– Lag=7	–			*–				*+	0.92	0.89	1.50

Civil research and development

Equation	Constant	W	CivR&D	Gr	D	T	R^2	$AdjR^2$	DW
(10)	+	–	*–	–	*–	+	0.91	0.88	1.54
(11)	+	*–	+ Lag=4	–	–	*+	0.91	0.89	1.22
(12)	+	*–	*+ Lag=5	–	*–	*+	0.94	0.92	1.70

* significant at five per cent level.

The entries in each cell are derived as explained under Table 5.2, and statistical tests used are the same.

year. Moreover, it should be borne in mind that there is no unambiguous definition of research and development. It would not be unreasonable to argue that much of the work which is regarded as 'development' ought to be reallocated to production costs. Given these substantial constraints, the following analysis concentrates on aggregate government military and civil research and development.

Table 5.3 presents equations relating investment and growth to military expenditure and other variables. The equations in the following sections are estimated using data for 1961–87, against the period of 1960–87 for the results in Tables 5.1 and 5.2.

The first equation in Table 5.3 (equation 5) explains investment share in terms of defence research and development, growth, prices, unemployment and GDP per capita. The coefficients of defence research and development, prices, unemployment and GDP per capita are significant at the five per cent level. Defence research and development has a negative coefficient, consistent with the military expenditure results. However, unlike the coefficient of military share in equation 1, the coefficient of defence research and development in equation 5 is significant at the five per cent level. An equation incorporating the government dummy variable (equation 6) also has a negative and significant coefficient for defence research and development, but with a low Durbin Watson statistic. This equation is very similar to the equation incorporating military share and a government dummy (equation 2).

It might be suggested that defence research and development spending takes several years to have an impact on the investment share, since research projects tend to have a long gestation period, which is considerably lengthened by the succeeding development phase, and the need to transfer technology between the military and civil sectors. Equations 7 to 9 have defence research and development lagged by periods from one to seven years. The number of observations limit the length of lag that can be considered. Results are shown for lags of one, six and seven years, the only years in which the defence research and development variable is significant. In the sixth and seventh year the defence research and development variable is negatively related to investment share in the UK. If the relationship is causal, this evidence offers some support for the crowding out hypothesis. Also, the coefficient of other defence spending is significant and negative throughout (equations 7–9).

Equations 10–12 substitute government civil research and development for defence research and development. With lags of four and five years government civil research and development is positively and significantly related to investment share, although the Durbin Watson statistics are indeterminate. When civil research and development is lagged the coefficient becomes positive (equations 11 and 12), unlike military research and development which remains negative (equations 7–9).

76

Table 5.4
International comparisons of the determinants of investment

Country	Years	Const	W	Def R&D	Def Oth	Gr	T	R^2	Adj R^2	DW
UK	1961–1987	+	−*	+*	−*	−	+	0.93	0.91	1.53
USA	1963–1985	+	−	−	−*	+	+	0.72	0.63	1.33
France	1963–1985	+	−*	+	−	−	+	0.43	0.26	2.74
WG	1963–1985	+	−*	−*	−*	−	−	0.88	0.84	1.92
Japan	1963–1985	+	−*	−	+	−	−*	0.82	0.76	1.67
NL	1963–1985	+	−	+	−	+	−*	0.82	0.76	1.29

* significant at the 5 per cent level.
WG = West Germany; NL = Netherlands

Questions arise as to whether the defence relationships estimated for the UK apply to other nations. Here, a model based on Fagerberg (1988) was used to look at some of the possible determinants of the share of investment in GDP for a number of countries (equations 14–18 in Table 5.4). Contrary to expectations, in the Fagerberg formulation the defence research and development variable for the UK is positively and significantly related to the investment share, while the series 'other defence expenditure' is negatively related to the investment share. A possible causal relationship involves UK military research and development generating substantial technological spillovers for the rest of the economy. Such a conclusion would be somewhat premature. Firstly, the Durbin Watson statistic for the UK is in the indeterminate range. Secondly, running the same equation for five other countries over a slightly different period (due to data difficulties) produces only one further country, West Germany, which has a significant defence research and development variable, and this has the opposite sign to the UK variable. It would appear that the results are highly sensitive to the selection of countries and to the selection of the other variables in the equation. A different investment share equation for the UK generates a negative but insignificant defence research and development variable. The sensitivity of the results to the form of the equation and to the data used suggests that caution should be exercised in drawing conclusions from such analysis.

Conclusion

As with previous analysis of the relationship between defence spending and economic performance, there is no convincing evidence that military expenditure has a marked effect on investment and hence growth, whether positive or negative. Extending the analysis to the less direct impact through research and development variables does not alter the picture, although the serious data problems must be acknowledged. The most likely interpretation of the results is that both military expenditure and the welfare variable are influenced by other factors including cycles, government priorities, the performance of the economy, the perceived security threat and the age and size of the population.

It has been suggested that military expenditure has a more significant and negative effect on investment than that of welfare (Fagerberg, 1988, p 362). Our results in Table 5.2 suggest that military expenditure has a negative impact on investment whereas both NHS and education have a positive relationship. Where welfare and defence are included in the same equation (Table 5.3) the impact of welfare spending and other (non–research and development) defence spending is negative, with defence having the larger effect. Defence research and development has a positive impact in the first year, but negative in subsequent years. Again, the impact is larger than that of welfare.

The analysis presented in this paper has extended the approach adopted in previous studies to include measures of welfare expenditure and by considering the impact of research and development expenditure rather than defence as a whole. The results do not provide conclusive evidence to either support or refute the crowding out hypothesis. The possibility remains that the mechanism linking military expenditure and other economic variables is not a simple causal relationship. The analysis needs to be extended to incorporate defence and other spending into a properly specified economic model which can then be subjected to rigorous empirical testing.

References

ACOST (1989), *Defence R&D: A National Resource*, Cabinet Office, London.

Adams, G. and Gold, D.A. (1987), 'The economics of military spending: is the military dollar really different?', in Schmidt, C. and Blackaby, F. (eds), *Peace, Defense and Economic Analysis*, Macmillan, London.

Benoit, E. (1973), *Defense and Economic Growth in Developing Countries*, Lexington Books, Massachusetts.

Benoit, E. (1978), 'Growth and defense in developing countries', *Economic Development and Cultural Change*, vol. 26, no. 2, pp. 271–80.

Chalmers, M. (1985), *Paying for Defence: Military Spending and British Decline*, Longwood, London.

Chester, E. (1978), 'Military spending and capitalist stability', *Cambridge Journal of Economics*, vol. 2, no. 3. pp 293–9.

CSS (1986), *UK Military R&D*, Council for Science and Society, Oxford University Press, Oxford.

Fagerberg, J. (1988), 'International competitiveness', *Economic Journal*, vol. 98, pp. 355–74.

Greenwood, D. (1987), Note on the impact of military expenditure on economic growth, in Schmidt, C. (ed.), *The Economics of Military Expenditure: Military Expenditures, Economic Growth and Fluctuations*, Macmillan, London.

Grobar, L. M. and Porter, R. C. (1989), 'Benoit revisited: defense spending and economic growth in LDC's', *Journal of Conflict Resolution*, vol. 33, no. 2, pp. 318–45.

De Haan, H. (1987), 'Military expenditure and economic growth', in Schmidt, C. (ed.), *The Economics of Military Expenditures*, Macmillan, London.

Hartley, K. and McLean, P. (1978), 'Military expenditure and capitalism: a comment', *Cambridge Journal of Economics*, vol. 2, no. 3, pp. 287–93.

Kaldor, M., Sharp, M. and Walker, W. (1986), 'Industrial competitiveness and Britain's defence', *LLoyds Bank Review*, vol. 162, pp. 31–49.

Kirby, S. and Hooper, N. (1991), *The Cost of Peace: Assessing Europe's Security Options*, Harwood Academic Press, Reading.

Russett, B. M. (1970), *What Price Vigilance? The Burdens of National Defense*, Yale University Press, New Haven and London.

Smith, D. and Smith, R. P. (1983), *The Economics of Militarism*, Pluto, London.

Smith, R. P. (1977), 'Military expenditure and capitalism', *Cambridge Journal of Economics*, vol. 1, no. 1, pp. 61–76.

Walker, W. (1988), *UK Defence Electronics: A Review of Government Statistics*, ESRC, London.

6 Home ownership, wealth and welfare: New connections

S.G. Lowe

In the 1980s Britain matured as a nation of home owners. On average nearly 70 per cent of households now live in owner occupied dwellings compared to about 30 per cent in 1950. Over the last four decades owner occupation has grown steadily by about one per cent per annum relative to the rental sectors. But the distribution of home ownership by social class, age and geography is very uneven and this has led some scholars to argue that the impact on society as a whole of this change is limited. Because it is so numerically dominant home ownership, so it is argued, simply reflects the heterogeneity of modern society as a whole (Forrest, Murie and Williams, 1991). This chapter argues, on the contrary, that the changing pattern of housing tenure is itself the source of fundamental changes in the nature of our society. There are two strands to this argument. Firstly, the potential over the last two decades to accumulate capital through home ownership and for these assets to become available for spending has accelerated rapidly. The new affluence of the home owning society is more equally spread within the social structure of the nation and this is a trend which will strengthen in the next few decades. The second strand concerns the impact that the creation of a nation of home owners has had on people's access to welfare services and more fundamentally on the nature of the welfare state. The era of privatisation of services and welfare restructuring are closely connected to the rise of home ownership. This can be demonstrated empirically, particularly in relation to services for elderly people, and in relation to comparisons between societies with and without high levels of owner occupation (Kemeny, 1981; 1991).

The protracted growth of home ownership in Britain is closely connected to the conditions in which public services have come under pressure and private forms of welfare have become more prominent. The reasons for this are complex but are to do partly with a new link that has been created between individual households and the wider macro–economy arising from housing wealth, and partly with the more individualised nature of a society of property owners. The emphasis in this chapter is on the former issue. The chapter describes the growth of housing as a form of popular investment from the early 1960s and focuses on the more recent advent of equity withdrawal, the process by which housing assets can become 'spendable'.

Housing as an investment

Households are increasingly able to use housing to accumulate capital and to make this capital spendable through the process of equity withdrawal. It is now widely accepted that home ownership creates 'real' capital gains, although how this gain is measured and its social and geographical distribution are complex. This section outlines the key variables involved and suggests that several of the academic orthodoxies have become very questionable.

A major inflationary trend in house prices developed in the early 1960s and it is from this period that the rates of capital gain accelerated dramatically. Average house prices rose in the 20 years between 1970 and 1990 from £5,000 to £65,000, an increase of 1,200 per cent. The reasons for this relate to problems of demand and supply in the housing market, inflation in land prices, growing real incomes, and interest rate instability from the early 1960s onwards (Holmans, 1986). Two important policy decisions in the early 1960s also had an impact on the housing market. First, the abolition in 1963 of the schedule 'A' taxation of owner occupiers (the tax on the imputed rental income of home owners) in the context of the continuation of mortgage interest tax relief effectively created an incentive to home owners to use their housing as an investment. Secondly, in 1964 the Labour government exempted profits from the sale of first homes from capital gains taxation, further underpinning home ownership as an investment. What were in effect large scale state subsidies to owner occupiers became capitalised into house prices.

The measurement of capital gain through home ownership depends on a variety of assumptions which have to take into account the costs of owning and transacting a house sale as well as the tax advantages. Table 6.1 shows a number of calculations of the investment return on owner occupied dwellings from the 1960s using different assumptions and also compares the rate of return with other types of investment. The first line shows the simple average annual increase in house prices, including an adjustment for exemption from capital gains tax. The second line shows the rate of return including transaction costs (estate agents' fees, stamp duty etc.) and gross repayments of a mortgage calculated on a 25 year repayment period. The third line shows the net rate of gain including an adjustment for mortgage interest tax relief.

Table 6.1
Rate of return from owner occupied dwellings

Measures of capital gain in owner occupied housing	Date of purchase				
	1960 %	1965 %	1970 %	1975 %	1980 %
Annual house price change to 1985	11	12	14	12	9
Average gross return on a house sold in 1985*	12	13	15	11	−1
Average net return on a house sold in 1985*	13	14	17	15	5
Other investments to 1985					
Building society ordinary shares	9	10	11	12	11
Tax free national savings	6	7	8	9	9
Gold	13	17	23	17	6
FT ordinary shares	5	6	8	12	19
Retail prices index	9	10	11	10	7

* indicates that the house was bought with a 25 year repayment mortgage.

Source: Nationwide Anglia Building Society, Bulletin, April 1985.

The table shows that with the exception of the short term (that is, houses bought less than five years ago) buying a house with a mortgage provides a good annual rate of return which usually exceeds the retail prices index and compared with other forms of investment is outperformed only by gold which is not a commonly used type of investment. The short term loss is mainly a function of transaction costs. The figures deliberately do not include the data on the recent boom and slump cycle from the late 1980s because it is intended here to show the long run trend rather than the short term changes, given that house prices are notoriously unstable.

The early 1960s was an important period in the development of home ownership because at this time it became a source of very considerable capital gain mainly due to rapid house price inflation. Previously house prices had risen slowly, more or less in line with general inflation. As we have seen, the acceleration in house prices was considerably stimulated by policy decisions, and saw the emergence of an all–party consensus on the primacy of owner occupation. Not only were home owners nearly a majority of the electorate at that time, and an outright majority in many constituencies in the south of England, but the development of the notion of housing as a source of investment gain became a key part of the state ideological structure that promoted the further expansion of home owning. A political trade–off between the increasingly powerful electoral base represented by home owners and the escalating cost of the highly regressive and increasingly inequitable tax concessions cemented home ownership into the fabric of the social, economic and political structure. From this period onwards the expansion of the tenure and the notion of home ownership as a source of investment gain have been closely connected.

A particularly important change took place in the early 1980s as a result of the liberalisation of the financial markets. The growth in capital accumulation in housing had been rapid and continuous since the 1960s, but due to major structural changes in the financial markets the accumulated equity became more spendable in the 1980s through the process of equity withdrawal, discussed in detail in a later section. A crucial connection was made, therefore, between individual households' housing wealth and the macro–economy. This link resulted from two closely related features of the financial structure that underpinned owner occupation in this period. Firstly, rapid house price inflation had decreased the outstanding mortgage debt relative to the current value of the house. For most people income also increased so that the cost of owning the increasingly valuable housing asset diminished. Secondly, the amount of mortgage finance available increased dramatically in the early 1980s as a result of the liberalisation of the money markets. More, and more readily available, mortgage finance made access to home ownership easier.

The abundance of mortgage finance was also the key to the growth of massive scale equity withdrawal from housing described later in the chapter. The next section describes the changes in the mortgage industry at this time because they are central to the growing impact of owner occupation on the macro–economy and also to the social policy issues arising from the advent of Britain as a nation of home owners.

The liberalisation of the financial markets

In the 1970s and more so in the 1980s the major banks needed to diversify their interests as a response to the general decline in the British economy. One approach was to rebuild their base in the personal lending market, including mortgage finance. For most of the post–war period building societies had been the major source of mortgages. But in the early 1980s the banks' share of the mortgage market surged, peaking at 40 per cent of new lending, and has subsequently settled down to about 20 per cent. The volume of money available for mortgages greatly increased as a result of this development. Changes in the financial regulations in the early 1980s allowed the building societies to generate more of their funds from the wholesale money markets, and for quite long periods of time it was cheaper to buy money in this way than to raise it through their retail activities (principally over the counter from small investors). This also increased credit for home purchase, ending the queues for mortgages and allowing the lenders to increase the size of the loans available to customers.

In addition, during the 1980s, a series of new lenders entered the market, often backed by overseas money or insurance interests. These new lenders operated very distinctive methods of funding and servicing mortgages, which can be most closely linked to the mortgage market in the USA. There the processes of originating, financing and servicing the mortgage are undertaken by different companies, unlike the typical British building society which carries out all three functions. In a highly competitive market the institutions with the best specialist knowledge in each of the three main areas of mortgage financing (originating, financing and servicing) are likely to be most successful, and not necessarily the traditional building society covering only moderately well all three activities.

The growth of the 'secondary' mortgage market arising from the recognition of this potential has been a major change in the structure of British housing finance in the 1980s. During 1985 and 1986 at least five new mortgage lenders were established, all raising their funds from the wholesale markets. Since then they have captured 10–15 per cent of the market, especially at the more expensive end of the mortgage range. British mortgage lending is an exceptionally secure form of investment, backed by the value of the property and by the borrower's income. Even in a slump in the housing market the companies are secure because borrowers of more than 80 per cent of the value of the property have to buy a one–off insurance premium for the outstanding amount. In addition the social security system supports borrowers by paying the interest on outstanding mortgages after the first 16 weeks of unemployment, during which time income support pays 50 per cent of the interest. Despite the rapid increase in mortgage default and arrears during 1991 the building societies and banks can easily absorb losses that may be incurred.

The mortgage market is now almost unrecognizable from the days when building societies were almost the only actors on the stage of house purchase. In order to compete the societies themselves have had to diversify their activities into mainstream banking and several major lenders have found it necessary to keep control of the origination function by opening chains of estate agencies. The rapid growth of endowment mortgages has allowed them to generate new finance from insurance company commissions, and this form of mortgage currently accounts for over 75 per cent of all new lending. Financial liberalisation and the new competitive environment in the mortgage industry created conditions in which the supply of mortgage backed credit has been superabundant. The new affluence generated through home ownership has been entirely dependent on these changes in the mortgage industry. The next section shows how mortgage finance combined with the growth in the value of housing assets to create circumstances in which housing equity can be 'leaked' into the economy.

Equity withdrawal from the housing market

Muellbauer observes, '... not only did financial liberalisation help drive up house prices but it made housing wealth more spendable than ever before' (Muellbauer, 1990, p. 5). The main way in which this spending occurs is through the process of equity withdrawal and a number of associated forms of borrowing, notably the increasing trend for households to remortgage their house (that is, to increase their mortgage by topping up an existing loan or paying off an existing debt and taking on a new and higher one due to the increase in the value of the property). Equity withdrawal from housing occurs when part of the asset value of the property is replaced by new borrowing, thus spendable cash is generated. There are a variety of circumstances when this occurs, but the two largest sources are the proceeds arising from house purchase transactions, typically when an existing home owner retains some of the proceeds from selling the house and taking a bigger mortgage upon moving to the next property, and secondly, from housing inheritances. Here the proceeds of the sale are distributed to the beneficiaries while the new lending is incurred by the purchasers. Similarly outright owners can move and buy a cheaper house without themselves incurring any mortgage debt. This is quite typical of what happens during a move associated with retirement from work.

There have been various attempts to calculate the level of equity withdrawal, most recently by Carruth and Henley (1990). Using various assumptions they focus particularly on equity withdrawal by movers, showing that with about 15 per cent of the total owner occupied housing stock being traded in 1988, with an average rate of equity withdrawal of 12 per cent then consumer spending increased by about £12 billion in that year. The best estimates are those made by A.E. Holmans, Chief Economic Adviser in the Department of the Environment. He examined all the main sources of equity extraction, including sales of rented accommodation by local authorities and by private landlords (Holmans, 1986). Holmans' estimates were for the period from 1977 to 1984. Results of calculations based on a reworking of his figures but using more recent accounting identities are shown in Table 6.2. This compares the two major categories involved, inheritors and movers with mortgages and shows a net equity withdrawal from those sources of some £16 billion in 1988 alone, and in the five years between 1984 and 1988 a total in excess of £53 billion.

Table 6.2
Equity withdrawal by inheritors and movers with mortgages

	1982	1983	1984	1985	1986	1987	1988
Inheritors	2,988	2,998	3,965	3,562	4,304	5,545	5,545
Movers	3,393	4,780	4,165	4,552	4,905	6,621	10,088
Total	6,381	7,778	8,130	8,114	9,209	12,166	15,633

Source: Lowe and Watson, 1989.

Housing inheritance has been the focus of several major studies, and a whole book devoted to the evaluation of this type of equity withdrawal has recently been published (Hamnett, Harmer and Williams, 1991). This issue is certainly very important but the main impact of housing inheritance is likely to occur after the year 2000. This is due to the facts that, as Table 6.3 shows, home owning is not yet the majority tenure of the over–60s and that it is among the younger age groups that owner occupation is most densely concentrated and has grown most rapidly during the 1980s.

After the age of 60 the rate of home ownership is inversely related to increasing age. It is clear that over the next 20 years or so owner occupation among the elderly will increase markedly. In their study Hamnett et al. argue against the notion that money from housing inheritances is equalising the pattern of wealth distribution by showing that people in the higher social classes are four times more likely to inherit such money than households in the manual worker strata. But given the age distribution of owner occupation and the rapid increase in home owning among middle aged people over the last 20 years this result largely arises from its historical context. They do not rule out the possibility that there might be a greater degree of filtering down in the future. For example, other things being equal, new wealth will be enjoyed by the beneficiaries of the one and a half million council tenants who bought their house during the 1980s under the 'right to buy' legislation. A very high proportion of these people were skilled manual workers.

Table 6.3
Proportion of owner occupiers among heads of
households by age in 1971 and 1986

Age of head of household	1971	1986	Increase
	%	%	%
24 or under	31	35	13
25–29	52	65	25
30–44	56	73	30
45–59	48	70	46
60–69	48	56	17
70–79	46	51	11
80 or over	43	45	5

Source: General Household Survey, 1971; 1986.

As can be seen from Table 6.2 in the period from 1984 to 1988 movers with mortgages accounted for the biggest share of equity withdrawn (Lowe, 1990). The figures demonstrate the very large magnitude of equity being extracted in the process of moving. They fluctuate more than the figures for housing inheritances because the number of transactions taking place reflects the state of the housing market at any one point in time. 1988 is clearly a boom year for the market, and the number of moves and the house price cycle have turned sharply downwards since then. A downturn in the cycle does not, however, imply that equity withdrawal stops and it certainly does not follow that the process goes into reverse and that equity is invested. Recent experience of the difficulty of controlling consumer spending suggests that in a slump there is no equivalent reduction in spending and increase in saving. The scale of equity withdrawal in a slump is likely to be affected only by the decline in the number of transactions taking place.

The uses of equity withdrawn from housing

One of the concerns about the growth of equity withdrawal from housing in the 1980s has been its impact on the macro–economy, particularly by stimulating consumption. The evidence from the inheritance studies and what little is currently known about movers suggests this impact is more muted than might have been expected in theory. The empirical findings of the study by Hamnett et al. concern the use made initially of the bequests. They show that 21 per cent of inheritors used most of their money on property related spending, either to buy (presumably paying off the mortgage) a first home, moving up–market or buying a second home. Six per cent used most of the money on home improvements. Nearly half the households put most of the cash into some form of financial investment; 27 per cent putting money into building society deposits, and the rest divided between banks, shares, unit trusts and other forms of investment. Only 24 per cent used most of their inheritance in general consumption; for holidays, car purchase and other consumer goods. Because this research shows only the first usage it is not possible to show the long term impact. It is clear, however, that a high proportion of housing wealth finds it way back into the savings market and is not used for consumption.

At the moment there is no reliable or systematic information about the uses to which equity extracted by moving households is put. It is probable that a considerable amount of this cash is spent on the furnishing and decoration of the new house, and there is limited evidence of this (OPCS, 1983). It seems unlikely that the same pattern of initial use shown by Hamnett et al. for inheritors will be replicated by movers who extract equity by increasing their borrowing. This money is much less likely even in the short term to find its way back into savings. Cash from last–time sales by elderly owners, who are a major category within the movers definition, is frequently used to pay for private sector residential care. There is also some evidence that equity withdrawn during a move is used to restructure debts (NCC, 1987; Berthoud and Kempson, 1991).

Home ownership and society

Capital accumulation through home ownership has created an expansion of wealth in society and through the process of equity withdrawal these assets are more easily available for consumption and underpin the financial security of millions of households. It is, however, very important to be clear about the distributional consequences of this new wealth. There are, for example, differences between equity released to the beneficiaries of housing inheritances and to movers. As we have seen Hamnett et al. suggest that housing inheritances do not at the moment serve to redistribute wealth in society. This is not likely to be the case with movers who are drawn from a much broader cross section of the population than the current beneficiaries of housing inheritances. As a wealth creator housing has grown from about 25 per cent of net disposable assets in 1960 to over 50 per cent at the end of the 1980s, reflecting the growing number of home owners relative to the other tenures and the increasing real value of housing equity.

There are two main interpretations about the distributional consequences of this in society as a whole. In their recent book about home ownership Forrest et al. argue that owner occupation in the late 1980s is socially heterogeneous and the experience of home owners in different parts of the country and sub–markets is very varied (Forrest et al., 1991). They show that the rate of capital accumulation is very diverse depending on region and particularly on the time at which the owner entered the housing market. It is clear from the earlier section in the chapter that this much is valid. But in the wider context there is a second and countervailing view of the development of the tenure.

A key point here is that the growth of home ownership in the last 20 years has been particularly rapid among skilled manual workers and this would suggest that relatively there has been a filtering down of housing wealth into the working classes. Owner occupation is no longer exclusively middle class (and it should be added, in some parts of the country, notably the north west and parts of Wales, it never was). Saunders' study of home owners in three towns in England concludes that manual worker owner occupiers made rates of gain in the accumulation of value in their property at a similar rate to all home owners (Saunders, 1990). Of course it is the case that owners of more expensive houses in some parts of the country will gain in absolute value more, and at certain points in time may even have lost, but the fact that there are variations and differences does not invalidate a reasonable generalisation. As Saunders suggests, while all owners are clearly not in the same position, it is nevertheless possible '... to generalise about the experience of the great majority of owners who do make substantial sums as a result of purchasing their housing' (Saunders, 1991 p. 145).

Table 6.4 shows that in the late 1980s the major social divide based on tenure occurs *within* the manual worker strata. Nearly two–thirds of skilled manual workers are home owners compared to less than 30 per cent of unskilled workers and are thus more closely aligned to the middle classes as owners rather than renters of housing. The table also shows that comparing the early 1970s with the mid–1980s the greatest rate of increase in home ownership was among the manual social strata with the largest change occurring among skilled manual worker households.

The significance of this is that in general terms the skilled manual worker social strata are through their housing increasing their disposable assets and in this respect are more closely aligned with the non–manual social groups. The patterns of gains and losses clearly are very complex. An old terraced house in the south east of England owned by a manual worker may have far greater monetary value than a large modern detached house owned by a professional household in the north. By the same token the fact that the main division of the nation by tenure occurs within the manual worker social strata also highlights a major structural change to society arising from this pattern of growth of home owning among skilled manual workers in recent years. The social and economic 'residualisation' of council housing is well documented (see Forrest and Murie, 1988 for the most comprehensive overview) and it is apparent that this largely manual worker social base is increasingly pauperised. The advent of a housing tenure division between a relatively affluent body of home owners and a state dependent minority of tenants in social rented housing may be as important a measure of real living standards as any general social stratification based on occupation or income since 1945.

Table 6.4
Tenure of household by socio–economic group

	1973		1980		1986		percentage change of owner occupiers 1973–86
	00 %	T %	00 %	T %	00 %	T %	
Professional	81	19	85	15	90	10	11.1
Employers/managers	77	23	82	18	83	17	7.8
Intermediate	58	42	73	27	68	32	17.2
Skilled manual	46	54	54	46	63	37	45.7
Semi–skilled manual	30	70	37	63	39	61	30.0
Unskilled manual	23	77	28	72	29	71	26.0
All heads of households	49	51	54	46	63	37	28.6

Note: OO – owner occupier; T – tenant
Source: General Household Survey, 1973; 1980; 1986.

This is not to suggest, as has been made clear already, that all owner occupiers gain. Indeed, some lose both through limited opportunities to move and as a result of the declining value of their property. The recent increases in the scale of mortgage repossessions and arrears can be cited as a major social issue arising from the exigencies of home owning. In the long run, however, the number of households involved in repossession is tiny relative to the vast majority of home owners with mortgages. The problem is partly a function of the house price cycle (when people buy into the market or trade up in a boom period, only to find the value of the property declining during the trough) and does not invalidate the general picture of widespread financial gain experienced in the last two decades by the majority of owners.

The growing quantities of wealth accumulated in home ownership and its potential as a source of investment gain has in the course of the last three decades underpinned the continuous expansion of the tenure relative to the rental sectors. Moreover, the long term processes associated with capital accumulation through owner occupation, far from merely reflecting the greater diversity of experiences of home ownership, have had irreversible impact on the core social structure of the nation.

Home ownership and the welfare state

The second and closely related consequence of the growth of home ownership over the last two decades within the dominant notion of housing as an investment is the effect it has had on the structuring and restructuring of the welfare state. The social cleavage between owners and tenants may be intensified if the resources available through home ownership are utilised in provisioning private welfare. There are several examples of new large scale private services which are directly related to the increasing capital value of owner occupied dwellings. A very large proportion of the cash from last-time sales by elderly owners has been used to underpin the rapid expansion of private sector residential care and nursing homes. Moving into private sheltered housing has also become increasingly common in the last five years. From the initial ideas of the developers Macarthy and Stone for cheap retirement homes, there is now a diverse range of products from retirement homes for early retired 'empty nesters' to supervised accommodation for frail elderly people, all based on the ability of owner occupiers to utilise their housing equity. Some 60,000 units of private sector sheltered housing have been built in the last five years or so. Equity is often leaked during moves to private sheltered housing and helps to provide a nest egg for future use, although it may be consumed by service charges (Williams, 1986; Oldman, 1990).

Another growing source of spendable cash are the annuities and interest only loans available to elderly owner occupiers to enhance their income or pay for housing repairs. There have been a number of problems with such schemes, particularly the cost of paying the interest (Leather and Wheeler, 1988). But new products now enable the borrower to 'roll up' the interest into the debt which is paid off when the property is eventually sold. The package offered by the Nationwide Anglia building society allows a loan based on 15 per cent of the value of the house and guarantees that at least 25 per cent of the value of the property will revert to beneficiaries on sale. In the provision for elderly people in particular there is a direct connection between the growth of some forms of private service provision and the use of capital accumulated in housing.

However, in terms of the debate about the nature of welfare provision a more important point than direct evidence of how housing equity withdrawal is spent is the relationship of the growth of home ownership to the ideologies of welfare. Kemeny's comparison of Sweden, Australia and Britain and his exploration of comparative social theory reveals for the first time the intimate connection between individualised and collectivised forms of housing provision and the stability or fragility of welfare states (Kemeny, 1991). In Britain the growth of home ownership has been accompanied by a gradual destabilisation of public welfare, and the two things are highly contingent.

The point here is that home owning is an individualistic way of satisfying housing needs and coupled with the evidence of capital gain and large scale equity withdrawal creates the conditions in which the privatisation of welfare provision is more easily accomplished. Home ownership is a source of wealth for millions of households, and increasingly so for skilled manual workers. This filtering down of new resources may broaden the choices available to these people. It may make it possible for households to buy private services, or at least give them the option of choosing private provision if the public sector is not satisfactory. As the examples above show, particularly in relation to elderly people, important services have developed in the 1980s which are dependent on using housing equity. To the extent that home ownership makes these new services available then tenants, without command over such resources, are disadvantaged. Home ownership has become in the 1980s a major source of wealth and may increasingly influence the ways in which households can defend or satisfy their welfare needs. The privatisation of welfare is connected, therefore, to the growth of home ownership. Moreover, whether for good or ill, it is in the private domain of the owner occupied dwelling that the values of privatism are nurtured.

References

Berthoud, R. and Kempson, E. (1991), *Credit and Debt in Britain. First Findings from the PSI Survey*, Policy Studies Institute, London.

Carruth, A. and Henley, A. (1990), 'Spending and saving, and the housing market' in *Economic Review*, September, pp. 16–20.

Forrest, R. and Murie, A. (1988), *Selling the Welfare State: The Privatisation of Public Housing*, Routledge and Kegan Paul, London.

Forrest, R., Murie, A. and Williams, P. (1991), *Home Ownership: Differentiation and Fragmentation*, Unwin Hyman, London.

Hamnett, C., Harmer, M. and Williams, P. (1991), *Safe as Houses: Housing Inheritance in Britain*, Paul Chapman Publishing, London.

Holmans, A.E. (1986), *Housing Policy in Britain*, Croom Helm, London.

Kemeny, J. (1981), *The Myth of Home Ownership*, Routledge and Kegan Paul, London.

Kemeny, J. (1991), *Housing and Social Theory*, Routledge, London.

Leather, P. and Wheeler, R. (1988), *Making Use of Home Equity in Old Age*, Building Societies Association, London.

Lowe, S. and Watson, S. (1989), *From First-time Buyers to Last-time Sellers: Equity Withdrawal from the Housing Market 1982-1988*, Report to the Joseph Rowntree Memorial Trust, University of York.

Lowe, S. (1990), 'Capital accumulation in home ownership and family welfare'in Manning, N. and Ungerson, C. (eds), *Social Policy Review 1989-90*, Longman, Harlow.

Muellbauer, J. (1990), 'The great British housing disaster and economic policy', *Economic Study*, no. 5, pp. 1-28.

NCC (1987), *Security Risks: Personal Loans Secured on Homes*, National Consumer Council, London.

OPCS (1983), *Recently Moving Households*, HMSO, London.

Oldman, C. (1990), *Moving in Old Age: New Directions in Housing Policies*, HMSO, London.

Saunders, P. (1990), *A Nation of Home Owners*, Unwin Hyman, London.

Saunders, P. (1991), Review of Forrest et al. (op. cit.) in *Housing Studies*, vol. 6, no. 2, pp. 145-146.

Williams, G. (1986), *Meeting the Needs of the Elderly : Private Initiative or Public Responsibility?* Department of Town and Country Planning, Occasional Paper 17, University of Manchester.

7 Young people in the 1980s: New opportunities or new constraints?

S. Hutton

Introduction

Political, demographic and economic changes over the past three decades have altered the experience of young people making the transition from home and school to work and independence. Compared with the 1960s, there have been positive changes for young people which have led to wider ranges of options within family life and education. Economic changes, however, and the rise in unemployment among young people in particular, have introduced new constraints. This chapter discusses whether it has become more difficult to achieve financial and domestic independence. The first section describes the changes over the past thirty years in family life. The last two sections cover the transition from school to work, and the move from the parental home to an independent household.

Changing patterns of family life

As a result of changes in legislation and attitudes, a wider range of choices of family arrangements has become acceptable, including stable unmarried relationships, later marriages, and more frequent divorces. The role of young people within the family has changed: 'teenagers' have been discovered and have more say within the family. Smaller families and married women going out to work have become more usual. Thus most of the families that children grow up in now no longer fit the traditional mould of a male breadwinner, a housewife, and dependent children.

Changes in legislation and attitudes

The late 1960s and 1970s saw a battery of legislation relating to the family, marriage and sexual mores. The following are among the most influential in changing family life:

(i) the Family Planning Services Act 1967, which set up family planning clinics and made the oral contraceptive available through the NHS;

(ii) the Divorce Reform Act 1969, which made 'irreversible breakdown of marriage' grounds for divorce;

(iii) the Matrimonial and Family Proceedings Act 1984, which allowed couples to petition for divorce after one rather than three years.

The ability to control fertility, changing aspirations of women and changes in the law have all contributed. The oral contraceptive became widely available in the 1960s and reduced the risk of pregnancy to minimal levels. Halsey (1986) states, 'Virtually all can now choose the timing of their parenthood. This is as important a feature of social change as any I could mention' (p. 105).

This has clearly created opportunities, particularly for women. Women can now plan their families and take advantage of openings in the labour market. Until the late 1970s, the demand for women to work outside the home was high. The women's liberation movement was also important in initiating and demanding change within the family. Many more, mostly women, are bringing up children on their own now mainly because of marital breakdown. Thirty seven per cent of recent marriages will end in divorce and in 60 per cent of divorces there are dependent children who will generally remain with their mother (Haskey, 1989; Millar, 1988).

Effect on the family

In spite of the changes in legislation and attitudes, by the late 1970s, marriage was still popular, 95 per cent of women married at some time, and 30 per cent were married by the age of 20. Although there were differences between social groups in attitudes to sex and contraception, final family size and aspirations for family size were similar for all groups (Dunnell, 1979). The trend, however, is for women to be older when they marry.

Reduced hours of work since the 1960s, longer holidays, and owner occupation have meant that men spend more time at home with their wives than ever before, although there has been little reduction in the sexual division of labour. Women still tend to have responsibility for child care and housekeeping (Pahl, 1984). A study of newly–weds by Mansfield and Collard (1988) showed that a gendered division of labour, unequal resource allocation and differential control is part and parcel of the lives that 'modern' couples construct for themselves. Other evidence suggests, however, that marriage has become more equal (Allan, 1987).

Thus, despite the many changes in the law and increasingly liberal attitudes, the idea of marriage and the family remains remarkably intact. These changes have, however, widened the choice in family arrangements available to young people (see recent work by Kiernan and Wicks, 1990), and the constraints of early and untimed pregnancy and strict divorce laws have been removed. It should be easier now than in the 1960s for young people to find the sort of family life which suits them. While they are still in the parental home, however, life may be more constrained. Recent high levels of unemployment have meant added strain, the presence of an unemployed adolescent in the family can cause friction, and more so when the parent is also unemployed (Allan, 1987).

The transition from school to work

School is the first step to independence from the family. The changes in Britain's schools in the thirty years since the 1960s mean that those who left school in the 1980s will have come from a different background to those who left in the 1960s. New opportunities have arisen with the introduction of the comprehensive system after the 1970 Education Act, and the expansion of higher education. On the other hand, more young people are staying on in school to avoid the dole, and the motivation for education provided by the prospect of work has been eroded. Leaving school is the next stage in growing up, and this section discusses the routes from school to work. In the 1960s, the great majority of young people who did not continue in higher education went straight into work, but in the 1980s, only a minority made this transition directly. Difficulty in this transition was one of the main constraints for young people in the 1980s.

Demographic changes

Demographic change often underlies social change. The number of 16 year olds reached a peak of 932,000 in 1980–82 and will reach a trough of 620,000 in 1992–93. The effects of changing numbers depend on other circumstances and the context in which they occur. For example, the two increases in the numbers of 16–24 year olds in the early 1960s and late 1970s were regarded very differently in the light of current labour market conditions. The rising numbers of young people in the early 1960s were viewed as an affluent consumer group because of their access to earnings, and those of the late 1970s as a disturbing labour problem (Kiernan, 1986).

Changes in education

Partly as a response to rising youth unemployment, but also to create a better educated workforce to compete with foreign industry, the school leaving age was raised from 15 to 16 in 1973. The numbers staying on in education beyond the compulsory leaving age of 16 grew throughout the late 1970s as an alternative to unemployment. Girls were more likely to choose to stay on at school. By 1982, 25 per cent of 16–19 year olds were in school; six per cent in further education; four per cent in higher education; six per cent in government training schemes; and 42 per cent employed (Bradshaw, Lawton and Cooke, 1987). The peak (50 per cent) of 16 year olds staying on in education was reached in 1983; the subsequent decline is possibly associated with the greater availability of training schemes. By the late 1980s, however, Gray and Sime (1989) suggest that a considerable majority are still in some form of education or training until seventeen–plus.

The first concern, perhaps, was the problem of motivating older pupils in school as it became clear that education was highly likely to lead straight to the dole queue for many of them. Empirical evidence (Brown, 1987) suggested, however, that although many 'ordinary kids' do not conform to the school ethos, they are willing to make the effort to gain qualifications. They could not imagine that the future would not include work, and, having spent so much time in school, they felt they might as well have something to show for it.

The expansion of the universities and the polytechnics came after the Robbins Report of 1961, and in 1963 many colleges were upgraded to polytechnics. New universities, such as York, Sussex, Stirling and East Anglia were set up around this time. By the late 1970s, a likely long term downward trend in the numbers of 18 year olds coincided with the Conservative government's demands for reduced expenditure, so the expansion of higher education was halted. Although it is true that the number of 18 year olds was declining, the birthrate of those in social class

I and II has risen since the 1960s, so the group from which the universities traditionally draw students was not smaller. Also Britain sends a much lower proportion of its eighteen year olds into higher education than other European countries and North America. Thus it is debatable that this reduction in higher education was in response to a fall in demand (see Briggs, 1987; Marwick, 1982; Hill, 1983; Halsey, 1986). The expansion of higher education, although giving more opportunities than the 1960s, has not been as great as it might have been.

Effects of background on the move from school to work

Class and cultural background are dominant in deciding what happens to school leavers. Willis (1977) points out 'The difficult thing to explain about how middle class kids get middle class jobs is why others let them. The difficult thing to explain about how working class kids get working class jobs is why they let themselves' (p. 1). Other studies considered whether finding work depended on how far individuals thought it was up to them, to others or to chance (Banks, 1989). Thinking it was up to the individual was associated with academic success and finding work, whereas those who had been out of school longest were more likely to attribute success to chance. Of course, the state of the labour market also has a major influence on attitudes and routes into employment: attitudes in a more buoyant labour market were more conformist and committed to finding work than those in areas of high unemployment (Day, 1987).

Routes to employment

The government responded to youth unemployment with initiatives to raise the skills of young people. The Employment and Training Act of 1973 established the Manpower Services Commission. Although most initiatives were for adults, the Work Experience Programme (WEP) started in 1976, was replaced by the Youth Opportunities Programme (YOP) in 1978, and finally led to the creation of the Youth Training Scheme (YTS) in 1983. The common paths or 'trajectories' from school to work can be summarised as follows: academic; other educational; straight from school into work; two stages via YTS to work; unemployment; and other more complex routes (Roberts and Parsell, 1988). Analyses of the Youth Cohort Study (Courtenay, 1989) discuss in detail the routes into employment, either directly from school at age 16, or after staying on at school, or through the YTS, or after higher education. One of the controversial conclusions from this study was that YTS made little difference to chances of employment or to the kind of work obtained after taking account of the differences due to gender and qualifications. Staying on at school also did not greatly increase the likelihood of finding work, partly, it is claimed, because of employers' poor regard for lower grade academic qualifications (Raffe and Courtenay, 1988). Young people might be more likely to get work by going on the dole for a while rather than staying on at school although this choice is no longer available to 16 and 17 year olds. Work from the Economic and Social Research Council 16–19 Initiative also concludes that the best route into employment is straight from school with relatively high academic qualifications; YTS was little more successful than unemployment as a first step (Bynner, 1989; McGurk, 1988). Kiernan (1988) uses data from the 1981 Labour Force Survey to describe the transitions in young adulthood and, in particular, the transition from 'Education to Job' as part of a more complex set of changes. She notes that men and women make this transition at approximately the same age, but women subsequently move out of the labour market as they move through their twenties.

An integral part of the route to employment is the adjustment to the opportunities available in the labour market. For example, failure to get a job after participation on a YTS led to disillusion and depression. A common reaction, after being in work for a while, was the downward adjustment of aspirations, both about the type of work and the rate of pay (Bates, 1988; Main and Shelley, 1988). Wallace (1986) found that 'the stick' that finally beats young people into submission in seeking work is the long term reproduction of the domestic life cycle which is more obvious by the time young people have reached their twenties than at 16. By this time marriage and setting up home has led to a greater preparedness to accept what the young people in her survey described as 'shit jobs'. The most striking pattern she observed amongst her sample of school leavers on the Isle of Sheppey was the increasing divergence between those who had been regularly employed and were therefore able to accumulate possessions and purchase a home, and those who were excluded from this process through unemployment.

Thus those who made the smooth transition from school to work in the 1960s are likely to have been able to establish themselves more easily than their contemporaries in the 1980s. Even research undertaken during the economic revival suggests that the new routes into employment established in the early eighties have not fundamentally altered the prospects for young people. Staying in school and government training schemes are talked of in terms of 'warehousing' and 'cooling-out' aspirations (Roberts, Parsell and Siwek, 1989).

Leaving home

The age at which young people leave home is likely to be influenced by social and demographic circumstances, the availability of both suitable housing and an independent income either from employment or other sources. Before discussing the changes in the timing of leaving home and family formation, the availability of housing and support from the social security system is considered.

Housing

If young people are to leave the parental home, there must be other accommodation for them to go to. Fluctuations in house building and measures to encourage either owner occupation or, in the final years of the eighties, private renting, are the themes of changes in the housing market since the 1960s.

Changes in tenure At the beginning of the 1960s, the move to home ownership was under way, the Conservative government had committed themselves to building 300,000 new houses a year in 1951, mostly for owner occupation. From the 1950s to the 1970s both labour and conservative governments regarded state housing provision as residual, concerned with replacement and provision for the elderly. The 1970s saw reductions in public spending on housing (Leather, 1981). This decline can be dated back to 1975–76 as a lagged response to the 1973 oil shock (Rees, 1987). However, by 1977, there was no longer a national shortage of houses and the Tory government felt free to introduce measures which led to council house building being stopped in 1980. The present government has reduced the amount of local authority housing even further through sales to tenants. Sales of council houses peaked in 1982–83, and ten per cent have transferred into private ownership. The overall subsidy to housing has declined less than might otherwise appear, because of the transfer from capital funds to rebates as a result of legislation in the 1965 Rent Act which established fair rents, the 1967 Rating Act which introduced rates rebates and the 1973 Housing Finance Act which introduced rent rebates. Changing attitudes to subsidies for rents and rented accommodation has been a theme in the rented sector. The implications of changing patterns of leaving home for housing single, mobile young people are set out in recent work by Jones (1987). This study showed that young people from the middle classes were more likely to have an intermediate home with friends before marriage whereas the first home of those from a working class background was more likely to be with a partner. The need for suitable housing prior to establishing a family home was identified.

Thus, although there was a numerical surplus of houses, the accommodation available did not necessarily match well the households needing to be housed. First-time buyers have always been particularly vulnerable to changes in interest rates and house prices and the move to owner occupation meant a wider range of young people were affected.

Recent changes Rents for new lettings were deregulated in the 1988 Housing Act and the 'assured rent' was introduced. The policy aim is to move towards market rents to make letting more attractive financially, and increase the supply of rented accommodation. Housing associations are being asked to undertake a major role in social housing. The movement is concerned, however, that the discontinuation of fair rents will mean that many of their traditional tenants will no longer be able to afford the accommodation offered. Young single people fall into this category. They are particularly vulnerable both as a result of the changes in rent levels outlined above, and because of changes in social security benefits.

Unemployment was rising rapidly at the same time as it was claimed that the housing market moved into surplus. So, although accommodation was available, and fair rents and rebates were in place, lack of income and lack of appropriate accommodation led to the problems of homelessness which featured so prominently in the late seventies and eighties. In the 1977 Housing (Homeless Persons) Act local authorities were required to help priority categories of the homeless, but these excluded young, non–disabled, single people. Homelessness doubled over the past decade. Reports by Shelter and the National Association of Citizens Advice Bureaux (NACAB) describe cases of extreme hardship and destitution arising from the lack of housing and changes in benefit regulations (Pollit, 1989; NACAB, 1989).

Social security

In times of fluctuating labour markets, and changing family patterns the social security system can ameliorate some of the worst effects of these changes. If income from work is not available for a young person to use to set up their own home, how far does social security help?

Young people were among those most affected by the changes to the social security system in the 1988 Social Security Act. The government no longer considers it appropriate to provide benefit for fit young people who should be encouraged to take work even at low rates of pay. Benefit is lower for single young people under 25 years than other single claimants. Sixteen and 17 year olds cannot claim income support in their own right, except in some rather specialised circumstances, such as disabled young people, and, since July 1989, those who are estranged from their parents can claim at the same level as 18–25 year olds (Lakhani, Read and Wood, 1989; Roll, 1990). The

101

government has in effect introduced workfare for these young people in that the only benefit to which they are entitled is the Training Allowance payable on participation in a Youth Training Scheme. All 16 and 17 year olds are entitled to a place on a Training Scheme.

The social security system was giving very different signals to young people in the 1980s and since from those it gave in the 1960s. At that time young people had the same claim on the system as adults, but this is no longer true.

The timing of leaving home and family formation

For many young people leaving home means leaving home to marry and start a family of their own, so leaving home and family formation are the same event, and are discussed together. Sex, social class, labour market conditions and education levels all affect the timing, sequence and interrelation between transitions in young adulthood and this is as true of these final transitions as of earlier stages.

Patterns on leaving home reflect patterns on leaving school. The academic stream who go into higher education in effect leave home at 18, and for this group, finding work and setting up a household generally take place later and in that order. Those who leave school and go straight into work are more likely to leave home to marry or set up a separate family although some will marry and return to live in the parental home.

Leaving home may not take place at one step. Many young people return to the family home after a period of independent living before leaving home permanently. Work in the USA and Canada (Johnson, 1989) has coined catchy labels, such as 'boomerang kids', for these young people. It is not possible to follow progress from the parental home with cross–sectional surveys but Kiernan (1988) has analysed cohort data from the National Childhood Development Survey. The main reasons given for leaving home were for marriage or further education. Marriage was likely to be a permanent move whereas education may mean a return home. Also, the sequence of the transitions, education to work, to leaving home, to marriage, was found to be quite ordered for those who have made all the transitions by their early twenties. For those completing the sequence when older, leaving home and marriage were likely to be separated. Women left home earlier than men, in general at ages 19–23 compared with 20–25. Over the age of 20 most women were likely to be living with a spouse whereas this was not true for men until their late twenties. The different ages men and women leave home may have something to do with the different way they are treated in the parental home. Girls are kept more dependent compared with the greater scope for independence available to boys at home. It seems the only way girls can achieve a similar level of independence is to leave (see Kiernan, 1988; Wallace, 1987).

The age at which young people leave home is critical for the rate of household formation. An EEC study using data for 1982 (Kiernan, 1986) showed that by age 19, less than half of Danish women lived at home compared with 66 per cent in the UK, and 80 per cent elsewhere. For those who leave school and go into unemployment or temporary work the timing of leaving home and even establishing a stable relationship may be difficult. The traditional view is that high unemployment is likely to delay marriage and child rearing. In addition, it has been suggested that better family planning will mean that family formation may (in future) be more directly related to current social and economic background (Social Trends, 1973). An example of this is found in work which suggests that, as an alternative to life on the dole and having to live in the parental home, some girls find marriage and child care the only available 'career' (Wallace, 1987; Allan, 1987). Although there is debate about the details, the link between the labour market and family formation seems to be agreed. The consequences of this link could be serious. It has been suggested that high unemployment could lead to the 'long–term undermining of family patterns and work motivations' (Roberts, 1987, p. 92).

Overall, then, the trend towards greater independence among young people throughout the 1970s, as a result of the affluence of the 1960s and liberalisation of attitudes, gave young people the chance to try their wings earlier. By the 1980s, however, unemployment and changes in social security provision flung them back into dependence on their families, with all the constraints which this implies. Despite the considerable house building programme undertaken over the past 30 years, changes in the housing market have not been entirely to the benefit of young people, and by the 1980s the combination of fewer houses to rent, removal of rent controls, and lower benefit incomes resulted in considerable homelessness among young people. Thus more young people in the 1980s than the 1960s, were likely to experience difficulty in leaving home and establishing an independent family. The phenomenon of structured dependency of young people on their parents emerged in the 1980s (Stewart and Stewart, 1988).

Conclusion

In this overview of the changes affecting the process of becoming an independent adult over the past 30 years we have seen how unemployment has constrained each transition. In the move from school to work the available choices have become more restricted with fewer opportunities for changing jobs, and people having to accept jobs which fall short of their ideal. Opportunities for higher education, and, to some extent, training, have offered some compensation. In contrast, in the transition from the parental home to an independent household, the 1970s liberalisation in the laws and attitudes has increased the choices available. The ability to exercise these choices, however, is constrained by unemployment and changes in the benefit system. Also, despite the greater supply of housing in the 1980s than in the 1960s, there was, and is now concern that young people will not be able to afford it.

The 1980s was a frustrating time to be young. Young people could see the opportunities people of the same age had had in earlier times, and they had the liberal ideas and desire for independence generated in the 1970s, but unemployment meant these opportunities and ideas were not for them. It seems that the 1990s will be little different as the current recession continues to constrain the aspirations of young people.

Note

The study, to which this work contributes, is funded by the Economic and Social Research Council.

References

Allan, G. (1987), 'The family' in Causer, G. (ed.), *Inside British Society: Continuity, Challenge and Change,* Wheatsheaf Books Ltd., Brighton.

Banks, M. H. (1989), 'Beliefs about economic success', *ESRC 16-19 Initiative Occasional Papers,* Social Statistics Research Unit, The City University, London.

Bates, I. (1988), 'Culture, curriculum and caring: an exploration of economic socialisation of YTS girls', *ESRC 16-19 Initiative Occasional Papers,* Social Statistics Research Unit, The City University, London.

Bradshaw, J., Lawton, D. and Cooke, K. (1987), 'Income and expenditure of teenagers and their families', *Youth and Policy, no. 19, pp. 15-19.*

Briggs, E. (1987), 'Education' in Causer, G. (ed.), *Inside British Society: Continuity, Challenge and Change,* Wheatsheaf Books Ltd., Brighton.

Brown, P. (1987), *Schooling Ordinary Kids:Inequality, Unemployment and the New Vocationalism,* Tavistock Publications, London.

Bynner, J. (1989), 'Transition to work: results from a longitudinal study of young people at four British labour markets', *ESRC 16-19 Initiative Occasional Papers,* Social Statistics Research Unit, The City University, London.

Courtenay, G. (1989), *The Youth Cohort Study: The Survey and Some Findings,* Social and Community Planning Research, London.

Day, B. (1987), 'Rites of passage: education policy from the perspective of school leavers', *Policy and Politics,* vol. 15, no. 3, pp. 147–55.

Dunnell, K. (1979), *Family Formation,* Office of Population Census and Surveys, HMSO, London.

Gray, J and Sime, N. (1989), 'Extended routes and delayed transitions among 16–19 year olds: national trends and local contexts', *ESRC 16–19 Initiative Occasional Papers,* Social Statistics Research Unit, The City University, London.

Halsey, A. H. (1986), *Changes in British Society,* Oxford University Press, Oxford.

Haskey, J. (1989), 'Current prospects for the proportion of marriages ending in divorce', *Population Trends,* 55, Spring, pp 34–37.

Hill, M. (1983), 'Trends in social policy' in Stewart, A. (ed.), *Contemporary Britain,* Routledge and Kegan Paul, London.

Johnson, L. (1989), 'The new extended family, patterns of youth employment and family configuration in three Canadian cities', in Pijl, M. (ed.) *Changing Patterns of Work,* Council on Social Welfare, The Hague.

Jones, G. (1987), 'Leaving the parental home: an analysis of early housing careers, *Journal of Social Policy,* vol. 16, no. 1, pp. 49–74.

Kiernan, K. (1986), 'Research notes. Leaving home: living arrangements of young people in six West–European countries', *European Journal of Population,* no. 2, pp. 177–84.

Kiernan, K. (1988), 'Transitions in young adulthood', National Child Development Study User Support Group, Working Paper no. 16, Social Statistics Research Unit, The City University, London.

Kiernan, K. and Wicks, M. (1990), *Family Change and Future Policy,* Joseph Rowntree Memorial Trust and Family Policy Studies Centre, York and London.

Lakhani, B., Read, J. and Wood, P.L. (1989), *National Welfare Benefits Handbook,* Child Poverty Action Group, London.

Leather, P. (1981), 'Housing and public policy: a review article', *Policy and Politics,* vol. 9, no. 2, pp. 227–34.

Main, B. G. M. and Shelly, M. A. (1988), 'School leavers and the search for employment', *Oxford Economic Papers,* no. 40, pp. 487–504.

Mansfield, P. and Collard, J. (1988), *The Beginning of the Rest of Your Life? A portrait of Newly–wed Marriage,* Macmillan, Basingstoke.

McGurk, P. (1988), *What Next? An Introduction to Research on Young People,* ESRC, London.

Marwick, A. (1982), *British Society Since 1945. The Pelican Social History of Britain,* Pelican Books, London.

Millar, J. (1988), 'The costs of marital breakdown', in Walker, R. and Parker, G. (eds), *Money Matters,* Sage, London.

NACAB (1989), 'Income support and 16–17 year olds'. NACAB, 115–123 Pentonville Road, London, N1 9LZ.

Pahl, R.E. (1984), *Divisions of Labour,* Basil Blackwell, Oxford.

Pollit, N. (1989), *Hard Times,* Shelter, London.

Raffe, D. and Courtenay, G. (1988), '16–18 on both sides of the border', paper presented to seminar on The Youth Cohort Study, University of Sheffield, December.

Rees, A. M. (1987), 'Housing', in Causer, G.A. (ed.), *Inside British Society. Continuity, Challenge and Change,* Wheatsheaf Books, Sussex.

Roberts, K. (1987), Discussion in White, M. (ed.), *The Social World of the Young Unemployed*, Discussion Paper no. 19, Policy Studies Institute, London.

Roberts, K. and Parsell, G. (1988), 'Opportunity structures and career trajectories from age 16–19', *ESRC 16–19 Initiative Occasional Papers,* Social Statistics Research Unit, The City University, London.

Roberts, K. Parsell, G. and Siwek, M. (1989), 'Britain's economic recovery, the new demographic trend, and young people's transition into the labour market', *ESRC 16–19 Initiative Occasional Papers,* Social Statistics Research Unit, The City University, London.

Roll, J. (1990), *Young People: Growing Up in the Welfare State,* Family Policy Studies Centre, London.

Social Trends (1973), *Central Statistical Office,* HMSO, London.

Stewart, G. and Stewart, J. (1988), '"Targeting" youth or how the state obstructs young people's independence', *Youth and Policy,* no. 25, pp. 19–24.

Wallace, C. (1986), 'From girls and boys to women and men: the social reproduction of gender role in the transition from school to (un)employment', in Walker, S. and Barton, L. (eds), *Youth Unemployment and Schooling*, Open University Press, Milton Keynes.

Wallace, C. (1987), 'Between the family, and the state: young people in transition', in White, M. (ed.), *The Social World of the Young Unemployed,* Discussion Paper no. 19, Policy Studies Institute, London.

Willis, P. (1977), *Learning to Labour: How Working Class Kids Get Working Class Jobs,* Saxon House, Aldershot.

8 Prosperity, alcohol and crime: A need for new policies?

T.R.A. Ensor and C.A. Godfrey

Introduction

During the 1980s there was an emphasis on the importance of fewer regulations both for individuals and enterprises in an attempt to encourage wealth creation. The rising affluence has, however, been thought to threaten social cohesion. One example which gave rise to considerable public concern was alcohol related violence and public disorder. The emergence of the 'lager lout' in the summer of 1988 brought inevitable demands for policy action. There have been several initiatives, including the banning of alcohol at football matches and schemes banning drinking in public places, which may be thought to impinge upon individual liberty. There is, therefore, some question about the balance between wealth creation and the policies which may be necessary to restrict some of the harmful consequences of individual 'greed'.

As with other social problems, one reaction has been to look for single causes. The debate about the relationship between alcohol and criminal behaviour is no exception. Similarities in trends between the number of offences and alcohol consumption are used as evidence of a link between alcohol and crime. However such crude correlations may be misleading because they do not take account of other factors that may be important. There is, therefore, a need for research which attempts to control for the many factors which may influence alcohol consumption and criminal

107

behaviour, and which examines and tests causal links. Only from such research would it be possible to make predictions about the likely effects of changing social conditions, such as increasing affluence, and of different policies which may be proposed to tackle undesired consequences.

Economists have long been interested in the determinants, including income, of alcohol demand. The factors which may influence levels of crime are varied and investigations of criminal behaviour can be considered from a number of different disciplinary perspectives. Economists have developed models of the supply and demand of crime and have attempted to determine the effectiveness of different enforcement policies. In this chapter, the preliminary results from a research project designed to construct and test economic models of the interactions between alcohol consumption and criminal behaviour are considered. The aims of this research are threefold. The first aim is to consider the difficulties of specifying, estimating and statistically testing economic models of alcohol and crime. The second aim is to evaluate the contribution of the economic research in establishing causal links between alcohol and crime. Finally, the policy implications of the models and empirical estimates are evaluated.

The implications of the research for understanding potential conflicts between rising affluence and the levels of social problems are examined in this chapter. First, the possible relationships between alcohol consumption, income and crime, are briefly examined. This is followed by a description of the main features of the economic models developed to consider the interrelationships between alcohol and crime. In the third section some preliminary results derived from testing these models are presented.

Alcohol, income and crime

There have been few studies which have attempted to consider simultaneously the potentially complex interrelationships between alcohol, income and crime. Existing research is generally divided into three separate subsets of these relationships, namely the links between income and alcohol; alcohol and crime; and income and crime.

The role of income in determining alcohol consumption

Most studies of the determinants of alcohol consumption have found significant and sizable income effects, although the importance of the influence of income varies between different alcohol beverages and across different studies, (Godfrey, 1989). A useful way of comparing results from different studies is to calculate elasticities. An income elasticity is defined as the ratio of the proportionate change in demand to the proportionate change in income, for example an income elasticity of one for wine would imply that a one per cent increase in income would result in a one per cent increase in the demand for wine, all other factors remaining unchanged. Some examples of income elasticities obtained from studies of the determinants of alcohol consumption in the UK are given in Table 8.1. Even estimating the effects of income on alcohol consumption provides problems for economists and, as seen in Table 8.1, results vary between studies. However, some conclusions can be drawn from these results. A general rise in affluence and in consumers' personal incomes is likely to lead to considerable increases in alcohol consumption, particularly of wines and spirits. Predictions from such elasticity estimates, however, assume other factors such as price levels remain unchanged. Changing tastes and lifestyles may also alter the pattern between income and alcohol consumption in the longer term.

Table 8.1
Examples of alcohol income elasticities

Details of study	Income elasticities
Spirits:	
Walsh (1982)	0.99 to 1.20
McGuinness (1983)	1.54
Duffy (1983)	1.60
Godfrey (1988)	0.60 to 2.76
Baker and McKay (1990)	1.00
Wine:	
Walsh (1982)	0.49 to 0.51
McGuinness (1983)	1.11
Duffy (1983)	2.20 to 2.50
Godfrey (1988)	1.10 to 2.53
Baker and McKay (1990)	1.61
Beer:	
Walsh (1982)	0.12 to 0.13
McGuinness (1983)	0.13
Duffy (1983)	0.80 to 1.10
Baker and McKay (1990)	0.89

The relationship between alcohol and income is not necessarily constant across various social and demographic groups and the differences may be important in examining the links between alcohol, income and criminal behaviour. Surveys of drinking indicate that, for both men and women, the 16 to 25 year old age group drinks considerably more on average than other age groups (Goddard and Ikin, 1988). Income may be a more important determinant of alcohol consumption among these groups than for the older age groups (Godfrey and Posnett, 1988).

Evidence linking alcohol and crime

Many claims are made linking alcohol consumption with crime and indeed alcohol was reported to be one of the factors explaining the increase in reported crime between 1988 and 1989 (Kirby, 1990). There have been a number of research reports which would seem to support such claims. The results include the following findings: that levels of alcohol consumption are correlated with the number of offences; offenders are more likely to have consumed alcohol before crime; many prisoners have alcohol related problems; moderate and heavy drinkers are more likely to commit offences than abstainers or light drinkers; and some offences are clustered around drinking locations or peak shortly after the end of permitted drinking hours. Reviews of these studies have questioned the methodological basis of using such results to deduce some sort of causal link and suggest that any relationship between alcohol and crime may be complex (Mott, 1989; Hore, 1988).

To attempt to build models of the relationships between alcohol and crime, some distinction between direct and indirect effects may be necessary. Alcohol may directly affect behaviour and the likelihood of an individual committing a crime. A number of studies, for example, have examined the links between alcohol and aggression, although results have been mixed. The effect of alcohol on aggressive behaviour may be short term and disappear on abstinence (Hore, 1988). A number of psychological disorders were described by Pernanen (1981) which are associated with drinking but may also lead to the propensity to violent crime. Chronic drinking may affect the functioning of the brain and lead to changed behaviour.

Another type of interaction between alcohol and crime may involve interactions with the criminal justice system. For example, offenders who consume alcohol prior to a crime may be more likely to be caught, or offences arising from public disturbances near public houses or city centres may be self–detecting, unlike other acts of violent crime or criminal damage.

The interrelationships between the place where alcohol is consumed, cultural attitudes and individual behaviour are complex but may account for some of the observed links between alcohol and crime. The study of drinking and disorder in non–metropolitan areas undertaken by the Home Office illustrates some of the factors that influence outbreaks of disturbances (Tuck, 1989). Weekend drinking among young people in 'entertainment centres' was found to be a well established cultural pattern. (This norm may have been created after increases in affluence among young people in previous generations.) Most incidents of disorder occurred outside rather than in public houses. There were differences between the small group of participants in disorder and other young people. The participants were more likely to drink heavily (the most marked difference), to have left school at 16 or 17, and to be unemployed, or semiskilled or unskilled manual workers. The findings from this research suggest that at an individual level the link between affluence, alcohol and crime is not proven.

Indeed it was found in this study that the more affluent young tended to go on to night clubs where closure around 2 a.m. was associated with fewer problems than the closure of public houses at 11 p.m. The location of public houses, fast food outlets and other points in towns where people congregate are factors associated with disturbances along with the management of public houses and policing practice. Simple correlations or measures of associations which take no account of intervening factors may give a misleading picture of the links between alcohol and crime. Investigating the different ways in which alcohol interacts with crime, the criminal justice system and other social and cultural factors may clarify understanding.

Crime, affluence and unemployment

Increasing affluence may be hypothesised to have two conflicting effects on crime. Increasing wealth may increase the potential rewards for some crimes such as burglary. On the other hand, if individuals can earn more in legitimate ways, the rewards of crime may seem of less value and the cost of arrest and punishment appear higher. A review of the wide range of literature about the links between crime and unemployment is outside the scope of this paper. Existing studies do indicate the complexities of estimating and testing causal relationships (Carr–Hill and Stern, 1979) – a feature common to other studies on links between alcohol, crime and income.

Developing economic models linking alcohol and crime

There are several different methodologies which could be adopted to provide more evidence on the potential links between alcohol and crime. Specifying and testing economic models of crime and the criminal justice system is one approach and the development of models which include the effects of alcohol are described in this section.

Economic models of crime

The basic assumption underlying economic models of crime and criminal behaviour is that offenders will respond to incentives, both negative and positive, and the criminal market can be modelled in a similar way to the markets for other goods and services. It is important to note that for economic models of behaviour to be useful they have to act only as adequate approximations of actual behaviour. Hence it is not necessary that every offender responds to incentives.

Within economic models of crime, the costs and benefits to the offender of committing crime are considered with the interaction between the offender and the criminal justice system. The expected costs to the offender are hypothesised to depend on the costs of punishment (length of sentence, size of fine etc.), the prospects of being detected and the likelihood of successful prosecution. Included in the 'costs' of a crime is the time or labour cost involved in undertaking the activity. This labour has an opportunity cost in terms of foregone legitimate activity and/or leisure. The benefits of crime may be financial or more intangible.

If the behavioral assumptions about incentives are generally predictive, then economic models may help trace out the variety of factors which may influence levels of crime. For example, an increase in the level of unemployment reduces expected legal wages and the value of time in work or leisure will be smaller which may result in an increase in the expected marginal benefits of crime. However, if there is simultaneously an increase in sentences or increasing numbers of police the expected benefits of crime may fall. A number of factors which may be expected to influence crime and the criminal justice system could be interrelated. For example, an increase in crime may lead to changes in the number of police and average sentences.

In testing models it is important to take all the factors and possible simultaneities or feedbacks into account. Typically, economic models of crime have consisted of three interrelated basic or structural equations: first, a function linking the rate of crime with incentives and deterrence variables; second, an equation linking the probability of arrest and punishment with resource inputs and other determinants of law enforcement productivity; and finally, a demand for law enforcement equation linking spending on law enforcement with the determinants of intervention which may include the rate of crime (Ehrlich, 1973).

Introducing alcohol into economic models of crime

It is clear from the brief review of the previous section that alcohol could be introduced into different parts of these types of economic models of crime.

112

The first aspect to consider is the introduction of alcohol in the equation of the determinants of the level of crime. Alcohol may play a part in altering the values individuals place on the costs and benefits of crime. Alcohol may reduce inhibitions which is equivalent to a fall in the perceived costs of crime or an increase in adrenalin after drinking might raise anticipated benefits of an offence. However, the context of drinking may be important, and drinking in public houses might be more stressful, possibly leading to aggression, compared with drinking at home. While the level of alcohol consumed may be used as a reliable indicator of criminal activity, it is not necessarily useful for predicting the effectiveness of some policy options if place of drinking is impurtant. It may therefore be necessary to augment the way alcohol enters the level of crime equation by considering, for example, the proportion of alcohol drunk in on–licensed premises. The role of alcohol or other factors in determining levels of crime is unlikely to be constant across different types of crime. Some crimes such as drunkenness or drink driving offences cannot be committed without alcohol consumption. For other offences it could be predicted that, for example, petty thefts and vandalism are more likely to be linked to alcohol than bank robberies. More generally, consumption of alcohol is only likely to change the likelihood of crimes which need little other inputs to the criminal production function, for example planning time, equipment etc., and are more likely to be committed on impulse. Also, because alcohol may lead to individuals heavily discounting future costs, it could also be the case that those crimes most affected by alcohol consumption may be the least responsive to deterrent measures such as policing or sentencing.

Alcohol, as well as entering as a variable in the level of crime equation, may also have effects on the probability of detection. The full effects of alcohol can only be extended by tracing out its different influences for all equations. Income is also likely to enter the system of relationships in a number of ways, as shown below.

The basic model

Building on previous models of crime and criminal behaviour, the specification of our general model of alcohol and crime was as follows:

$$
\begin{aligned}
\text{CRIME} &= f\,(\text{ALC, SENT, PROB, PDI, OUT, POLICE}) \\
\text{PROB} &= f\,(\text{ALC, POLICE, CRIME, POLEXP}) \\
\text{POLICE} &= f\,(\text{CRIME, POLEXP, PROB, PDI}) \\
\text{ALC} &= f\,(\text{PRACL, PDI, ON, OFF, PROB, SENT})
\end{aligned}
$$

where

CRIME	=	number of offences per capita
PROB	=	a proxy for the probability of being found guilty

POLICE = the number of police per capita
ALC = per capita consumption of alcohol
SENT = expected sentence
PDI = personal disposable income per capita acting as a proxy for different factors in different equations
OUT = a measure of the outside wage, i.e. the opportunity cost to the offender of committing a crime
POLEXP = police expenditure per member of the police force
PRALC = real price of alcohol
ON = number of on-licences
OFF = number of off-licences

The first equation describes the influences on the level of crime, namely the level of alcohol consumption, the possible costs in the form of the probability of being caught and expected sentence, the opportunities for crime measured by the general level of income, the opportunity cost to the criminal in terms of the outside wage, and the level of policing. Income was used in this study as a proxy for the opportunities for crime. Other studies have used measures such as indices of property values (Carr–Hill and Stern, 1979), but this type of measure was not available for the period of study.

The proxy for the probability of being caught is specified as being dependent on the level of crime, the level of policing and the resources devoted to policing as well as alcohol consumption. The variable PROB is a conventional proxy for a probability (being defined as the ratio of the number sentenced to the number of recorded crimes) but is not subject to the same bounds as a true probability. It may be the case that the resources devoted to crime depend on the level of activity and crime detection rates, and so the third equation specifies the influences on the number of police per capita. Clearly a potential influence on the resources devoted to crime prevention is general wealth and hence increasing affluence may allow more resources to be spent on detecting and preventing crime. The final equation specifies a demand for alcohol equation which allows for price, income and availability and the probability of being involved in criminal activity to influence demand.

Clearly this basic model could be further refined. For example, the place where alcohol is consumed, as well as the amount, may be a determinant of the level of crime, and such variants were tested in the empirical work. Separate effects for different types of alcohol were also considered. An amended version of the model was developed for drink–driving offences.

Empirical testing of the model – some preliminary findings

Data requirements

There are considerable problems involved in testing the empirical validity of the above model. In particular, it is difficult to find adequate data for some of the variables. Principally this difficulty occurs because many of the variables, particularly the number of offences, are unobservable. The available recorded crime figures are significantly lower than the number of actual crimes. Carr–Hill and Stern (1979) report a number of studies which suggest that over 90 per cent of offences go undetected. Bottomley and Coleman (1981) describe a number of factors which may affect the ratio of recorded to actual crime. These factors are likely to be similar to those affecting actual crime rates and there are, therefore, considerable difficulties in being able to separate out effects. The results reported below are derived using reported crime figures and therefore have to be interpreted with care. For example, some results may indicate that an increase in police expenditure increases crime. This effect may, however, obscure an increase in the detection rate and therefore would not imply an increase in actual crime. There is a similar problem with the variable measuring the probability of detection.

Problems arise in finding adequate proxies for the expected costs of being sentenced. In this study, the average length of sentence multiplied by the probability of being imprisoned was used. This proxy for expected costs is subject to some limitations, for example it takes no account of the levels of fines and other sanctions.

There are also different types of data. One option is to use time series observations, but there can be difficulties in finding consistent series over periods of time long enough to provide sufficient data to test the model adequately. Geographical coverage of data series also varies. In economic series for example, personal disposable income and alcohol consumption are published for the UK as a whole. Criminal statistics are published separately for England and Wales, Scotland and Northern Ireland because of differences in the legal systems.

It may be possible to obtain adequate time series models that describe the factors influencing national patterns. However, within England and Wales there are regional differences in policing practices, and possibly drinking and criminal cultures. While there are insufficient regions to permit a cross sectional analysis for a particular year, data for several years can be pooled. Other insights could be obtained by finer geographical breakdowns or in depth analyses of particular locations – such analyses were unfortunately outside the scope of the present study.

Statistical framework

Several further steps are required before the model outlined above can be tested empirically. The first step is to consider a mathematical form. There were no theoretical reasons for favouring any particular functional form. In these preliminary tests, a double logarithmic form of the equations was used. Because of the possible feedback effects between crime, alcohol, probability of detection and level of policing, it is necessary to use appropriate estimation techniques to estimate the parameters of the model. Ordinary least squares (OLS) regression will yield biased and inconsistent estimates if such feedback effects exist. The two stage estimator (2SLS) of an equation produces consistent estimators and was used to test the different equations of the system by applying appropriate statistical checks of their validity. The two checks used for the time series models were a test for serial correlation of the error term and a general misspecification test (Godfrey, L, 1988).

Coefficient estimates were obtained for the model for all crime and different types of offences using time series (1960–1987) and pooled regional time series data (standard regions, 1980–1987). There were some theoretical and empirical variations in the different models tested. A separate analysis was made of drink–driving offences.

Preliminary findings

The preliminary findings on testing this general model with both time series and the pooled time series/regional data illustrate the difficulties of obtaining useful model estimates for the aggregate crime time series model. Adequate specifications of the equations for the level of crime, the probability of detection and alcohol consumption were obtained. While many of the coefficients had the 'right sign', they were poorly determined and therefore no strong conclusions can be drawn on the precise effects, for example, of alcohol on crime. In Table 8.2, estimates of the level of crime equation disaggregated for the crimes of criminal damage, burglary and violent crime are given. There is indication of residual serial correlation in the criminal damage equation and the burglary equation has evidence of misspecification. There is, however, no evidence of misspecification of the violent crime equation. The results suggest that alcohol consumption and the number of police both have a positive effect on the level of recorded violent crime.

In Table 8.3 the estimates for the equation for the determinants of PROB, the proxy for the probability of detection are given. This equation satisfied the two specification tests and alcohol is also seen to have a positive effect on the probability of detection.

The equations in Tables 8.2 and 8.3, combined with the aggregate demand for alcohol and policing equations give the full set of structural coefficients. The interpretation of the estimated coefficients of the structural equations requires some care. For example, the estimated coefficient of the income variable PDI in the CRIME equation does not give a measure of the full effect of an income change on CRIME. Income changes have effects on endogenous variables that appear as regressors in the CRIME equation (e.g. ALC) and so have what might be viewed as indirect effects. In order to discover how each endogenous variable responds to changes in nonendogenous variables, it is necessary to obtain the reduced form system that links each endogenous variable only to the full set of nonendogenous variables. Reduced form coefficient estimates can be obtained in two ways.

Table 8.2

Estimates of disaggregated crime equations

Regressor	Type of crime		
	Criminal damage	Burglary	Violent crime
PROB	−2.16	−4.84	−0.55
	[−3.70]	[−1.13]	[−0.76]
ALC	5.18	2.02	1.97
	[3.34]	[1.26]	[2.73]
OUT	3.03	−8.74	−0.14
	[0.47]	[−1.05]	[−0.69]
PDI	−2.63	3.05	−0.32
	[−0.57]	[0.60]	[−0.08]
POLICE	−2.74	0.32	1.09
	[−1.20]	[0.14]	[2.30]
CON	23.62	−9.90	0.76
	[5.20]	[−1.20]	[0.21]
Misspecification test	4.20	8.68	0.76
(critical value)	(7.82)	(5.99)	(5.99)
Serial correlation test	21.84	1.96	0.15
(critical value)	(3.84)	(3.84)	(3.84)
Sample size n	27	27	27

Note: Figures in square brackets are t−statistics

117

Table 8.3
Estimated equation for variable PROB

Regressor	CRIME	POLEXP	ALC	POLICE	CON
Estd. coeff.	0.89	−0.20	1.94	0.74	1.62
t–statistic	[−2.14]	[−0.43]	[2.46]	[1.43]	[0.75]

Misspecification test	2.12	Serial correlation test	0.48
(critical value)	(9.49)	(critical value)	(3.84)

The estimated structural equations can be solved to obtain the derived reduced form estimates implied by the two stage least squares results. Alternatively, each reduced form equation can be estimated by OLS to obtain the unrestricted reduced form system. If the sample is large and the structural model is correctly specified, the estimates for the derived and unrestricted reduced forms will be similar. In fact, the two sets of reduced form results were quite different when applied to the models reported, but both approaches produced estimates with high standard errors. Given the low precision of estimates, large differences between derived and unrestricted estimates are not unexpected.

In the regional analysis it was generally found necessary to disaggregate alcohol consumption into separate effects for beer and spirits and wine. Some evidence of a link between the level of violent crime and, in particular, beer consumption was found.

Conclusions

Estimating the interactions between alcohol consumption, income and the criminal justice system using economic models poses a number of problems. Difficulties have been found in finding precise estimates of the different effects on the level of crime and criminal behaviour. The results do confirm, however, that reliance on simple correlations between levels of crime and alcohol consumption could be misleading if used for predicting the results of policy alternatives. The research outlined in this chapter could be usefully extended by employing data disaggregated by police areas and across a number of different types of crime. No published data are available for alcohol consumption by area but the use of commercial and trade surveys could be investigated in future research.

The preliminary results from our study support the view that alcohol may play a part in determining both the level of some recorded crimes and the probability of detection. This finding when combined with the well established dependence of alcohol consumption on income suggests that

118

patterns and levels of crime may vary in responses to increases in income. These relationships are not straightforward as illustrated in this chapter and in other more general research on the links between economic prosperity and levels of crime (Field, 1990). Economic models are one means of illustrating these complexities but other complementary research is required to inform policy makers of the efficiency and acceptability of policies which may contain harmful consequences at the expense of curtailing some individual freedom.

Note

The authors gratefully acknowledge the support of the Home Office in undertaking this research.

References

Baker, P. and McKay, S. (1990), *The Structure of Alcohol Taxes: A hangover from the past?* IFS Commentary No. 21, Institute for Fiscal Studies, London.

Bottomley, K. and Coleman, C. (1981) *Understanding Crime Rates: police and public roles in the production of official statistics*, Gower, Farnborough.

Carr–Hill, R.A. and Stern, N.H. (1979), *Crime, the Police and Criminal Statistics*, Academic Press, London.

Duffy, M. (1983), 'The demand for alcoholic drink in the United Kingdom, 1963–1978', *Applied Economics*, vol. 15, no. 1, pp. 125–140.

Ehrlich, I. (1973), 'Participation in illegitimate activities: theoretical and empirical investigation', *Journal of Political Economy*, vol. 81, no. 3, pp. 521–565.

Field, S. (1990), *Trends in Crime and Their Interpretation*, Home Office Research Study, No. 119, HMSO, London.

Goddard, E. and Ikin, C. (1988), *Drinking in England and Wales in 1987*, HMSO, London.

Godfrey, C. (1988), 'Licensing and the demand for alcohol', *Applied Economics*, vol. 20, no. 11, pp. 339–343.

Godfrey, C. (1989), 'Factors influencing the consumption of alcohol and tobacco', *British Journal of Addiction*, vol. 84, no. 10, pp. 1123–1138.

Godfrey, C. and Posnett, J. (1988), 'Alcohol consumption and young people: the impact of prices and incomes', Paper presented to the Economic and Social Research Council Conference, Alcohol Abuse and Young People, December, London.

Godfrey, L.G. (1988), *Misspecification Tests in Economics: The Lagrange Multiplier Principle and Other Approaches*, Cambridge University Press, Cambridge.

Hore, B.D. (1988), 'Alcohol and crime', *Alcohol and Alcoholism*, vol. 23, no. 6, pp. 435–439.

Kirby, T. (1989), 'Crime hits record levels as burglaries increase by 21%', *Independent*, 28 March, p. 5.

McGuinness, T. (1983), 'The demand for beer, spirits and wine in the UK, 1956–1975', in Grant, M. Plant, M. and Williams, A. (eds), *Economics and Alcohol*, Croom Helm, Beckenham.

Mott, J. (1989), 'Alcohol and crime in the United Kingdom', Paper presented at the Society for the Study of Addiction to Alcohol and Other Drugs Conference, Addiction and Crime, November, Leicester.

Pernanen, K. (1981), 'Theoretical aspects of the relationship between alcohol use and crime', in Collins, J.J. (ed.), *Drinking and Crime*, The Guilford Press, New York.

Tuck, M. (1989), *Drinking and Disorder: A Study of Non–Metropolitan Violence*, Home Office Research Study No. 108, HMSO, London.

Walsh, B.M. (1982), 'The demand for alcohol in the UK: a comment', *Journal of Industrial Economics*, vol. 30, no. 4, pp. 439–446.

Part Three
USING NEW TECHNOLOGY

9 Medical technology assessment: Necessary discipline or barrier to progress?

J. Hutton

Introduction

Increased expenditure on health care, in absolute terms, and as a proportion of national income, has been a feature of the economies of the developed world during the period of almost continuous economic growth experienced by these countries since the end of the second world war. Such increases in expenditure on health care have had wide popular support and, in the context of this volume, could be regarded as channelling the benefits of economic growth towards one of the most needy groups in society – those with ill–health. However, the expansion of the health sector has been accompanied by technological advances, and the practice of modern health care has become dependent on sophisticated instrumentation for many diagnostic and therapeutic procedures. The medical supply industry has expanded accordingly, and has a direct interest in the continued expansion of health care expenditure to increase sales and profits. Although the medical supply industries are research intensive, and re–invest much of their profits in developing new techniques and equipment, a feeling has grown that continued technical advance of this kind may not always be the best way to maximise health benefits. Rather than meeting important health needs, there is a danger that increased expenditure on health care is feeding the greed of the technologically dependent medical specialisms and the medical supply industry.

123

The response of the academic research community and health policy makers during the 1980's has been the development of an activity called medical technology assessment (MTA). This is a process by which a decision is reached on the appropriate use of a technology in a particular social and organisational context. In principle MTA could be used to demonstrate the need for rapid diffusion of an effective technology, but in the context of moves by many governments in the 1980's to contain the growth of health care expenditure, it has more often been seen as a means of restricting the spread of expensive technologies.

This chapter examines the potential policy conflict between the desire to allocate existing health care expenditure efficiently and contain costs, and the desire to increase the general level of health care expenditure to introduce medical advances, and benefit disadvantaged groups. Better information about the benefits and costs of technologies, and more open discussion of priorities and the value judgements on which policy decisions are based, are essential to the resolution of this conflict. MTA is an activity designed to address these issues. The following sections examine the elements of MTA; how it might influence the technological development process; and whether the resources devoted to such forms of evaluation are justifiable, if the aim is to achieve the best possible allocation of resources across the whole economy.

Medical technology assessment

Acceptance of the term MTA to describe the process of evaluating medical technologies is relatively recent, but specific aspects of the activity itself have been carried out independently for much longer. The first academic journal devoted explicitly to MTA appeared in 1985 (Jönsson and Reiser, 1985) but in the UK economic evaluation of medical technologies and procedures began in the 1960's (Drummond and Hutton, 1987). The most comprehensive description of the elements of MTA is to be found in Institute of Medicine (1985).

The approach must be multidisciplinary as technical, clinical, economic, social and ethical issues are addressed, and concentration on just one of these areas gives too narrow a view. For those technologies requiring capital equipment the MTA must review engineering design and performance. The clinical effectiveness of the technology in diagnosis or treatment must be demonstrated. This, by itself, is not sufficient to justify diffusion as consideration needs to be given to the resource costs, both direct and indirect, of using the technology. If the most effective technologies are also the most expensive their use may not be appropriate. Technologies cannot be assessed without taking account of the social context of their use, the patient groups for whom they are designed and the type of health care organisation through which they will be provided. Potential benefits may not be achievable without changes in social attitudes and institutions. Some advances in the technical capabilities of medicine pose serious ethical issues, particularly those concerning birth and death.

The general growth of interest in MTA has resulted from pressures arising in each of the multidisciplinary areas. Rapidly expanding technical capabilities continue to produce an extended range of diagnostic and therapeutic methods from which doctors can select treatment for their patients. The doctor's interest in the appropriateness of technology is more related to individual patient needs than overall social consequences, but the twin pressures of malpractice suits and constrained budgets (even in the USA) have increased concerns over the identification of effective and efficient care.

Faced with these expanding technical capabilities and pressure from clinicians to have available the latest equipment, those responsible for the funding of health services have sought mechanisms for prioritising demands for resources. Unlimited commitments to provide all health services demanded have not proved possible in either insurance–funded or tax–funded systems. Citizens in the role of taxpayers or insurance premium payers are less willing to demand unlimited provision of the best possible health care than in the role of patients.

Social pressure is not always for the greater use of medical interventions and technologies as is shown by the debate over prenatal care (Banta et al, 1985). In some circumstances the provision of care in a situation less dominated by clinical technology has been preferred by certain sections of society, for example home births and the use of hospice care for the terminally ill. Other technologies have been pushed to the attention of decision makers as much by social pressure as by the demands of clinicians. The provision of better screening services for breast and cervical cancer comes into this category.

The ethical aspects of the use of certain technologies have led to detailed assessments of the implications of their use, and often quite strict regulations. The development of in vitro fertilisation (IVF) techniques raised hitherto unasked questions about the rights of women to have children, and also the separate issue of the use of embryos for research purposes. Advances in neonatal intensive care have made possible the survival of premature infants previously not considered viable. Screening techniques can now detect foetal abnormalities more accurately. Parents and doctors are now faced with decisions which previously did not arise, and society may take a view on how those decisions should be made.

Economic evaluation

For all the reasons outlined above the unfettered development, diffusion and utilisation of new medical technology may lead to socially undesirable outcomes. This chapter will concentrate on the economic aspects of technology assessment, not because the other dimensions are considered unimportant by the author, but because the policy debate on many technologies is focused on the economic factors, and it is with this policy debate we are concerned. Economic evaluation is concerned with the costs and benefits of a technology and, hence, is dependent on good clinical information about effectiveness as well as assessment of the direct and indirect resource requirements (Drummond, 1987).

The scope of the economic evaluation must be defined in each case, which requires consideration of social, ethical and organisational aspects of the use of the technology. For example, from whose perspective is the assessment of costs and benefits being made – the patients' or society in general? MTA is generally seen as an aid to social decision making, but an understanding of the motivations of patients, and the incentives to which they might respond, could influence the ability of policy to achieve a perceived socially desirable outcome. Cultural and ethical factors may also influence the acceptability, and hence the effectiveness of some technologies, for instance the use of birth control and termination of pregnancy may be rejected by some religious groups. These wider social aspects must be taken into account if the results of MTA are to be generally applied, and they must be considered from the outset when feasible policy options for evaluation are being identified.

The economic evaluation technique of cost effectiveness analysis provides a good framework within which trade–offs between costs and benefits can be set out. The valuation of health benefits in financial terms was rejected early on in the development of economic evaluation of health care because of dissatisfaction with productivity–based methods of valuing the saving of human life (Mishan, 1971; Mooney, 1976). A further problem was the difficulty of obtaining financial measures of the benefits of avoided morbidity, although this debate has recently been revived (Johanesson and Jönsson, 1991). Most studies now attempt to use utility–based measures to assess the benefits of health care interventions and technologies (Torrance, 1986). These can be adapted to enable comparison of the cost effectiveness of different technologies through presentation of cost per quality adjusted life year (QALY) gained (Williams, 1985). The QALY combines the two main health benefits, increased survival and improved quality of life during survival, into one index using weights derived from empirical studies to score the dimensions of health states. Benefit arises, that is 'QALY gain', if survival is increased in the same health state; if patients are moved to a higher valued health state for the same survival period; if the length of increased survival at a lower health state is sufficient to offset the loss of quality value; or if patients are moved to a sufficiently higher valued health state to offset any reduction in the survival period. The relative benefit from different interventions can be shown by dividing the QALY gain by the extra cost of obtaining it, to produce a cost per QALY ratio for each intervention. While most health economists agree on the conceptual approach the practical application of the cost per QALY measure is fraught with difficulties. Apart from concerns over the QALY measure itself – are the dimensions of quality of life appropriate, do the weights reflect social values – there is a need for good clinical data on the outcomes of the use of technology, and cost data, both of which should preferably come from controlled trials.

The important thing to remember is that the results of cost effectiveness and cost utility analyses are relative and not absolute. They do not show whether an activity is worth pursuing per se, but provide a ranking of the options analysed. The interpretation of 'league tables' of medical technologies and procedures based on cost per QALY rankings, such as that in Maynard (1991), must be done carefully. There is a tendency for technologies with a high cost per QALY ratio to be labelled expensive, when the correct judgement should be that they are expensive relative to the other technologies which have been evaluated. The list in Maynard (1991), for example, is far from comprehensive, and it is quite possible that there are several medical procedures, routinely undertaken, the value of which no one has questioned, which might have even higher cost per QALY ratios (Neumann and Weinstein, 1991).

There is always a tendency for new technologies to be subjected to more intensive evaluation than established ones. This may not be a problem if the new technology is designed to replace existing methods of treatment or diagnosis for a specific condition. Provided that the existing and the new technologies are assessed on the same basis, a partial analysis can inform the decision to introduce the new method or not. However, if the new technology offers the possibility of treating hitherto untreatable conditions, that is, there is no obvious candidate for replacement, the cost per QALY data is less helpful. In such circumstances comprehensive information on the cost effectiveness of all activities is necessary, before the new technology can be ranked. In other words a zero–based approach, rather than an incremental approach, to evaluation and resource allocation is necessary, and this would be very demanding of evaluation resources (Merewitz and Sosnick, 1971). Knowledge about the costs and effectiveness of technologies is slowly expanding, as more rigorous studies are carried out, but resources are not made available at present to evaluate all new procedures let alone the backlog of unevaluated standard interventions.

Technological research and development

The main thrust of MTA, and particularly its economic components, has been to identify the appropriate use of technologies as they have been made available for general use. In state funded health care systems with fixed annual budgets, such as that in the UK, the evaluation has generally been regarded as an instrument for delaying or controlling the diffusion of technology, although there have been cases where extra funding has been provided after favourable assessments, as in the case of heart transplantation (Buxton, 1987). The flow of innovations has been to some extent taken for granted, and the potential effect of more rigorous assessment of technologies on the willingness of companies to invest in research and development has often been ignored. Brazier et al (1990) have argued that the financial arrangements most likely to produce a cost effective use of existing technologies involve constraining the overall health system budget. It is particularly difficult to combine this with a policy of expanding the overall scale of health sector activities to meet social demands for new or better services.

Those who believe that priority should be given to the latter objective have challenged the use of MTA in two ways: accuracy and scope. Several authors have contended that so-called 'expensive' medical technologies, for example diagnostic equipment such as computed tomograpy (CT) scanners and magnetic resonance imagers, and lithotripters for the treatment of kidney stones, actually reduce health care costs. Although the initial capital cost is high, this can be offset by cost savings from reduced need for other procedures and shorter hospital stays as a result of faster diagnosis and more appropriate treatment (Halfpap, 1986; Maly, 1987). Some authors have even suggested that technological advances will soon reduce the overall cost of health care (Duckworth, 1989). This is an interesting modern version of the view held by many in 1948 that the improvement in health as a result of the creation of the NHS would ultimately lead to reduced need for expenditure on health care.

There are several problems with analyses which attempt to show cost savings resulting from the introduction of new technology. Often the figures are based on hypothetical estimates of changes in medical practice, which assume the abandonment of many current techniques, although in practice they may continue to be used alongside the new technology. Another problem is the use of average costs to measure savings rather than the avoidable marginal costs. When the number of procedures is reduced the only immediate savings may be reduced use of consumables, for example, x-ray film, electricity, drugs. Staff time savings may not be easily allocated to new tasks and staff reduction cannot be achieved immediately. Only when a whole department can be closed can the average cost per procedure be used to measure savings. This error often occurs in the context of insurance–funded health care systems where prices charged for procedures are used as proxy measures for costs. Comparison on a patient by patient basis may show the potential for cost saving in individual cases, but is a poor guide to overall service costs. Capital equipment and trained manpower no longer required for one group of patients, are often transferred to other groups of patients who previously did not receive a service. In such cases no cost savings are made but health benefits may be produced if the new treatment is successful.

Even when cost savings estimates are made from actual data this is rarely from randomised, controlled trials, but more often from retrospective comparison. Such studies are often carried out in specialist teaching hospitals where the caseload and clinical practice may not reflect the generality of health service experience. The difficulties of this type of study are well illustrated by Moore et al (1987) in a study which found that the annual financial savings from using a CT scanner were three times the annual equivalent cost of purchasing and operating the equipment. On checking some of the figures for savings from cessation of other investigations they found that the estimated number avoided was greater than the actual number carried out before the installation of the scanner. Prospective study designs would avoid such over estimations.

The second, and more important, line of criticism of MTA has been over its scope, not just in focusing primarily on costs and effectiveness, but in restricting the viewpoint to that of the health care system rather than the whole of the economy and society. Decisions made by the health care system on the acquisition of technology do not only affect patients and health care workers. They can have serious implications for those working in the industries which manufacture and supply medical products. Those involved in the development of new technologies are often convinced of the value of their innovations and become frustrated if health service authorities are slow to share their view (Young, 1988). The economic value of having a strong domestic medical supply industry has often been argued in the UK. Proposals have been made to increase expenditure on capital equipment by the NHS to stimulate growth and research and development activities in the UK medical equipment industry (ACARD, 1986).

This raises difficult conflicts between the objectives of achieving cost effective health care provision in the NHS, and meeting the objectives of industrial policy, which have been discussed in detail elsewhere (Hutton, 1991a). Whether the use of MTA can help to resolve these conflicts is discussed in the following section.

Incentives to innovate

Successful innovation of medical technology is of interest to the supplying industry and to the policy makers controlling the health care system. To gain an understanding of the forces influencing innovation it is necessary to clarify the objectives of each group and the characteristics of technologies likely to succeed. Figure 9.1 gives a simple diagrammatic representation of three key influences on industrial decision making with regard to innovation. The technical problem must be solved first, but the resulting product must be in a form acceptable to potential users and society in general. The technically feasible and socially acceptable product must also be marketable at a price which produces profit for the company (after the recovery of the research and development costs). Economic viability is crucial to the commercial organisation and whether the market is in the public or private sector does not matter as long as sales can be made at the right price.

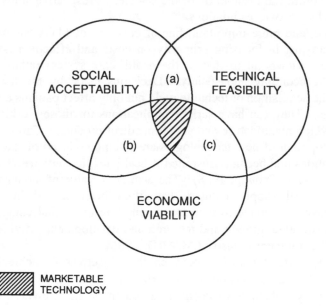

Figure 9.1 Diffusion model (from Hutton, 1991b)

The shaded area in Figure 9.1 represents marketable technology for which the three criteria apply. The greater the convergence the more likely is innovation to take place. Industry itself can exert most influence over technical feasibility through research and development activities, but these may expand the feasibility set overall without increasing the area of convergence. Social acceptability is less easy to influence by direct means and is more dependent on longer term trends in social attitudes. Economic viability depends on the ability of the producer to control the costs of production and the willingness of potential users to pay for the product. Marketing can exert some influence here and, in the medical context, the role of clinicians in determining the pattern of product diffusion makes them a prime target for the industry's sales effort. The implications of this model have been explored in more detail in Hutton (1991b).

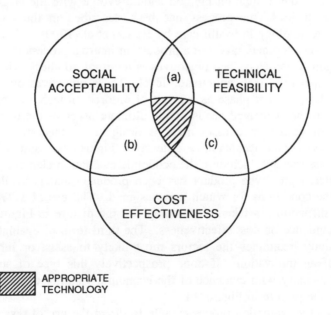

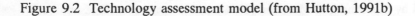

Figure 9.2 Technology assessment model (from Hutton, 1991b)

The perspective of the public sector decision maker is shown in Figure 9.2 in which the shaded area represents appropriate technology from the perspective of society in general. The difference is that the third characteristic is cost effectiveness rather than economic viability. Many products have diffused successfully in world markets without clear evidence of their cost effectiveness, and demonstration of cost effectiveness does not guarantee a market. A mutually satisfactory outcome can occur if an innovation is shown to be cost effective and economic viability is ensured by the willingness of health care providers to buy the technology. Properly conducted technology assessment can facilitate the identification of such products.

The role of evaluation

One of the problems of working in a multidisciplinary environment is the potential confusion of terms and concepts between disciplines. This applies to MTA particularly between engineers and economists over the concept of evaluation. Timing is all important in the evaluation of a developing technology and the evaluation method should evolve with the stage of the product life cycle. This process has been described in the context of information technology in health care by Hutton et al (1990).

During the development phase of a product an internal process of checking progress against predetermined objectives is required, to check whether the product will perform to its anticipated level. These objectives may change during the development phase as a result of unforeseen technical problems or changes in the perceived needs of the ultimate users of the technology. This form of constructive assessment is designed to meet the technical feasibility and social acceptability criteria of Figures 9.1 and 9.2. Full technology assessment, including the economic evaluation elements, is only possible after a prototype product has been produced and is available for testing in the conditions for which it is designed. The use of MTA before significant diffusion has taken place completes the picture in Figure 9.2 by providing evidence on cost effectiveness. The third form of evaluation, the diffusion study, examines the factors most likely to assist or inhibit the diffusion of an innovation. If done prospectively this type of study can supply the industry with evidence of the economic viability of innovations, completing the picture in Figure 9.1.

Used correctly evaluation processes help to direct the use of research and development resources to those areas most likely to produce appropriate medical innovations. Unfortunately the systematic use of MTA has been slow to develop. In the UK the first detailed argument for MTA was put forward by Stocking and Morrison (1978) and in spite of a large number of independently generated studies, formal arrangements for assessment in the NHS have yet to be developed. Writing on the topic very recently Stocking commented, 'better technology assessment information is essential for local decision–makers if they are to assess trade–offs in the care they are providing' and noted that of the European countries only Sweden and the Netherlands had satisfactory arrangements for MTA (Stocking, 1991, p. 134). The new proposals for reorganising research funding by regional health authorities in England may go some way towards filling the gap if MTA is given sufficient priority (NHS Management Executive, 1991).

Discussion

To return to the underlying theme of this book, it is possible that MTA has indeed slowed the diffusion of medical technology and provided governments and insurance funds with arguments to justify the containment of overall expenditure on health care. The question remains – has this prevented the meeting of legitimate health needs or inhibited the greed of those with a financial interest in the diffusion of medical technology, regardless of its social value?

Producers of medical products have a clear financial interest in increased health care expenditure, but this does not mean that they do not genuinely believe in the value to patients of the products they develop and sell. Clinicians also derive financial rewards from the use of new medical technology indirectly through enhanced professional status; or more directly when payment systems are on a fee per procedure basis. However, clinical advocates of new technology may wish to acquire technology solely for the potential benefits it may bring to patients. As long as such interests are clearly stated, and known to decision makers they need not undermine a rational decision process. The more such interest groups are constrained to present the information to support their arguments in a standardised form, the easier it will be for decision makers to separate good evidence from special pleading.

In many countries the regulatory authorities require evidence of safety and efficacy before granting product licences to drugs and medical devices. In 1990 the Australian government introduced a requirement for evidence of cost effectiveness to be produced before approving re–imbursement for new medicines in the public health system (Drummond, 1991a). If other countries follow suit and pressure for MTA continues to increase, the supplying industries will be forced to seek innovations which are cost effective in order to achieve economic viability. This will reduce the potential conflict between industrial and health service objectives.

Most of the MTA resources in developed countries have been devoted to high profile, high technology forms of health care, which tend to capture the public imagination and therefore the attention of policy makers. Such technologies may take up as little as one per cent of health sector budgets (Maly, 1987). Inducing more caution in decisions to acquire such technologies may not lose many health benefits, but equally may not save many resources. If MTA can encourage the industry to pay more attention to the cost effectiveness of products, without reducing the effort put into research and development, the extra cost of more evaluation may be justifiable.

Pharmaceutical manufacturers are supporting an increasing number of economic evaluations of their products and it is likely that the other medical supply industries will follow suit. It is important that such studies are methodologically sound to avoid accusations of bias in the results (Drummond, 1991b).

The main focus of this chapter has been on the need to take account of the wider context of MTA and its influence on industrial innovation as well as health policy. In the changing field of health policy priorities the increasing emphasis on health promotion and disease prevention poses new challenges for MTA. Like many other countries the UK is developing a health stategy which acknowledges that many of the major influences on health are beyond the control of the health care system (DH, 1991). Improved policies in relation to accidents, dietary habits and environmental pollution may offer greater potential health gains than increased spending on treating the ill–health which results from these factors. This opens up the debate to the level of intersectoral allocation of resources, rather than consideration of the efficient use of resources within the health care sector itself. If sensible decisions are to be taken at this level, a consistency of approach to evaluation between sectors in relating health benefits to social costs will be essential.

Conclusion

Scepticism about the benefits of high technology medicine is not confined to economists; clinicians themselves have highlighted the problems (Jennett, 1986). Equally, concern over use of NHS resources for less cost effective activities does not automatically lead to the conclusion that health care expenditure should not be increased in other areas. Politically, there is a danger that a health sector which is too scrupulous about evaluating its own activities could lose out, in the allocation of public sector resources, to other government departments. The answer to this problem is an all round improvement in public sector evaluation practice, rather than a reduction to the lowest common denominator.

All the arguments lead to the conclusion that more and better evaluation is required and this implies greater allocation of resources for such activities by government, health services and the suppliers of medical technologies. Economic evaluation will continue to be a central part of the assessment process, but must take account of the equally valid contributions from other disciplines and recognise the broader scope of the policy issues behind individual evaluations. This breadth of scope must match the broadening context of the health policy debate, as increasingly, matters traditionally dealt with by other government departments are assessed for their health effects.

The need for this broadening of outlook has been recognised within the technology assessment community and is reflected in the changes of title given to the discipline over the years. This chapter began with the original and probably still most familiar title – medical technology assessment. In recognising the involvement of professions other than medicine in the delivery of care this was often changed to health care technology assessment. The modern trend is to use the term health technology assessment, indicating a role for those not involved in health care provision in improving health. The next challenge for all these groups is to develop techniques which assist policy makers to decide the most appropriate size of the whole health sector, without undermining the current use of micro–economic techniques within that sector. The problem has been recognised but no easy solutions have been found.

References

ACARD (1986), *Medical Equipment*, Advisory Council on Applied Research and Development, HMSO, London.

Banta, H.D., Houd, S. and Suarez Ojeda, E. (1985), 'Prenatal care – an introduction', *International Journal of Technology Assessment in Health Care*, vol. 1, no. 4, pp. 783–788.

Brazier, J., Hutton, J. and Jeavons, R. (1990), 'Evaluating the reform of the NHS' in Culyer, A.J., Maynard, A.K. and Posnett, J. (eds), *Competition in Health Care*, Macmillan, London.

Buxton, M. (1987), 'Problems in the economic appraisal of new health technology' in Drummond, M.F. (ed.), op. cit.

DH (1991), *The Health of the Nation*, Department of Health, HMSO, London.

Drummond, M.F. (1987) (ed.), *Economic Appraisal of Health Technology in the European Community*, Oxford University Press, Oxford.

Drummond, M.F. (1991a), 'Australian guidelines for cost–effectiveness studies of pharmaceuticals', Discussion Paper no. 88, Centre for Health Economics, University of York.

Drummond, M.F. (1991b), 'Economic evaluation of pharmaceuticals: science or marketing', Discussion Paper no. 91, Centre for Health Economics, University of York.

Drummond, M.F, and Hutton, J. (1987), 'Economic appraisal of health technology in the United Kingdom' in Drummond, M.F. (ed.), op. cit.

Duckworth, E. (1989), 'Space age cost–cutters', *Health Service Journal*, vol. 99, no. 5133, p. 47.

Halfpap, B. (1986), 'What does health really cost?' *Electromedica*, vol. 54, no. 1, pp. 19–30.

Hutton, J. (1991a), 'The conflict between industrial and health policy in the UK medical equipment market' in Hutton, J., Hutton, S., Pinch, T. and Shiell, A. (eds), *Dependency to Enterprise*, Routledge, London.

Hutton, J. (1991b), 'Medical device innovation and public policy in the European Economic Community' in Gelijns, A. and Halm, E. (eds), *The Changing Economics of Medical Technology*, National Academy Press, Washington, DC.

Hutton, J., Fagnani, F., Jorgensen, T., Persson, J. and Saranummi, N. (1990), 'Assessment of information systems and technologies in health care' in Monteagudo, J.L., de la Concha, S., Garcia de Vinuesa, S. and Soriano, S. (eds), *Proceedings of the AIM Euroforum*, Ministerio de Sanidad y Consumo, Seville.

Institute of Medicine (1985), *Assessing Medical Technologies*, National Academy Press, Washington DC.

Jennett, B. (1986), *High Technology Medicine: Benefits and Burdens*, Oxford University Press, Oxford.

Johanesson, M. and Jönsson, B. (1991), 'Economic evaluation in health care: is there a role for cost–benefit analysis?', *Health Policy*, vol. 17, no. 1, pp. 1–23.

Jönsson, E. and Reiser, S. (1985), Editors' introduction, *International Journal of Technology Assessment in Health Care*, vol. 1, no. 1, pp. 1–2.

Maly, W. (1987), 'Expensive health technology and the cost of health care', Paper presented to the 14th European Health Policy Forum, Brussels, 12 June.

Maynard, A.K. (1991), 'Developing the health care market', *Economic Journal*, vol. 101, no. 408, pp. 1277–86.

Merewitz, L. and Sosnick, S. (1971), *The Budget's New Clothes*, Markham, Chicago.

Mishan, E.J. (1971), 'The value of life', *Journal of Political Economy*, vol. 79, no. 4, pp. 687–705.

Mooney, G.H. (1976), *The Valuation of Human Life*, Macmillan, London,

Moore, A.T., Dixon, A.K., Rubenstein, D. and Wheeler, T. (1987), 'Cost–benefit evaluation of body computed tomography', *Health Trends*, vol. 19, no. 3, pp. 8–12.

NHS Management Executive (1991), *NHS Research and Development Strategy: Guidance for Regions*, NHS Management Executive, London.

Neumann, P.J. and Weinstein, M.C. (1991), 'The diffusion of new technology: costs and benefits to health care' in Gelijns, A. and Halm, E. (eds), *The Changing Economics of Medical Technology*, National Academy Press, Washington DC.

Stocking, B. (1991), *Factors Affecting the Diffusion of Three Kinds of Innovative Medical Technology in the European Community Countries and Sweden*, Kings Fund Centre, London.

Stocking, B. and Morrison, J. (1978), *The Image and the Reality*, Nuffield Provincial Hospitals Trust, Oxford.

Torrance, G. (1986), 'Measurement of health state utilities for economic appraisal', *Journal of Health Economics*, vol. 5, no. 1, pp. 1–30.

Williams, A.H. (1985), 'Economics of coronary artery bypass grafting', *British Medical Journal*, vol. 291, no. 6491, pp. 326–329.

Young, I. (1988), 'Time to bring on the scanners', *Health Services Journal*, vol. 98, no. 5123, medical technology supplement, pp. 1–2.

Figures 9.1 and 9.2 reprinted with permission from *The Changing Economics of Medical Technology*, c. 1991 by the National Academy of Sciences. Published by National Academy Press, Washington, DC.

10 Community alarms services: Who needs them?

P. Thornton

Introduction

Community alarms are a recent innovation. A survey in the late 1970s of housing departments and social services departments in England and Wales aimed to identify innovative ways of enabling elderly people to remain in the community (Tinker, 1984). 'Alarms' schemes emerged from that study, along with good neighbour/personal care schemes, as of 'greatest potential interest'. Yet, of the five alarms schemes chosen for case study investigation only one employed the kind of telephone based communication technology that dominates current alarms provision. Now an estimated 850,000 households (including those in sheltered housing) in the UK have some sort of technological device for calling for help, a larger number than any other country (Fisk, 1990). It has been estimated that about 20 per cent of alarms users live in ordinary, mainstream housing, with the rest in sheltered, grouped or amenity housing (Fisk, 1989b).

What is a community alarm? Briefly, it is a technological device which allows its user to call for help via a telephone by pressing a remote control trigger carried on the person. When pressed, the trigger, usually worn as a pendant, activates a special telephone (the 'home unit') which sends signals to a permanently staffed external 'control centre'. A computer tells the operator who is calling and, in most cases, a speech link is opened between the operator and the caller. If physical help is wanted, the control centre staff will alert someone to respond in person. The respondent may be a warden employed for that purpose, or a relative, friend or neighbour previously nominated by the user. Less commonly, other agency staff or volunteers may be respondents. The control centre will alert an emergency service if that appears to be needed.

Most control centres have been set up by and are managed by housing authorities. There are some private sector control centres. A very small number are run by social services departments and some are run by consortia of statutory and voluntary agencies. There are now over 300 control centres in the UK. Alarms users either purchase the equipment outright, or lease it, paying a fee for the link to a control centre, or they receive a free or subsidised service with the costs borne by their social services department, housing department or, unusually, health authority.

The need to call for help

What are community alarms for? The answer depends on limits imposed by the agencies involved and on the willingness of the user to define functions for him or herself. Typically, alarms use is limited to emergency situations where the user needs physical help. Usually, an 'emergency' is taken to mean a fall where the person cannot right her or himself without physical assistance from another person, sudden illness or accident needing medical attention, or other life or property threatening events such as fire, flood or break-in. Users are normally allowed some latitude in defining 'emergency'. The strictures of one scheme, despite the name 'Care Link', are among the most extreme. According to its advertising leaflet:

> The alarm is intended for use only in emergencies. Its purpose is to save lives and bring the appropriate assistance to seriously distressed older people. Anyone using the alarm for other reasons will detract from its effectiveness and could even cause loss of life by delaying emergency services.

In the same advertising leaflet that scheme offers 'the care you need when you need it', 'security and peace of mind' and 'help to older people in difficulty whenever and wherever a problem arises'.

Some providers of alarms services do recognise that anxiety, depression or feeling unwell are legitimate reasons for calling help. The implications for the respondents to the calls are always a consideration, however. A minority of alarms agencies acknowledge a need to respond to physical care needs. An independent scheme in Tower Hamlets stressed its function in filling a gap in the out-of-hours and weekend care services. It claimed a large proportion of calls at those times 'are not concerned with emergency physical injury calls, but the need to be put to bed or to be taken to the commode or lavatory' (Pellow, 1987, p.108).

Some alarms devices include a surveillance function. Inactivity within a given period triggers the alarm. Some agencies offer a daily telephone checking service and routine visiting as surveillance alongside the response service. Alarms may also be used for communication between the control centre and the user. Such communication use is obviously not specific to alarms and could occur via the telephone if a central communication point existed. But the majority of alarms are provided with reactive rather than interactive functions in mind.

Apart from these primary functions – 'emergency' response, surveillance and communication – alarms are said to 'reduce isolation', 'provide peace of mind' and 'help elderly people maintain their independence'. Once viewed as byproducts, such claims are now often cited as primary functions. In Fisk's view, (1989b) '...the main benefit of alarms is now increasingly seen as providing reassurance rather than in obtaining help in the event of an emergency'.

There has always been a recognition that some people will need to call for help, if not regularly, at least from time to time. A common response has been to offer such people alternative accommodation – notably sheltered housing – which will meet that need as well as others. For people for whom moving is not an option, solutions have been restricted to

telephones;
rudimentary signalling systems, such as knocking on walls, flashing
external lights;
surveillance systems, such as telephone check networks, neighbourhood
watch;
increase in interpersonal contact time, by maximising home help or
other domestic support.

Such possibilities have always had a marginal position in the array of support options. In the absence of a mainstream service which addresses the needs of people who, from time to time, need urgent help from someone else, the tendency has been to move the person to accommodation – sheltered housing or residential care – where both the means of summoning and the help itself are integral to the support system.

The development of alarms technology has coincided with a shift away from investment (both ideological and financial) in sheltered housing. The scarcity of sheltered housing, an increasing recognition that tenants value the housing features more than the extras, and ideological commitment to community care rather than residential care have together combined to raise again the question of how to meet the needs of people who have to call for

140

help. The 'problem' of people who fall cannot be solved now by residential care alone. Community based means have to be found.

Whose needs?

Surprisingly, given the prevalence of community alarms systems, questions are rarely posed about who benefits and whose needs they meet (Fisk, 1989a). These questions have to be asked if, as the community care legislation proposes, services are to be shaped by the needs of those who will use them (DH/DSS/Welsh/Scottish Office, 1989).

I want to argue that the potential of community alarms services as a contribution to meeting community care needs has not been realised. The increasing evidence from research (Thornton, 1992) indicates that community alarms services have an important role to play in supporting vulnerable people in ordinary housing. That potential has not been realised, I suggest, because of a fundamental conflict between the needs of those who promote alarms systems and the needs of those users who stand to benefit most. The dominance of the needs of the promoters and providers leads to false assumptions about who 'needs' alarms. Their dominant values, moreover, affect the manner in which community alarms are provided, leading to disillusion over their effectiveness. At the core of the problem is a conflict between neoliberal ideals of 'independence', which assume that, once allocated the service is in the control of its users, and the obligations on the provider, either because of accountability or a commitment to intervention to ensure that the service is used appropriately and to the advantage of the consumer.

Community alarms are unusual among community care options in being viewed differently depending on where you stand. They are rarely seen as a social service with specific community care objectives. Community alarms do not immediately spring to mind as one of the range of service options available to support vulnerable elderly people at home. Scan the practitioner literature and you will be surprised to find any reference to community alarms. There is a dearth of both research and critical writing on the subject. The knowledge base is limited – there are no aggregate data on the scale and spread of provision, on the agencies operating schemes or on the ways in which community alarms services operate.

It is interesting to speculate on why community alarms have such a low profile as a service. The answer lies in part with the drawing power of the technology. An emphasis on the technology tends to ignore the human components needed to let the system function. It also tends to ignore the fact that the technology has human beneficiaries. It is not uncommon to read articles or listen to presentations which make no reference to the users of the technology. (An irony is the highjacking of the term 'user' to refer to the agencies employing the technology: 'users groups' consist of agency representatives.)

But a more significant explanation is that a view of alarms as a social service has to compete against other more dominant perceptions. To understand the relatively marginal place of alarms as a social service, it is important to understand how that style of application fits with other current models of alarms provision. This conceptual unravelling is important not just for an understanding of the potential of alarms as a service. It also has considerable relevance to the future of service provision when changes in community care policy take effect. There are four ways of conceptualising the ways in which alarms are made available. Each has associated with it distinctive values. Organisational practices are imbued with these values.

Alarms as a commercial enterprise

The dominant perception of the alarm is as a consumer good. Perceptions are heavily influenced by manufacturers' promotion of the home units. Advertisements in 'up–market' magazines emphasise that vulnerability and dignity can be combined in (usually affluent) old age. It is up to the consumer to identify him or herself as a potential user. Consumer choice is facilitated by guides to 'best buys', concentrating on technical reliability and ease of use of the equipment (Which? 1986; 1989). Arrangements for the response to an alarm call are at the discretion of the user and not seen to be problematic: adverts suggest that once the alarm has been activated the problem has been dealt with. As with other consumer durables, the providers have no interest in the use the individual consumer makes of the alarm.

The dominant values in the commercial model are those of choice, retention of control by the consumer and consumer sovereignty. The themes of independence and reassurance are marked in manufacturer led promotions.

The alarm as a consumer good is useless unless it is linked to a monitoring centre which will handle the emergency calls. Monitoring is a commercial enterprise, with fees of around £2.00 per week payable for monitoring only. More is charged if the monitoring centre provides the response to the call. Monitoring is offered by private sector and charitable organisations. Increasingly, local authority housing departments are marketing monitoring services as a way of generating an income from surplus capacity at their control centres. A further commercial development has been local authorities marketing their own alarms service to people in their locality. For a rental charge, home units and monitoring are provided; some offer a warden response service. More unusually, routine visiting is also part of the deal. Such enterprises are intended either to run alarms services at a profit or to subsidise services to other local users. There are no eligibility criteria other than ability to pay. It is not uncommon for marketed services to be promoted under a 'community care' banner.

Alarms as a property feature

Alarms are also commonly perceived to be a feature of property occupied by elderly people. Housing authorities are now promoting alarms as a feature of improved public housing for 'special needs' groups. Sometimes these are presented as all–purpose intruder, smoke detector and 'care' alarms. Accommodation typically occupied by older people is earmarked for alarms installation. Occupants may be given little real choice as to whether they want this 'improvement'. Subsequently, when the property falls vacant, it is reallocated as elderly persons' accommodation. Some local authorities aim to house all elderly tenants in 'appropriate' accommodation equipped with alarms. The management, financial and political imperatives are intertwined in a complex way. Management of housing stock, maximising sources of central government finance via housing benefit, and the search for a role in times of severe constraint on housing departments' activities all have a part to play.

The rationale for installing alarms as a housing improvement has its origins in sheltered housing. Purpose built 'special needs' housing included a range of features to make the accommodation manageable, sociable, accessible and within range of help. But, by osmosis, the defining features of the property have turned into defining features of its occupants. Thus, when housing providers claim to extend one of the features of sheltered housing to elderly people in ordinary housing they assume that because people belong to the category 'potential sheltered housing occupant' they are natural candidates for alarms. This transference of the notion of alarm *availability* as a feature of a type of *property* to alarm *need* as a characteristic of a type of *person* underlies much of the expansion by local authorities into alarms provision beyond special housing. Alarms are also being installed in newly built or improved housing by private developers and housing associations. They too appear to share the assumption that all potential occupants are, by definition of being elderly, natural alarms users.

Such blanket applications aimed at improving housing amenity have no interest in assessing the effectiveness of their provision.

Alarms as an aid

I turn now to applications of community alarms which have some sort of 'welfare' intent. Within social services departments, alarms are likely to be classed as 'aids and adaptations' and viewed as an updated telephone. Alarms unit users are now receiving financial support under the provisions of the

Chronically Sick and Disabled Persons Act, 1970, previously directed to support telephone users.

Jones, Baldwin and Hirst, in the following chapter, point to the dual image of the telephone as a consumer good and as a service. Social services departments, in intervening to support financially telephone installation and rental, view the telephone as a social necessity with a role in improving quality of life. The role of the agency is to improve access to it for people disadvantaged through disability and low income. But the use to which the phone is put is immaterial to the agency.

The shift in financial support assumes an equivalence between the telephone and the community alarm which ignores the service elements arguably essential to the effectiveness of community alarms.

Jones, Baldwin and Hirst are posing one view of the telephone as something that is accepted as necessary to provide access to basic levels of functioning and basic participation in society. But if the claims made for it are to be believed, the alarm is of a different order of social service. The alarm is a means of calling on a service, whenever the alarm user decides is necessary. That service may be negotiated with informal contacts or provided by agents of a statutory body. The physical presence of a supportive person is as much part of the service as the system which enables the call to be made.

Alarms as a service intervention

This brings us to the final model which views community alarms provision as a service intervention.

In England and Wales, alarms provision is claimed by housing authorities to demonstrate their capacity as welfare providers. Indeed much of the provision of alarms services to elderly people in ordinary private housing is managed by housing authorities, resulting from their traditional involvement in provision of sheltered housing and associated warden services to older people. (Most control centres were established to provide out-of-hours cover for sheltered housing wardens, or to replace resident wardens altogether. The existence of the facility with almost limitless capacity led many authorities into this new welfare role.)

Not surprisingly, given the history, housing agencies acting as providers can lack clarity about the aims of their interventions. Notions of appropriate service recipients are driven more by the need to ration limited resources than by considerations of who might benefit. Eligibility formulae are fairly standard – often limiting applications to the very elderly, people living alone and housebound and socially isolated. People who are confused or suffering from dementia are usually excluded. Because they are rarely providers of other home based services to people in the community, housing authorities

144

are effectively providing an 'add on' service to people who may receive statutory services from social services or health authorities. They are rarely able to integrate their service with those others.

Social services alarms agencies are thin on the ground. There are few authorities which design and manage alarms services and retain control over the processes of delivery. Commonly, the functions of assessment of need and service delivery are split between agencies. While a social worker can assess individual need and create with the client an appropriate 'package of care' including an alarms service, typically another agency takes over responsibility for the processes of installation and service delivery. Increasingly, housing authorities are providing an alarms service to social services departments and health authorities who nominate their own clients. Thus the social worker has little knowledge of or control over the components of the service arranged for the client.

Provision in practice

These four categories are analytical rather than operational. In practice, the world of community alarms is much messier. Attributes and values spill over from one model to another. Housing authorities in the business of property enhancement also market a service and attempt to implement interventionist welfare services. The White Paper on community care, in its only reference to alarms, surprisingly treats them as housing 'adaptations', along with hand rails and stair lifts, rather than as a service (DH/DSS/Welsh/Scottish Office, 1989). The majority of services end up as uneasy compromises between 'stand alone' alarms, with the service user responsible for use decisions, and 'social service' alarms where the agency takes responsibility for enhancing use. Here, the tension is most clear between market imperatives (to leave the consumer to his or her own devices) and recognition of accountability (to ensure an appropriate and adequate service). It is this half–heartedness that leads to disillusionment.

Creating need?

Two interlinked forces lead to the unwarranted assumption that 'need' for alarms is widespread: the market; and 'special needs' policies.

Market strategies have two targets: the users and the agencies which recommend and promote alarms among potential users. Direct marketing has become restrained in recent years in the wake of censure over the portrayal of unnecessarily frightening scenarios. The targets for persuasion are as much the concerned relatives as the elderly user. A telephone survey of elderly people provided with an alarm via Help the Aged found the largest proportion (24 per cent) reporting that it was 'first suggested' by a son or daughter; and that it was 'most wanted' not by the alarm user (37 per cent) but by 'others' (56 per cent, 45 per cent of whom were their children) (Breen, 1990). Local authorities are the principal targets for promotional activity. Manufacturers argue the benefits in terms of costs saved in not providing specialised housing. They also attempt to convince health authorities of savings in nursing home places and hospital bed occupation.

These arguments are premised on the assumption that if people happen to be in need of some care, suffering ill–health, or just old, they then 'need' an alarm service. By creating such defining categories, 'need' can be assessed. Thus, for example, a Canadian study (cited in Hobbs, 1991) estimated that '47 per cent of the elderly may be in need of a PRS [Personal Response System] (i.e., have a disability/age 75 and live alone)' (p.17).

The gap between 'need' and demand is then explained in US marketing terms of 'barriers to use'. Such barriers are thought to include 'denial of need', 'refusal to admit increasing frailty' as well as lack of awareness and cost (Montgomery, 1990).

In the UK, a similar set of assumptions is observable in housing led alarms provision. Just as it was assumed that tenants of sheltered housing 'needed' alarms (although research evidence suggested they were accorded low priority by tenants) now it is supposed that elderly people in mainstream housing 'need' a community alarm. Critics argue that allocation to subgroups of the population who are assumed to have 'special needs' because they are old or disabled is stigmatising and encourages negative images of dependent populations (Clapham and Smith, 1990). Clapham and Smith expand on the argument at length, in relation to housing policies in general and to community alarms services in particular. They, too, make the link between the influence of commercial companies who produce and market community alarms equipment and the presumption that older people, by definition, need a means of calling for help in an emergency.

An extension of the argument, discussed but rejected by Clapham and Smith, is to avoid the deleterious impact of special needs policies, and at the same time retain their value as a lever for resources, by widening the range of groups eligible to benefit from 'special' policies. This incremental approach is implicit in Fisk's advocacy of extension of alarms provision to other users (Fisk, 1990). But, as I shall go on to show, this proposition merely compounds the problems of inappropriate assumptions about 'need'. It demonstrates once more a reliance on the technology and a failure to understand the 'system' as a whole. The technology is only the *means* by which help is summoned.

Meeting individual needs?

It has been argued that the

> stereotyping of groups' requirements that is inherent in the 'special needs' philosophy also means that the amenities and services provided are standardised and packaged in ways which might be insensitive to individuals' needs and preferences (Clapham and Smith, p.197).

As I have shown, the majority of provision is allocated on the basis of either ability to pay in the market, or of occupation of a relevant housing type. In both those models of provision, the technology is emphasised and is available either as a consumer good or a feature of the property. This is also true in the model of an alarm as an aid. It is only when community alarms are viewed as a personal social service that the focus shifts and the technology is treated as a *means* to a service. Unless sources of help are in place in the system it is inoperable. And to be acceptable, help has to be individually negotiated and agreed with the service user (Thornton, 1992). This points to a need for commitment to enhance the effectiveness of the service to individual users, and a commitment to intervention.

Why intervene?

Community alarms services appeal to proponents of new welfarist ideology because of the strong element of self–determination. The user can choose when to use the service; it does not come to him relentlessly and against his will. But arguably, intervention is needed to bring the user to a point where he can exercise choice to his best advantage. The very fact that marketing of alarms is backed by notions of consumer autonomy, independence and the like masks the need for intervention. The research evidence to date suggests that effectiveness of community alarms is bound up with interventionist action to increase the user–friendliness of the alarms and the relevance of the components to their users. My contention is that the *processes* by which alarms are provided influence use.

At the most obvious level, it is important to ensure familiarity with the device and methods of operation. Home units can offer a range of features as well as a direct speech link to the control centre: programmed dialling to frequently used numbers; remote telephone answering via the portable trigger; with some, passive monitoring facilities involving a change of setting mode. The conjunction of such facilities on top of the crucial emergency link system can be difficult to assimilate on one briefing. A programme of instruction including hands–on experience can enhance familiarity and confidence in use. Such sustained 'educational' intervention is an uncommon feature, for the staffing resources of providing agencies are not designed to allow for much more than instruction around installation. Some enlist the support of other agencies: alarms agencies in West Glamorgan are backed by Age Concern Glamorgan's team of 'Lifeline Friends' – volunteers with the role of visiting users at the time of installation and after, to help them adjust to the new technology. These volunteers have a further befriending role and a special brief to pick up on unmet support needs that might be met by other agencies. Some schemes enlist the help of home care workers already visiting alarms users.

The impersonal nature of the communication may be a deterrent. Some schemes, through manipulation of staffing rotas, specially arranged visits, or at least photographs, try to ensure some familiarity between the client and the control centre operator. Schemes which incorporate a surveillance function may achieve some familiarity through routine phone calls from control centre staff.

Perhaps the biggest 'barrier' to use that requires interventionist strategies is the users' unwillingness to 'bother' the person who is to respond to a call for help. There are two principal types of respondent: those informal contacts nominated by the user; and wardens employed for that purpose. Supervision of nominated contacts again depends on the degree to which the providing agency is willing or able to try to enhance individual use. Only a small number of schemes have taken on board the Research Institute for Consumer Affairs' research findings that users were cautious of 'bothering' respondents (RICA, 1986), by vetting proposed respondents, ensuring that they were really available and knowledgeable about what was expected of them, or providing them with some preparation for their role. Some vetting of respondents was proved essential in research into one scheme. People nominated were traced and found to be unavailable during working hours, without transport and living at a distance, or themselves incapacitated and unable to cope (Birmingham Housing Department, 1986).

Wardens are employed on shifts. There is no guarantee that any one warden will respond to a call. Some schemes deliberately rotate geographical areas covered to ensure that all wardens are familiar to all clients. Others operate on a patch system. Increasing the familiarity between clients and wardens is expected to break down some of the barriers. On the other hand, it may have the opposite effect; overfamiliarity may change the relationship from that between professional and client to friendship.

Confidence in the appropriateness of the response is essential too. The operator has a pivotal role in the process of interpreting the situation and taking appropriate action to meet individual requirements. This includes sensitivity to individual interpretations of an emergency. Inappropriate responses from the control centre or from the person attending at the house can deter further use. After care is an almost totally neglected service area.

There is little evidence of schemes where staff routinely call on the user after a traumatic event to cope with possible after-effects.

Continuing involvement between the service providing agency and the service recipient may serve to enhance familiarity and to encourage the elderly person to use the service with confidence. It is also necessary to ensure that an appropriate response service is provided in emergencies. All central control computer data bases contain personal and medical information for each client, as well as details of next-of-kin, other contacts and routine service receipt. Typically, such information is entered at time of installation and updates are rare or irregular. The lack of up-to-date information on users' medical conditions and their consequences is a matter of concern. Control centre operators are responsible for making an appropriate assessment of the state of the caller, and wardens responding to a call must assess whether medical help is required.

Few control centres offer feedback on levels or patterns of use by individual clients. Computer software which can provide easy access to aggregate data exists but is little used. Consequently, few of those social services departments that pay housing agencies for a service to nominated clients receive any feedback on how their clients use the service. Such information should guide further service intervention and review.

There are schemes which demonstrate some of these service intervention strategies. No single scheme demonstrates all of them.

Conclusions

On the face of it, community alarms services are well placed to join other mainstream services which support vulnerable people in the community. The technology is advanced and the infrastructure is in place, yet alarms services are rarely used as a resource by those who help plan the care of vulnerable people in ordinary housing. Why should this be? One reason is that the technology and the infrastructure did not develop as a response to community care needs. Rather, providing for people in ordinary mainstream housing has been an additional commercial opportunity for manufacturers and another opening for beleaguered housing authorities. As a consequence, there is a poor fit between the service and the needs it is assumed to meet.

The main obstacle, though, has been the assumption that the technology can stand alone, a reluctance to recognise that it is only a *means* of getting help, and that it is the nature of that help that counts. This shortsightedness is unavoidable given the influence of the market model of alarms provision. Current government ideology supports notions of independence and non-intervention, strengthening definitions of alarms as 'aids', not services. Yet, pulling in the opposite direction are directives about flexibility of services and responsiveness to individual needs.

What does this mean for community care planning? The question of *who* should provide community alarms services is no longer on the policy agenda, despite Griffiths' comments on dissipation of responsibility for delivery of services and his recommendation that alarm services be provided and financed by social services authorities (Griffiths, 1989). The White Paper on Community Care, however, ignored the whole debate about who might be the best *provider* of services. It put the onus on social services departments to identify need and to buy in appropriate services from whatever agencies can provide them. Indeed, the White Paper suggests that, rather than encourage specialism in service provision, a range of competing providers should be stimulated (DH/DSS/Welsh/Scottish Office, 1989).

The prognosis is gloomy for community alarms as a social service. Unless a scheme is designed within a 'service' mould it is unlikely to have any incentive to introduce labour intensive, costly and individually tailored services. Where the service is operating within the mixed economy of the typical housing department, the case for enhancing individual effectiveness is weak. In a market system, service improvements are needed only if take-up is low; as a property feature, individual use is irrelevant. Unless the new purchasing authorities have sufficient financial power to specify the components of the service they wish for their clients, and have the knowledge to base their specifications on, interventionist services tailored to individual needs are unlikely to prosper.

Note

This chapter draws on research supported by the Joseph Rowntree Foundation.

References

Birmingham Housing Department (1986), *A Review of the Dispersed Alarm Programme for Elderly People,* Birmingham.

Breen, T. (1990), 'Community alarms: a non governmental perspective', paper presented to the First International Symposium on Emergency Response Systems for Frail Persons Living Alone, Washington DC.

Clapham, D. and Smith, S. (1990), 'Housing policy and special needs', *Policy and Politics,* vol. 18, no. 3, pp. 193–205.

DH/DSS/Welsh Office/Scottish Office (1989), *Caring for People: Community Care in the Next Decade and Beyond, Cm. 849,* HMSO, London.

Fisk, M.J. (1989a), *Alarm Systems and Elderly People,* The Planning Exchange, Glasgow.

Fisk, M.J. (1989b), 'Dispersed Alarm Systems', Social Care Research Findings No. 2, Joseph Rowntree Memorial Trust, York.

Fisk, M.J. (1990), *Dispersed Alarm Systems in the United Kingdom – A Listing of Central Controls and Appraisal of Current Issues,* The Planning Exchange, Glasgow.

Griffiths, R. (1989), *Community Care: Agenda for Action,* HMSO, London.

Hobbs, M.L. (1991), 'Product design in a personal response program', *International Journal of Technology and Aging,* vol. 4, no. 1, pp. 17–19.

Montgomery, C. (1990), 'Personal response systems in the US: promoting independent living', paper presented to the First International Symposium on Emergency Response Systems for Frail Persons Living Alone, Washington DC.

Pellow, J. (1987), *Keeping Watch: A Study of Caring for the Elderly at Home with the Aid of Electronics,* John Clare Books, London.

RICA (1986), *Dispersed Alarms: A Guide for Organisations Installing Systems,* Research Institute for Consumer Affairs, London.

Thornton, P. (1992), *Community Alarms and Community Care,* Social Policy Research Unit, University of York.

Tinker, A. (1984), *Staying at Home: Helping Elderly People,* HMSO, London.

Which? (1986), 'Sounding the alarm', *Which?,* July, pp. 318–321.

Which? (1989), 'Alarms for elderly people', *Which?,* November, pp. 552–555.

11 Meeting the telecommunications needs of people who are deaf

L. Jones, S. Baldwin and M. Hirst

Introduction

The telephone has become an essential part of modern, everyday life. It helps individuals to keep in touch with family, friends and other social contacts, to manage personal business matters, to obtain information, advice and make emergency calls and, in some cases to practice a trade or profession.

In recent years access to the telephone has expanded and technical advances have created new possibilities for telecommunication. Domestic use of the telephone has increased dramatically. According to the *General Household Survey*, 85 per cent of households had a telephone in 1988 compared with only 42 per cent in 1972 (Foster et al., 1990). In the commercial sphere, cell and car telephones now represent a growing consumer market for telecommunication equipment alongside conference and video facilities.

Increasingly, therefore, people see telephones as a basic need – something without which they cannot fully participate in the life of the community. Access to the telephone is not, however, available on an equal basis. This chapter looks at the effect loss of hearing can have on access to telephone services and the effects of this on people's lives. It also considers the policy implications of regarding deaf people as potential consumers excluded from a key public utility, or as disabled people with special needs.

Deaf people and the telephone

Deafness can limit access to the telephone by restricting an individual's ability to receive and understand messages. However the communication needs of people who are deaf vary greatly. There are people who are born deaf or who develop a hearing loss before they have learned to speak. This group of people, estimated at 50,000 in Great Britain, tend to use sign language. They are more likely to see themselves as part of the deaf community and to want to communicate with other signers. They may be defined as 'culturally deaf'. This group of people regard English as their second language and one which they may have difficulty in reading and writing.

There is a larger group of people who develop a hearing loss in adult life. According to the OPCS disability survey, there are around 2.6 million adults in Great Britain with some hearing loss, though this estimate includes many with relatively minor difficulties (Martin et al., 1988). They usually use speech and regard English as their first language though some may no longer speak clearly. Those with a more severe hearing loss often rely on lip reading or having things written down.

The telecommunication needs of deaf people are equally varied. For people with a less than severe hearing loss there is special equipment which can help them use the ordinary telephone, essentially by amplifying sound. For people whose hearing loss is more severe, there is a range of telecommunication equipment for transmitting text; that is, for typing calls rather than speaking and listening.

At present, there are two main text telecommunication systems for deaf people (Frederiksen et al., 1989). One is a text telephone with a keyboard and small screen. This allows direct or back–to–back text transmission. The user types in what she or he wants to say and receives the response back in text. Both parties require compatible equipment to send and receive calls in this way. By early 1990, it was estimated that between two and five thousand text telephones were being used in the UK (RNID, 1990).

The other text telecommunication system is a relay or link–up service that requires an operator to act as intermediary. The deaf person either speaks directly to a hearing person or types a message to an operator who passes it on verbally; to receive a reply, the operator types the hearing person's response for the deaf person to read at his or her terminal. This system makes telecommunication possible when one party, usually a hearing person, does not have a special text telephone or terminal.

In 1984, the Royal National Institute for the Deaf (RNID), a major voluntary organisation, set up an experimental text relay system known as the Telephone Exchange for Deaf People (TED). The aim was to gain experience of operating a relay service and to evaluate the costs and benefits to its subscribers. The RNID Exchange was designed to serve around 170 subscribers, mostly in Greater London (Martin et al., 1986). Initially, the RNID met most of the overheads and running costs of the TED service with the help of a government funded scheme to create jobs for unemployed adults on socially useful projects. When this came to an end in 1987, the RNID announced that without financial support from government, the Exchange would have to close. In the event, financial support was provided by the government departments of Health and Social Security, and Trade and Industry; and by British Telecom, the main UK telephone company, for a two year period ending in March 1990.

The long term future of the relay service was uncertain however. The RNID was keen to expand the service and put its funding on a more secure basis. British Telecom was itself not willing to provide such a service, arguing that it would not be commercially viable. The government's view was that before longer term decisions could be taken, reliable information was needed on the telecommunication needs of severely deaf people in general, and on the specific role of TED in meeting these. While the RNID link-up service was popular among its subscribers, it was not known how generally useful it might be among people with a severe hearing loss, or how effective it would be in meeting their telecommunication needs. Nor was it clear exactly what its benefits to current users were. The Social Policy Research Unit at the University of York was therefore commissioned to carry out a representative survey of deaf people's telecommunication needs.

The research

The design for the study included three elements: a structured interview survey of around 200 people with an acquired hearing loss, 30 of whom were subsequently re-interviewed in depth, and a separate qualitative study of 20 people whose preferred means of communication was sign language. The chief aim was to help assess the need for and likely benefits of access to text telecommunication, in particular the RNID relay service. Accordingly, the samples were stratified in each case between TED subscribers and non-subscribers who might be considered potential beneficiaries of text telecommunication. The latter group was therefore drawn to encompass deaf people who cannot use the ordinary telephone even with amplification, and those who might find text telecommunication more reliable or less stressful than using an ordinary telephone. Deaf-blind people often use text telecommunication but their particular needs were beyond the scope of this study.

Standard survey techniques had to be adapted for talking to respondents with a severe or profound hearing loss. In the case of people born deaf or deafened from an early age for example, interviews conducted in sign language were video taped and subsequently transcribed into English (Jones and Pullen, 1990; Hirst et al., 1990). Further details of the research, which was carried out in 1989, are given elsewhere (Baldwin et al., 1990; Hirst et al., 1991).

Deaf people's needs for telecommunication services

The study demonstrated very clearly that deaf people felt disadvantaged in their access to the telephone. Most of the people interviewed wanted to use the telephone more than they were able to within the systems available at present, and to do so more easily and more cheaply.

Regardless of the telephone equipment they had, most people in the study still had to rely on hearing people to make calls for them. In emergencies all would have had difficulty in getting help speedily. This reliance on hearing people caused problems. It unnecessarily complicated deaf people's relationships with relatives, friends and colleagues. It was also said to have affected employment opportunities – both in the kind of job people were able to take on and in their career prospects. It clearly contributed to the strong sense of isolation and vulnerability expressed by many respondents.

The deaf people in the study deeply resented the dependence created by their inability to use the telephone in the same way as hearing people. They frequently expressed guilt at the way this forced them to impose on other people, and anger and frustration that it was necessary to do so. Their response to these limitations on their ability to use the telephone was intensified by a strong sense of inequity. The effort and expense required for deaf people to obtain and use basic telephone services was seen as disproportionate to those of hearing people. Moreover, telecommunications technology was seen to be advancing rapidly but not addressing deaf people's needs to the same extent as those of hearing people. Many deaf people were excluded completely from access to telephone services while more and more sophisticated equipment was developed for people with hearing.

The RNID Telephone Exchange for Deaf People

The potential benefits of a relay service are clearly demonstrated by the RNID Telephone Exchange for Deaf People (TED). The overwhelming advantage of TED is the opportunity it creates for telephone contact with the hearing world. TED also offers the choice of conveying messages directly through speech or as text via an operator at the RNID Exchange. The Exchange was greatly valued by respondents who were TED subscribers, chiefly because it enabled them to use the telephone independently. Potentially, TED creates the opportunity to contact anyone with an ordinary telephone without relying on friends or relatives.

Access to the RNID link–up service was reported to have had a significant impact on subscribers' use of the telephone: they made calls on their own more often than non–subscribers. They were also more likely to use the telephone for other than purely social contact, to conduct their personal business for example. The link–up service was also reported to have improved subscribers' quality of life on a number of dimensions. The ability to use the telephone independently via TED was said to have enhanced subscribers' confidence, self–esteem, personal autonomy and well–being. It had also enabled subscribers to keep in touch more easily with friends and family, while for some it had encouraged or strengthened a commitment to voluntary or community activities. TED had also enabled some people to use the telephone independently in their work and by implication had helped them to obtain or retain better paid jobs. However, it was difficult to establish how generally the job prospects of those already in work or seeking paid employment had been improved by access to TED because of the small size of the sample.

The RNID link–up service was clearly very popular with its users. There was also a group of non–subscribers who indicated that they would like to know more about relay services and might be interested in using one. Their knowledge of relay services was limited, however, so we cannot estimate the potential size of this group.

The RNID link–up service does not provide a complete substitute for the ordinary telephone. Some of the reasons for this are inherent to relay systems. The most obvious one is that telephone messages are passed via an operator. This can create problems both for understanding and receiving information; it may limit the ability to convey meaning or feeling and is not ideal where privacy or confidentiality is required. Relay systems also rely on literacy. Relaying a message via an operator can be particularly difficult where the deaf person normally uses sign language or has limited skills in reading and writing.

Other limitations of the RNID link–up service included, above all, the problem of getting through to the Exchange. At the time of the study, the Exchange had only two operator stations, open between 9.30 a.m. and 9.30 p.m., and was closed on Sundays and public holidays. The Exchange was heavily congested most of the time. The cost of using the link–up service also placed TED subscribers at a disadvantage. They incurred two telephone charges when initiating a call via the Exchange; if they lived outside London, one or both calls would be charged at the higher, non–local, rate. The equipment necessary to use the Exchange was also expensive.

Thus, despite access to TED, most subscribers continued to rely on other people to make calls on their behalf via the ordinary telephone – both at home and in the workplace. In consequence, they were as likely to express frustration at their loss of control, privacy and spontaneity as non–subscribers. It was also apparent that the link–up service was less than satisfactory for use in emergencies or for more urgent calls, though many TED subscribers apparently regarded the Exchange as a lifeline. There was also some evidence that hearing people, the friends and relatives of TED subscribers as well as business contacts, were reluctant to use the RNID link–up service. TED subscribers said they initiated more calls than they received via the RNID Exchange, indicating that it did not readily promote reciprocal contact.

Most of these deficiencies reflected the practical limitations of what was essentially a demonstration or pilot project and could be overcome; TED subscribers themselves suggested several ways in which the service could be improved. But it was clear from the study that a link–up service on its own cannot do everything that users might want from a telephone system.

Text telephones

Most obviously, a relay service does not facilitate direct communication. Here direct–text telephones offer several distinct advantages over a link–up service. They are generally available and can be used at all times. In consequence, acquiring and using a text telephone is much more like getting an ordinary telephone than becoming a TED subscriber. Above all, text telephones provide direct, back–to–back communication allowing conversations to be completely private. They are cheaper to buy than the TED equipment; they are also cheaper to use, mainly because messages can be exchanged more quickly than via a relay system. Unlike the TED equipment, most text telephones are portable and can, for example, be used in public call boxes. Respondents who had a text telephone used them especially for keeping in touch with friends and family, and TED subscribers with text telephones reportedly used them as often as they did the RNID link–up service. Some respondents, TED subscribers and non–subscribers alike, also used a text telephone for work.

Text telephones are not, however, without their disadvantages. Like a relay service, their use demands literacy in a written language. In addition, text telephones can only be used to contact someone with compatible equipment. At present, they are not widely available within the hearing world nor in public services and similar agencies. This means that text telephones are of little value for conducting personal business, for contacting agencies offering information and help, or for emergencies.

Costs of text telecommunication

The costs of equipment required to use the RNID Exchange and the costs of text telephones and telephone aids and adaptations are potentially large, though extremely variable. According to this study, typical costs in 1989 for TED equipment, including necessary items such as flashing lights, were around £200 up to a maximum of £1000. The price of a text telephone was about £200. A significant minority had invested in both systems; most had purchased one or more aids or adaptations. The costs of special telephone equipment are therefore substantially more than those normally incurred by hearing people, and for some respondents were variously shared by family, and by statutory and other agencies.

To a degree, the amount of equipment individuals had obtained reflected their needs and preferences. As with all expenditure, however, what can be purchased is constrained by the income available. It cannot be assumed that the level of expenditure revealed by the survey estimates enabled the people in this study to assemble the telecommunications package that met all their needs. The costs of buying special telephone equipment have to be set within the context of deaf people's reduced purchasing power. Elderly deaf people are usually dependent on state benefits and deaf people below pension age are disproportionately found in manual occupations and are often underemployed (Jones et al., 1987; Jones and Pullen, 1989).

People who use sign language

Our interviews with people who are deaf and use sign language revealed that they have very different needs from people with an acquired hearing loss who are comfortable using English and will often want to use speech. Sign language users tended to see themselves as part of the deaf community and wanted to use the telephone particularly to communicate with other deaf people. They were thus not ideally served by either relay or text systems; both of these relied on the use of English, which was not regarded as their first language. English was seen as problematic because many culturally deaf people leave school with poor literacy skills. The presence of an observer, such as the operator in a relay service or a hearing person who did not understand that some deaf people had problems with English, was also problematic for some people.

In the long term, and to facilitate communication with other people using sign language, the videophone was seen as the ideal telephone. In the meantime, text telephones were regarded as providing an effective means of communication. They went further towards meeting the needs of culturally deaf people than relay services and were welcomed enthusiastically by this group. Another, smaller group of deaf people who used sign language found relay services more suited to their needs. These people tended to use sign–supported English rather than British Sign Language and to be more comfortable with English in its written form. The people in both groups welcomed new technology and felt that currently it was not being fully exploited to meet their needs.

Meeting needs for telephone services

The study clearly demonstrated that, like hearing people, deaf people have widely varying needs for telephone services. The choices they had made were, predictably, affected by factors such as their age; where they lived; the cost of different telephone systems and their ability to afford them; class and cultural attitudes to the telephone as a means of communication, and so on. These factors were, however, less salient than who deaf people wanted to communicate with and how they wanted to communicate. Some wanted to contact hearing people, others wanted to contact deaf people; some wanted to do both. Deaf people generally used the systems that catered for their particular needs, though there was a large group whose needs were met inadequately or not at all.

Their telephone 'systems' ranged from, at one extreme, nothing at all to a sophisticated and complex packaging of different kinds of equipment at the other. Thus a small minority in the sample had both direct–text and text relay systems, sometimes combining these with other telecommunication services such as facsimile transmission and electronic mail. Another group relied mainly on one of these systems, usually relay or direct–text. A third group had no access at all to text telephones or a relay service and access only to the ordinary telephone. People in this situation were forced to rely heavily on hearing people, had in general much less contact with friends and relatives and had even fewer options for dealing with emergencies than other deaf people. They were clearly disadvantaged by their lack of access to telephone services. This was sometimes the result of lack of information but more often related to the cost of buying and using special equipment. Many of the people in this group expressed interest in relay services or text telephones.

Thus the key distinction between respondents in the study was not between subscribers to the RNID link–up service and non–subscribers, but between respondents with a 'special' telephone system and those who had access only to ordinary telephones or none at all. People with access to any kind of text telecommunication were better off than those without a special telephone; those with a combination of text based systems were even more so. However even the most complicated of the systems described did not provide the perfect answer.

Discussion

The research project described in this chapter highlighted the exclusion of many deaf people from the easy and increasingly sophisticated telephone services on offer to the hearing majority. It confirmed the adverse effects this had on their lives and that they felt disadvantaged. Their expressed need for better access to the telephone was strong.

The situation of deaf telephone users has changed somewhat since the research findings were presented to the Department of Health. A Text Users Help Scheme was introduced in 1989. Funded by British Telecom and administered by the RNID, this scheme helps with the extra costs of text telecommunication by rebating 60 per cent of call charges up to a maximum of £160 a year. British Telecom has also provided £4 million over three years for the RNID to set up and run a national 24 hour relay service, and has donated 3,000 'discontinued' text telephones for the RNID to distribute at a token price.

These developments are welcome. However they also raise basic issues of principle. Where does responsibility for improving deaf people's access to telephone services lie? The latest developments can be seen as a benevolent gesture by a private sector entrepreneur at a time of high profitability, and administered by a charitable organisation – with all that implies for averting attention from service users' perceptions and wants. Institutional philanthropy does not really address the claims of deaf people to have access to a basic public utility like the telephone as of right. Are they better viewed as potential customers, currently excluded from the service (rather like people in the remoter parts of Britain who do not have access to mains sewerage or television), or as dependent people in need of special equipment and help with the extra costs of using the service?

Two distinct, but related, issues lie behind this question. One concerns the relative advantage of the status of customer as opposed to that of client. It is often argued that greater power and choice is available to disabled people when they can buy the goods and services they need in the market place rather than having to rely on welfare agencies or professionals' assessment to establish entitlement. Without the conditions to guarantee equal opportunity, however, treating deaf people purely as customers runs the risk of excluding their particular demands from the market process.

The second issue concerns the costs of improving deaf people's access to the telephone and whether these should be borne by government or by private sector providers of lines and equipment like British Telecom and Mercury.

In countries such as Sweden, Canada and the United States the view seems to have emerged that government and the private sector each have responsibilities and a role to play in improving deaf people's access to telephone services. Text relay services have been established as part of mainstream services to consumers, the costs being covered in various ways. In parts of the United States, for example, they are covered via a levy on all customers. Equipment too is often provided on a subsidised basis. In Denmark, for example, special equipment is developed by the telephone companies and provided free to people who are deaf; help with call costs is provided via the social security system. A different approach is used in Italy where a communication allowance is paid directly to deaf people to be used as they wish: for sign language interpreters or for telecommunications. In none of these countries, however, is the provision of telephone services for deaf people dependent on the goodwill of private sector companies or administered by charitable agencies.

In Britain, institutional arrangements for improving deaf people's access to the telephone remain unclear. Government departments, telephone companies, those who develop and manufacture equipment, statutory and voluntary agencies are all involved but none seems willing to accept full responsibility. The government's view at present seems to be that deaf people should be regarded as potential customers whom the telephone companies ought to enable to use this basic public utility. This view is clearly not shared by British Telecom for example, which sees itself primarily as a provider of the telephone network and, with firms like Mercury, of a range of customer services. As a profit making concern British Telecom admits no obligation to ensuring equal access though, as noted above, it is prepared occasionally to help deaf customers as a gesture of goodwill, via grants to the RNID. Helping with the extra costs that deaf customers face, whether for special equipment or calls, is felt to be the role of government departments in charge of policy on disability: Health, Social Security and Employment.

Our view would be that, as in countries like Denmark and Italy, public and private sectors each have obligations and should work together to provide access to the telephone for people who are deaf – on equal terms with hearing people and on the basis of entitlement rather than goodwill or patronage (Baldwin and Jones, 1990). There seems no good reason why the commercial sector should not develop and provide the necessary equipment on a subsidised basis, charging reasonable rentals and sharing any shortfall with government. In due course increased use of the telephone system might well cover any initial loss of revenue. Nor does it seem unreasonable that the extra costs deaf people encounter in using telecommunications services should be met from the social security system. Benefits which aim to cover extra costs are currently based on needs for help with physical functions and there are no plans to include communications costs (DSS, 1990). A communications allowance along the lines of the Italian model would redress the balance. An approach based on integrating public and private sector provision could enable deaf people to use the telephone on much the same basis as hearing people without polarising them as customers or clients. As in other fields of social policy, equality of access and of outcome requires positive and sensitive discrimination.

The technology already exists to provide telephone access for people who are deaf; the developments outlined here could be initiated almost immediately. The barriers have much more to do with responsibility and cost than with technical feasibility or, indeed, scruples about the form of access that is 'best' for deaf people. It is more than time that deaf people had the chance to use today's sophisticated telephone systems to meet their basic needs for personal autonomy and social participation.

Note

The research on which this chapter is based was funded by the Department of Health. The views expressed are those of the authors and are not necessarily shared by any government department.

References

Baldwin, S. and Jones, L. (1990), 'Poor connections', *New Statesman & New Society*, vol. 3, no. 125, p. 39.

Baldwin, S., Jones, L., Hirst, M.A., Pullen, G., Fothergill, B. and Thirlway, M. (1990), *Poor Connections: The Telecommunication Needs of People who are Deaf*, Working Paper no. 677, Social Policy Research Unit, University of York.

DSS (1990), *The Way Ahead*, Cm. 917, Department of Social Security, HMSO, London.

Foster, K., Wilmot, A. and Dobbs, J. (1990), *General Household Survey 1988*, HMSO, London.

Frederiksen, J., Martin, M., Puig de la Bellacasa, R. and Von Tetzchner, S. (1989), *The Use of Telecommunication: The Needs of People with Disabilities*, Fundesco and Telefonica, Madrid.

Hirst, M.A., Jones, L. and Baldwin, S. (1990), 'Communication skills and research', in Robbins, D. and Walters, A. (eds) *Department of Health Yearbook of Research and Development 1990*, HMSO, London.

Hirst, M.A., Baldwin, S. and Jones, L. (1991), 'Text telecommunication for people who are deaf: assessing the use of a text relay service', *British Journal of Audiology*, vol. 25, pp. 361–370.

Jones, L., Kyle, J. and Wood, P. (1987), *Words Apart: Losing Your Hearing as an Adult*, Tavistock, London.

Jones, L. and Pullen, G. (1989), *Inside We Are All Equal: A Social Policy Survey of Deaf People in the European Community*, European Community Regional Secretariat of the World Federation of the Deaf, London.

Jones, L. and Pullen, G. (1990), 'Doing deaf research', *Cash and Care*, Social Policy Research Unit Newsletter, no. 7, University of York.

Martin, J., Meltzer, H. and Elliot, D. (1988), *The Prevalence of Disability among Adults*, OPCS Surveys of Disability in Great Britain, HMSO, London.

Martin, M.C., Spanner, M., Warren, J. and Home, S. (1986), *RNID Telephone Exchange for the Deaf: progress report*, Royal National Institute for the Deaf, London.

RNID (1990), personal communication to authors, Royal National Institute for the Deaf, London.

12 Communication aid centres: Do they fulfil a need?

B. Leese, K. Tolley, K. Wright, S. Hennessy, M.A. Chamberlain, J. Stowe and C. Rowley

Introduction

The causes of communication disorders are many and varied and cut across all age groups, and socioeconomic and educational backgrounds. For most people, the development of speech and language occurs naturally during the infant years and is expanded throughout adolescence and adult life. However, a minority of young children have congenital problems such that they are unable to develop their language processes fully (for example in cerebral palsy). Other people acquire communication problems in later life often due to trauma such as stroke, head injury, laryngectomy, or a progressive disorder such as motor neurone disease (MND) or Parkinson's Disease. It has been estimated that 800,000 people in the UK have severe communication disorders (speech and language noticeably impaired) (Enderby and Philipp, 1986). Martin et al (1988) estimated that there were 1.2 million people with some sort of communication difficulty in Great Britain. Many of these people need help with their communication problems.

Speech therapists treat any person who has a communication disorder, and they have a range of intervention processes, including communication aids, which range from sophisticated but expensive computer and speech synthesiser systems, to low cost, low technology equipment such as picture boards or eye transfer frames. For present purposes a communication aid can be defined as 'any device or equipment used by a person whose speech is either absent or unintelligible, to communicate or facilitate communication with another person or persons'. The range of available equipment is vast (Rowley et al, 1986). People's requirements for communication equipment vary but principal considerations include accessibility, portability, flexibility (in order to respond to changing needs), cost, reliability, speed of output and motivation.

In the case of people with progressive disorders, the early introduction of communication equipment can maintain and extend the ability to communicate when physical function is severely impaired (Beukelman and Yorkston, 1989). Because of the increasing numbers and types of equipment available, professionals working with people with communication disorders have found their task of maintaining up-to-date knowledge about the assessment and provision of equipment becoming increasingly difficult, and this raises questions of how best to deliver a communication aid service.

Since 1983, some district health authorities have established their own Communication Aid Centres, for example in Leicester, Lincoln and Southampton. Most of the 33 Disabled Living Centres in the UK have a section devoted to communication equipment. Expertise in communication aid provision also exists in centres such as the ACE (Aids to Communication in Education) centre in Oxford. Little literature is available about the running of such centres.

In 1981, funding for six Communication Aid Centres (CACs) was provided by RADAR (The Royal Association of Disability and Rehabilitation) and the Department of Health and Social Security to meet an expressed need for specialist centres which would be concerned with all aspects of the supply of communication aids for speech impaired clients. The CACs have been operational since 1983, and were set up with four main objectives:

to assess patients with speech impairment for suitable aids;

to act as an information and resource centre;

to spread expertise to speech therapists;

to undertake evaluation and research.

In 1987 the Department of Health commissioned a study of the CACs from the Rheumatology and Rehabilitation Research Unit at the University of Leeds and the Centre for Health Economics at the University of York. The aims of this study were to assess whether the original ideals of the CACs were being achieved; to look at cost effectiveness; to examine client satisfaction and to measure the scope of the work carried out at each CAC. In order to help in the interpretation of the data, a group of clients was assessed from four districts which did not contain a CAC, namely Liverpool, Mid Surrey, Leeds West and Mid Staffordshire.

The six CACs were established in an attempt to cover the needs of children and adults and to give reasonable geographical spread. They are located at Frenchay Hospital, Bristol; in Birmingham (Sandwell CAC); in London (Charing Cross CAC, and Mecklenburgh Square Wolfson CAC); in Newcastle (The Dene Centre), and in Cardiff (Rookwood CAC). The Wolfson CAC sees only children and Charing Cross sees only adults while the others have a mixed caseload. This chapter assesses how far needs are met by a specialist communication aid service.

Methods

The study was conducted by means of questionnaires and interviews with staff and clients. An interview schedule was designed to elicit background information from staff on all aspects of the functioning of the communication aid service in CACs and non–CAC districts. Topics covered included staffing levels, referral, assessment and funding procedures, equipment available for demonstrations and loan, repair and adaptation facilities, and overall satisfaction of the staff with the service they were able to provide.

A one year prospective study looking at the day to day functioning of the communication aid service was also conducted, and this involved collecting data on all CAC and non–CAC district clients receiving a communication aid service. In addition, data were collected on aspects relating to caseload and workload, enquiries, feedback from courses held and the time allocation of staff involved in communication aids provision. Data collected included numbers of clients referred, numbers recommended an aid, and numbers provided with equipment; teaching commitments of staff; the extent of liaison with manufacturers and dissemination of information; as well as any research which might have been carried out. Data were collected in the same way from staff in the non–CAC districts.

Staff in the CACs were also asked to complete a questionnaire each month over a one year period to give an indication of the type of work undertaken. Information requested included data on the numbers of referrals from within and outside the districts as well as on the continuing caseload. A major part of the study involved assessment of the satisfaction of clients with the service they had received. All clients attending each CAC and non–CAC district over a year were followed up by the research team, provided client consent had been received. Of clients who had received equipment, a sample were personally interviewed and the remainder were sent a postal questionnaire. As the prospective year progressed it became apparent that some people had not received equipment several months after their initial assessment. To obtain information about their assessment, and to discover why they did not have communication equipment, a further postal questionnaire was sent.

Results and discussion

The focus of this chapter is on clients' views of the service they have received, in an attempt to assess whether the CACs do fulfil a need. However, before discussing client views, a brief outline will be given of some of the data collected directly from the CACs.

Service structure

The CACs are staffed in the main by a speech therapist with secretarial support. Part time assistance is usually received from a medical physics technician and both the Wolfson and Newcastle CACs employ a part time occupational therapist. The main departure from this arrangement occurs at the Sandwell CAC which is staffed by a team comprising two bioengineers, a psychologist, a speech therapist, and a secretary.

Variable amounts of information were submitted by the CACs so that direct and meaningful comparisons between them were not easy to make and should be treated with caution. In particular, because of staff shortages, Newcastle CAC was only able to supply retrospective data with much less detail than that supplied by the other five CACs.

Table 12.1 sets out the referral patterns and caseload of the CACs, and also shows the numbers of communication aids acquired during the study year, together with courses organised and attended by CAC staff.

CACs were much more likely to receive clients from outside their districts than from within them. For example, Sandwell received only two per cent of its clients from within the district. These figures reflect the fact that the CACs each serve a wide area of the country.

In many cases, where an aid was not recommended, this was because assessment was incomplete. This was particularly marked in Sandwell, where 81 per cent of clients not recommended an aid were still being assessed. This should be compared with Wolfson CAC, which treats only children, where all the clients who had not received an aid were in this situation for reasons other than because they were still being assessed. In Frenchay and Charing Cross approximately one third of clients not recommended an aid were still being assessed. Figures for Rookwood and Newcastle were higher at 60 per cent and 57 per cent respectively. These differences are a reflection of the autonomous nature of the CACs, each of which has its own pattern of service provision related to its history and to the needs of the population which it serves. In particular, Sandwell CAC undertakes a rigorous continuing assessment of clients, whereas in the other CACs an aid is frequently recommended after a single treatment session.

All six CACs acquired additional communication aids during the year. Frenchay acquired the largest number, whereas Rookwood reported only two

Table 12.1
CAC referral patterns and caseload

	Charing Cross	French-ay	New castle	Rook-wood	Sand-well	Wolfson
No. clients referred from within district	30	36	27	17	1	–
No. clients referred from outside district	102	56	70	48	58	90
Clients who had aid recommended	62	50	42	57	26	60

Continuing caseload

	Charing Cross	French-ay	New castle	Rook-wood	Sand-well	Wolfson
Under treatment	N/I	N/A	N/I	N/I	N/I	N/I
Reviewed	N/I	N/A	N/I	N/I	N/I	N/I
No longer wish to be seen	–	5	N/I	1	–	6
Been discharged	41	–	N/I	–	–	1
Died	13	6	4	–	5	2
Other	–	4	N/I	–	–	–

Clients with no aid recommended

	Charing Cross	French-ay	New castle	Rook-wood	Sand-well	Wolfson
Assessment incomplete	16	8	25	24	48	–
No aid required	8	3	12	3	5	–
No aid suitable/acceptable	14	6	–	5	3	–
Client did not attend	10	–	6	5	1	–
Other	–	3	1	3	2	31

Activities of CAC

	Charing Cross	French-ay	New castle	Rook-wood	Sand-well	Wolfson
No. aids acquired	30	56	32	2	27	37
No. courses organised	3	12	3	9	7	7
No. courses attended	7	7	4	6	8	4
Research activities	–	1	–	–	2	2

N/A = not applicable
N/I = no information

aids (plus a number of specially adapted switches). Acquisition of aids may be dependent on the CAC budget, and on the generosity of manufacturers. These communication aids are used during client assessment sessions, and in some cases for short term loans to clients.

In line with their stated aim of spreading expertise to speech therapists, staff of all the CACs were involved in teaching commitments which included lectures, talks and workshops to groups of students, speech therapists and related staff, and charities, as well as discussing aspects of their work with numerous visitors. In addition to teaching commitments, CAC staff also organised and attended a variety of courses. Courses were organised to update speech therapists, occupational therapists and other related staff such as general practitioners, physiotherapists and teachers about recent developments in the management of people with communication problems, and the appropriateness of aids. Courses were also organised to provide information on the role and function of the CACs. Staff of the CACs themselves attended courses organised externally to enable them to keep up with communication aids development, particularly where computers were involved. Research activities varied considerably between CACs. Three CACs did not report any research during the study year whereas Sandwell and Wolfson each had initiated two research projects.

In general, whilst the broad activities of all six CACs were similar, there were important differences according to the interests of individual staff and budget constraints. These were highlighted in an exercise carried out to assess the time allocation of centre based staff. CAC staff completed time allocation charts for between one and three working weeks. In particular, major differences were apparent in the amount of client contact time. Figures for Newcastle were particularly low, with only 14 per cent of staff time involved in direct client contact, but this could be due to the less reliable data obtained from this CAC. Wolfson, Frenchay and Rookwood CACs devoted a high proportion of their time to direct client contact (42 per cent, 39 per cent and 35 per cent respectively), but the reverse was true for Sandwell and Charing Cross where much client contact time was indirect, by telephone or letter. In the latter two CACs, direct client contact time accounted for 13 per cent and 21 per cent of staff time, respectively. In some cases, the client is assessed in a single session whereas in other cases the policy of the CAC is for a series of treatment sessions. These differences reflected the type and variety of services provided by the CACs, and the differing needs of the clients.

Table 12.2 shows the number of clients assessed at each CAC and non–CAC district during the one year study period. A total of 430 clients were seen, and 204 were followed up by the research team. However, information on only 24 clients from the four non–CAC districts was received, making comparisons between CAC and non–CAC services difficult.

Table 12.2

Clients seen at each centre during the study year

CAC	No. seen	Non–CAC district	No. seen
Charing Cross	115	Leeds West	13
Frenchay	72	Liverpool	5
Newcastle	78	Mid Staffs	1
Rookwood	46	Mid Surrey	5
Sandwell	56		
Wolfson	39		

A total of 226 clients were not followed up. The main reasons were that consent was not given (29 per cent) and non–return of the questionnaire from those assessed by post (17 per cent). It is inevitable in a population of moderately to severely ill people that a large number will either have died or be too ill to take part (13 per cent and 21 per cent respectively). Other reasons for non–follow up included factors such as the client having left the area, or moved abroad (three per cent).

Of the 204 clients who were followed up, 127 were interviewed and 77 were sent a postal questionnaire. Postal questionnaires were sent to all those who had not received their aids and occasionally to others with aids for whom it had proved impossible to arrange an interview.

268 of the clients seen by the CACs and non–CAC districts during the study year were male and 162 were female. As can be seen from Table 12.3, 43 per cent of the clients were aged at least 45 years, and only five per cent were in the age range 0 to 5 years.

Table 12.4 sets out the major diagnoses of the clients. Some had more than one problem recorded. Cerebral palsy and motor neurone disease (MND) were by far the most prevalent conditions. Those suffering from MND may find their ability to speak deteriorating relatively rapidly, so that referral, assessment and provision of an aid is necessary in as short a time as possible.

Table 12.3
Age distribution of clients receiving
communication aid services

Age range (years)	No. clients	% clients
0 – 5	23	5
6 – 18	84	20
19 – 30	64	15
31 – 44	56	13
45 – 64	105	24
65 and over	83	19
Not recorded	15	4
Total	430	100

Table 12.4
Diagnoses of clients referred for communication aid services

Diagnosis	No. clients with diagnosis	% of total clients with diagnosis
Cerebral palsy	144	30
Motor neurone disease	84	17
Stroke	42	9
Neurological disease	27	6
Multiple sclerosis	24	5
Laryngectomy	22	5
Learning difficulties	22	5
Head injury	18	4
Speech impairment	16	4
Language impairment	15	3
Parkinson's disease	10	2
Voice disorder	8	2
Visual/hearing impairment	8	2
Brain damage	5	1
Dementia	2	1
Other	35	7
Not known	3	1

Of the clients for whom information was available, 248 (63 per cent) had
their medical condition rated as severe, with a further 111 (28 per cent) being

rated as moderate. Only 35 clients (nine per cent) had their condition rated as mild by CAC staff. Many of these clients, therefore, were in considerable need of help with their communication difficulties.

Assessment usually took place at a CAC or a speech therapy department, and this was the case for 130 (64 per cent) and 23 (11 per cent) of clients followed up, respectively. However, where clients were unable to travel, assessment could take place at the normal place of residence of the client. This was the case for 26 (13 per cent) clients who were assessed at home. A further five clients were assessed at a day centre, and 20 clients were assessed elsewhere, for example, at a residential home or school. The service is flexible and able to respond to the needs of the client.

After assessment, there are a number of possibilities for the client including ongoing trials at which several aids are tested before a definitive choice is arrived at. Alternatively, an aid may be decided upon and loaned to the client, if the CAC has one available for this purpose, or a decision may be made on which aid would be most suitable and an application for funding made. Table 12.5 lists the most frequently recommended types of aids. It is quite possible that more than one aid may be recommended for a client. For example, a client who has had a laryngectomy may be recommended a voice amplifier and a telephone attachment which is programmed to speak short phrases on their behalf. For someone who is in a wheelchair, for example, perhaps with limited movement, special switches may be required to enable use of a computer to display text.

Table 12.5
Type of aid recommended to clients during the study year

Type of aid recommended	No. recommended
Letter display unit	100
Speech synthesis	61
Computer	30
Laryngectomy aid	13
Amplifier	34
Eye gaze/chart	55
Miscellaneous	184
Total	477

Aids may be given out on loan for a variety of reasons. The most frequent reason was that the device was on loan for a trial period to assess suitability. Some clients had an aid on loan while waiting for their definitive aid, and in other cases the situation was changing so rapidly that an aid was loaned for a short period and then the client was reassessed.

Table 12.6
Agencies expected to fund recommended aids

Agency	No. to be funded	% of total
Health authority	94	44
Charity	31	15
Self/family	23	11
Private sources	17	8
Social services department	17	8
NHS prescription	13	6
Education authority	6	3
Department of Employment	6	3
CAC	2	1
Manpower Services	1	0.5
Other	2	1
Total	212	100

Once a client has been recommended an aid, funding has to be considered. This can be a major problem even for low cost aids. Some of the computerised aids can be expensive, costing up to £3000. Another problem is that there is no recognised funding route and rarely a specific budget for communication aids. Table 12.6 lists the agencies expected to fund the recommended aids. In some cases, there was more than one stated agency. However, of the 430 clients referred to researchers as having been assessed for an aid during the study year, only 112 (26 per cent) had definitely received their aid by the end of the study period. A further five clients had received part of their aid, and no information was available on 173. There were 140 people who had not received equipment, of whom 40 were known to be waiting for equipment to be made up, and 25 were known to be awaiting funding. The major source of funding was the clients' local health authority, but there was a large input from charities (15 per cent) and many clients paid for their own aids (11 per cent).

Further questions were asked to determine why recommended aids had not been received by clients who were followed up. These reasons, where available, are listed in Table 12.7. More than one reason was frequently given. The major reasons cited for non–receipt of aids were that assessment was continuing or that funding was awaited. Communication Aid Centres

Table 12.7
Reasons for not receiving the recommended communication aid

Reason	No. clients giving reason	% of total
Still being assessed	21	21
Waiting for funding	18	18
Undergoing trial/review	15	15
Aid was not suitable	10	10
Recommended aid not available	8	8
No aid needed	8	8
None recommended	7	7
Waiting for adaptations	3	3
Other	10	10
Total	100	100

and the non–CACs provide a much needed service, greatly valued by clients, but follow up is frequently slow and uncoordinated, with funding being a particular problem. Nevertheless, the clients followed up during the study were asked to assess their overall impression of the centres on a scale in which 0 represented 'poor' and 100 represented 'excellent'. The results are presented in Table 12.8.

Table 12.8
Clients' overall impression of the assessment centre service

Rating	No. clients giving rating	%	Cumulative %
10–19	1	0.5	0.5
20–29	1	0.5	1
30–39	3	2	3
40–49	9	5	8
50–59	13	8	16
60–69	13	8	24
70–79	16	9	33
80–89	35	20	53
90–99	47	27	80
100	35	20	100
Total	173	100	100

Of the 173 clients who gave a rating, 35 (20 per cent) rated their assessment as 'excellent' and 67 per cent gave ratings of 80 or more, indicating a very high level of satisfaction by the clients with the service they had received from the assessment process.

Further efforts were made to assess client satisfaction with the process of acquiring a communication aid. When asked what they hoped the equipment would do for them, 79 clients said they simply wanted to be able to communicate better. Others had wanted the aid to help them at work or school, or had simply wanted to try out a number of aids. When asked if the equipment they had acquired had fulfilled their expectations, 108 responses were received. 71 (66 per cent) indicated that the aid had done what they had hoped it would do, and a further ten (nine per cent) said that this was partly the case. Only 27 clients (25 per cent) said that the aid had not fulfilled their expectations. Reasons for this included comments that the aid was not working properly; that it was unsuitable; or that more experience in using it was necessary. In addition, some displays were difficult to read.

The effect the aid had on the client's own rating of his/her quality of life was assessed and the results are set out in Table 12.9. Of 109 people assessed and who provided a judgement, 86 (79 per cent) stated that there was an improvement in their overall quality of life. Most of these (54) claimed a 'slightly better' quality of life, and the rest (32) thought their quality of life was 'much better' as a consequence of the communication aid. Twenty one per cent of clients assessed at a CAC felt that their quality of life had not improved.

Table 12.9
Clients' perception of the impact of the communication aid
on their quality of life

Effect	Number	%
Much better	32	29
Slightly better	54	50
No change	22	20
Slightly worse	1	1
Total	109	100

Are needs met?

The need for services for people who have difficulty in communicating has been amply demonstrated from this study. People were usually appreciative of the service they had received, though many were frustrated by the length of time they had to wait between the recommendation and receipt of an aid. This led to problems for CAC staff when deciding which aid to recommend to a client. One major factor was the likelihood that there would be a delay in the funding of expensive aids. The CAC service suffers from the lack of a standard mechanism for funding the purchase of communication aids for clients (a CAC budget or special consultant budget for communication aids). This is one of the major deficiencies of the CAC system, which could have been corrected when they were originally established. For example, the centres' objectives did not include being providers of aids, only assessors of need. At the time that this study was carried out, the onus of communication aid provision was on the client and the local speech therapist, or sometimes the consultant who referred the client.

Another problem faced by CAC staff is the urgency with which an aid is required by a client. For a client with, for example, motor neurone disease, the CAC staff had to reconcile the problem of urgent need for an aid which was appropriate, and the possibility that the aid, particularly if expensive, might not be immediately available. This also raises the problem that clients with less urgent needs might have to wait even longer for provision of an aid. These problems have been partially overcome by the development by CAC staff of a loans system, the aids sometimes being provided by manufacturers, or by recommending relatively low cost aids rather than other, more expensive, high technology aids. The establishment of a funding system that allows provision to follow assessment is urgently needed. This would do much to ease both the frustrations of the clients who, having been satisfied with the assessment process, find that the much needed aid is unobtainable because of lack of funding, and also of speech therapists trying to find their way round the system.

Speech impaired clients were generally satisfied with the service they received from the CACs. Once equipment had been acquired, most clients indicated their satisfaction that the aid had fulfilled their expectations. In terms of access to funding for aids, needs were not being fully met for some clients. Those who were more affluent could purchase their own aids, whereas poorer clients were dependent on funding being available, and frequently, this was not the case. A standard funding system for aids provision would lead to greater equity for clients, and would ensure that their needs were more likely to be met. The existence of CACs at only six locations in England and Wales means that some clients have to travel considerable distances to avail themselves of the specialist service. In some cases, this will involve high personal costs for the client and his or her family in terms of travel time, expenses and lost income. Again, this will be more of a problem for poorer clients, and is another example of lack of equity in provision. Since the CACs have evolved independently and provide different services, a client whose nearest CAC provides a 'continuous assessment' service might benefit more from the 'single assessment' model available at a more distant CAC. This again indicates that the needs of some clients are not being fully met.

In conclusion, the CACs provide a greatly valued service in assessing clients and recommending aids, and in this respect they do meet a need. There are, however, several factors which, if addressed, could lead to a more equitable service, which would go a long way towards meeting the needs of even more clients.

Note

This study was funded by the Department of Health.

References

Beukelman, D.R. and Yorkston, K.M. (1989), 'Augmentative and alternative communication application for persons with severe acquired communication disorders; an introduction', *Augmentative and Alternative Communication*, vol. 5, no. 1, pp. 42–48.

Enderby, P. and Philipp, R. (1986), 'Speech and language handicap: towards knowing the size of the problem', *British Journal of Disorders of Communication*, vol. 21, no. 2, pp. 151–165.

Martin, J. Meltzer, H. and Elliot, D. (1988), *The prevalance of disability among adults*, OPCS Surveys of Disability in Great Britain, HMSO, London.

Rowley. C., Stowe, J., Bryant, J. and Chamberlain, M.A. (1986), *Communication Aids Provision*, Rheumatology and Rehabilitation Research Unit, University of Leeds.

Part Four
ASSESSING NEEDS

13 Needs and resources in local government finance

P. Smith

Introduction

In April 1990 the United Kingdom government implemented a fundamental change to local government finance in England and Wales. The system of local property taxation, known as the rates, was abolished. In its place were put two new taxes. The local business rates were replaced by a national rate of business property taxation, set by the central government and levied at the same rate throughout the country. This new tax is known as the uniform business rate, or national non–domestic rate (NNDR). The yield from the NNDR is redistributed to local authorities in proportion to their adult populations. Domestic property taxation was abandoned completely, being replaced by a community charge (or poll tax) which is levied on all adults living in an area. With the exception of those on low incomes, who can claim rebates of up to 80 per cent, all adults in an area pay the same level of community charge.

The revision of the system of central government grants to local authorities was a third important feature of the reforms. Each local authority now receives a lump sum grant which is determined by central government's assessment of the level of needs in the area, and which is independent of the expenditure level adopted by the local authority. This means that a local authority's income from local business taxation and central government grant is fixed, so that the entire burden of its marginal expenditure is now borne

181

by local residents, in the form of the community charge. A fourth change, implemented simultaneously, but independent of the other reforms, was the simplification of the needs assessment procedures used to distribute central government grant.

The rationale for the reforms is set out in the Green Paper *Paying for Local Government*, and centres on the desire to enhance accountability in local government (DoE, 1986). The new taxes, in particular the community charge, provoked widespread public hostility, and many commentators cite the reforms as the main reason for the downfall of Margaret Thatcher in November 1990 (Gibson, 1990). Opposition political parties were committed to the abolition of the community charge, and in April 1991 the Conservative government announced its own proposals for a revised form of domestic property tax, known as the council tax, as a replacement for the community charge (DoE, 1991a). Although this chapter does not offer a comprehensive explanation of the failure of the poll tax, it presents data which cast some light on the regional implications of the tax, which made an important contribution to its unpopularity.

Implicit in the 1990 reforms was a dramatic change in the local resource base available to finance local government spending. In particular, the basis for local domestic taxation switched from property to adults, and this resulted in large swings in tax liability for individuals, households, and geographical areas. Elsewhere, Smith (1991) shows that, after rebates have been taken into account, the only income group as a whole that experienced a substantial change in tax liability was the top ten per cent income band, which on average enjoyed a considerable reduction in local tax bills as a result of the reforms. However within income bands there were large swings in fortune. The impact of the reforms on individual households is not considered further here.

Instead, the purpose of this chapter is to examine the geographical implications of the reforms for local domestic taxation. The focus of attention throughout the chapter is the average tax bill in a locality, before rebates have been deducted. In the next section, the system of finance introduced in 1990 is described, followed by an analysis of the geographical implications of the domestic sector reforms. Quite apart from the poll tax, the new system of measuring needs also resulted in considerable swings in tax liability between areas. The change to needs assessment procedures is therefore described next, and an estimate of its geographical implications presented. The chapter ends with an examination of the likely impact of the system proposed by the government as a replacement for the ill-fated community charge.

The 1990 reforms to local government finance

Underlying the system of local government finance prevailing before 1990 was the belief that a locality should be able to provide a standard level of service to its community at a standard rate of taxation, regardless of its resource base. The local tax yield varied considerably between areas when the standard rate of taxation was applied to the local property tax base (or rateable value). An important purpose of the central government grant was therefore to make up the difference between the yield from the standard tax rate and the standard spending requirement. A complicating factor is of course that the need for local government services also varies considerably between areas, depending (amongst other things) on local demographic and socio–economic circumstances. Central to this system therefore was the specification by central government of an estimate of the costs to a locality of delivering what it considered to be a standard level of service. This estimate was known as the locality's grant related expenditure assessment (GREA). The procedure for estimating GREAs was very complex, involving a variety of statistical techniques, and the use of over 100 indicators (Society of County Treasurers, 1989).

Once the GREA was estimated, it was possible to determine the level of central government grant, known as block grant. An authority's tax base comprised its domestic and business rateable value. If this is denoted in authority i by RV_i, and the national standard rate of taxation is g, then the identity $GREA_i = g.RV_i + BG_i$ gives the amount of block grant BG_i received by the authority when spending at its GREA. This mechanism for calculating central government grant support was known as needs equalization.

Moreover, the government chose to seek some form of equity between areas in the fiscal effort they required when spending varied from the GREA. This was achieved by setting a schedule of equal variations in the tax rate for equal per capita variations in spending away from GREA. As an authority's spending moved away from the GREA, its entitlement to block grant was altered so that it experienced a standard relationship between the per capita variation from GREA and the local rate of taxation. This procedure was known as resource equalization, and resulted in the following equation for local domestic taxation LDT

$$LDT_i = \left\{ \left[\frac{EXP_i - GREA_i}{POP_i} \right].\alpha + g \right\}.RV_i.DP_i \qquad (1)$$

where EXP is expenditure in area i, POP is the population, DP is the proportion of local rateable value in the domestic sector, and α is the national parameter determining the rate at which rates of local taxation varied as spending diverged from GREA.

The mechanism that replaced the rates system in 1990 is by comparison simple. Needs equalization is retained, although – as is explained later – the needs assessment procedures, and therefore the measures of need, have been altered. The new measure of the cost of delivering a standard level of service in a local authority (the replacement for its GREA) is known as its standard spending assessment (SSA). Central government grants are set so that, if an authority spends at its SSA, then it is able to impose the national standard community charge c. This secures needs equalization. However, because the tax base is population (albeit excluding those under the age of 18), the government decided that there is no need for any resource equalization of the sort employed under the previous system. Therefore, for any level of spending EXP, the local domestic taxation in authority i (LDT_i) – the community charge – is given by the equation

$$LDT_i = EXP_i - SSA_i + c.AP_i \qquad (2)$$

where AP is the adult population of authority i and c is the national standard community charge for spending at SSA. Notice that the entire burden of any spending over the SSA is borne by the local adult population in the form of an increased community charge bill. The remaining financing requirement in the local authority is made up by the central government revenue support grant and the authority's entitlement to non–domestic rates.

In general the two systems described above have very different implications for local domestic taxation. Suppose an authority spends at its needs assessment. Under the rates, a household's tax bill would then have been determined by the rateable value of its home. In contrast, the number of adults in the household is the determinant of the household's liability under the community charge. Clearly there might be an enormous difference between the two tax bills. In addition, if the local authority's spending varies from its needs assessment, the change in the tax bill also differs under the two systems. Equation (1) shows that, under the rates, for each £1 spent over GREA, the local domestic tax bill increased by an amount proportional to the per capita domestic rateable value in the area. Thus, households in areas with low domestic rateable values bore a relatively low proportion of the costs of extra spending. This variability between areas disappeared under the reformed system, with the adult population of all areas bearing the entire cost of extra spending under the community charge.

The government acknowledged the substantial shift between regions by introducing transitional arrangements to protect individual local authority areas from the immediate effect of the reforms. As originally envisaged, these took the form of lump sum transfers from net gainers to net losers equal to the per capita gains (or losses) in an area. In the first year such protection would be complete. It was then to be abated at the rate of 25 per cent per annum over a four year period. In the event, it was decided to allow gaining areas to retain the full extent of their gains after the first year of the new system, and the Treasury took on responsibility for funding the losers' safety nets.

In addition, the government later recognized that this safety net procedure did not protect individual households from large swings in fortune, so it introduced further specific temporary protection for some households suffering large losses under the reforms. This mechanism was extended to cover considerably more households in the second year of the new system. Moreover the government sought to reduce the impact of the reforms in inner London by the use of a variety of specific grants (the Association of County Councils (1991) gives details). These temporary expedients are ignored in the following analysis, which examines the long run effects of the changes.

Changes in tax bills arising from the 1990 reforms

This section presents estimates of the magnitude of the changes in local domestic tax bills that arise purely as a result of the 1990 reforms described above. It is assumed that everything remains unchanged other than the switch in resource base (from domestic property to adults), the nationalization of the business rate, and the consequent changes in entitlement to central government grant. The figures therefore indicate the long run impact of the reforms, assuming all other things are equal. They are based on 1989–90 budget data reported to the Department of the Environment on form ER90. Needs assessments and block grant are as set out in government reports (Association of County Councils, 1989). Non–domestic rates are derived from the Chartered Institute of Public Finance and Accountancy (1989).

In calculating the results, full account is taken of the fact that English local government is organized in tiers. The higher levels of local government (counties and joint authorities) make demands on the lower levels (districts), who are responsible for collecting local taxes. As a result, districts are not responsible for the entire tax bill they are required to collect. Nevertheless, the measure of political control used in this study is based on the state of political parties at the district level after the May 1989 elections. No account is taken of the political control of higher tiers, so the political control indicator should therefore be interpreted only as a guide to the political inclination of a locality. It is not intended to indicate the behaviour of local political parties. The 'other' political control category represents all authorities under no overall control, or third party control.

The geographical variation in taxation between areas is profound. Table

185

13.1 gives a regional summary. The standard community charge c is set to a value of £212.99 per adult, such that there is no change in the aggregate domestic tax burden in England.

Table 13.1
Change in local taxation per adult
resulting from switch from rates to community charge
(1989–90 base)

| | Local tax per adult | | |
	Under rates (£)	Under poll tax (£)	Increase (%)
North	233.02	288.11	23.64
Yorkshire & Humberside	224.55	284.96	26.90
North west	263.86	276.72	4.87
East midlands	249.17	253.30	1.66
East Anglia	246.34	214.93	−12.75
West midlands	268.78	228.61	−14.94
South east	298.42	227.14	−23.89
South west	245.45	233.14	−5.02
Greater London	283.93	359.51	26.62
Inner London	292.52	510.99	74.68
Outer London	279.19	268.88	−3.69
Metropolitan areas	257.19	282.37	9.79
Non–metropolitan areas	263.81	236.85	−10.22
Conservative	277.42	230.93	−16.76
Labour	259.91	309.07	18.91
Other	255.81	242.44	−5.23
England	265.17	265.17	0.00

The major losses resulting from the 1990 reforms occur in northern regions and inner London. The former is the result of the relatively low resource base (domestic rateable values) obtaining in northern regions, and therefore their relatively favourable treatment under the rates. The inner London effect is caused partly by the abandonment of the arbitrary arrangements whereby 29.3 per cent of the rateable value in inner London authorities was ignored for block grant purposes. The removal of this concession serves to disadvantage London under the new regime. The losses

186

in inner London are exacerbated by the high levels of spending in relation to GREA adopted by some authorities, particularly the Inner London Education Authority (ILEA). The high spending of ILEA in relation to GREA in the study year rendered it ineligible for government grant. As a result, all marginal expenditure was borne by local ratepayers. A high proportion of rateable value in inner London is in the business sector, so residents had to bear only a relatively small proportion of the overspending burden in the form of domestic rates. This subsidy from the business sector disappeared with the reforms.

The political analysis indicates strong gains associated with Conservative control, and comparable losses in areas under Labour control. Although some of this disparity can be accounted for by high spending in relation to GREA – particularly in Labour controlled inner London boroughs – the principal cause of this result is the relatively low domestic property resource base found in Labour controlled areas. It is noteworthy that intermediate political areas only derive modest gains from the reforms.

The reforms to needs assessment procedures

As noted above, estimates of spending needs are intrinsic to both unreformed and reformed systems of local government finance. The importance attached to measuring needs was indicated by the decision to overhaul the system of needs assessment procedures, even though such reform was not necessitated by the finance reforms. The ostensible reason for the change was the belief that the GREA calculations had become too complex, and were unstable from year to year. The new SSA system would 'reflect needs no less fairly than do the present [GREAs], but in a more understandable way' (DoE, 1987, para 15). In spite of pleas for a gradual approach (Bramley, 1987) the government implemented major reforms in introducing the new SSAs in 1991.

The GREA system, used between 1981 and 1989, is described in a series of technical documents (DoE, 1989; Society of County Treasurers, 1989). A detailed description is beyond the scope of this paper but the principle of the system was that aggregate cash limits were set centrally for each of the services provided by local government. Technical working groups then recommended methods of distributing the cash limited sum between authorities. This they did by examining appropriate indicators of need, and specifying a suitable model linking these indicators to the spending requirement of an authority. The methods employed range from the candidly judgemental in education (Taylor, 1989) to the deeply technical in personal social services (Derbyshire, 1987). The individual service allocations were determined by a series of 65 equations. The resulting service allocations for an authority were then aggregated to derive a total GREA.

Notwithstanding the objective of simplicity, the revised system of needs assessment, as embodied in the SSAs, is still fiercely complex (Society of County Treasurers, 1990). The same principles apply as in the GREA system, but there are now only 21 equations, many of which are simpler than hitherto. For example, the large category of 'other services' – which includes refuse collection and disposal, recreation, planning and development, and local tax collection – is allocated predominantly on a per capita basis. One key reform was the decision to include a factor to reflect the alleged extra costs of delivering services in the south east of the country. Under the GREA system only London enjoyed such treatment.

Analysis of the impact of changes in needs assessments on local tax bills is complex because no directly comparable measures of needs under the two systems have been published. However, it is possible to give an indication of the salient features of the change by comparing the GREAs for 1989–90 with the SSAs in 1990–91, and making some allowance for inflation and population change. This is not unreasonable as the base for many of the indicators used in both systems was the 1981 Census, and so many of the underlying needs data remained unchanged between the years. The principal changes relate to population size, and this is taken into account by adjusting the 1990–91 SSAs for changes in total population. In addition, the SSAs are deflated to 1989–90 prices by constraining their total to sum to the total of GREAs for that year.

The first column in Table 13.2 shows the change in government needs assessment implicit in the switch from the GREA to the SSA methodology. It indicates that, at the regional level, changes in assessed needs are modest. There is nevertheless a detectable shift towards London and the south east and away from the rest of the country, and at the level of individual local authority, some of the gains and losses are substantial..

Through equation (2) above, the changes in needs assessments give rise to changes in local poll taxes. Under the community charge, other things being equal, a £1 reduction in needs assessment gives rise to a £1 increase in local tax bills. Table 13.2 illustrates the consequences of the reformed needs assessment procedures for average poll taxes at the regional level. The basis for calculation is the same as that used in the previous section, except that the GREAs are replaced by the adjusted SSAs. As expected, London and the south east gain from the revised needs methodology at the expense of all other regions. The revisions to needs assessments therefore tend to reinforce the losses in northern regions noted in Table 13.1, but make a modest contribution to abating the losses in inner London resulting from the introduction of the community charge. Full analysis of the reasons for this finding is beyond the scope of this chapter. The interested reader is referred to the views of the local authority associations, reported in the Association

Table 13.2

Change in community charge
resulting from change in needs assessment procedures
(1989–90 base)

	Increase in needs estimate	Community charge		Increase
		Using GREA	Using SSA	
	(%)	(£)	(£)	(%)
North	−1.22	288.11	297.47	3.25
Yorkshire & Humberside	−1.66	284.96	297.50	4.40
North west	−1.38	276.72	287.90	4.04
East midlands	−1.65	253.30	265.03	4.63
East Anglia	−1.64	214.93	225.83	5.07
West midlands	−0.57	228.61	233.02	1.93
South east	2.04	227.14	209.33	−7.84
South west	−1.97	233.14	246.13	5.57
Greater London	2.54	359.51	341.46	−5.02
Inner London	2.47	510.99	488.71	−4.36
Outer London	2.48	268.88	254.28	−5.43
Metropolitan areas	−0.68	282.37	288.02	2.00
Non−metropolitan areas	−0.54	236.85	238.93	0.88
Conservative	−0.10	230.93	230.85	−0.03
Labour	0.68	309.07	304.38	−1.52
Other	−1.15	242.44	250.21	3.20
England	0.00	265.17	265.17	0.00

of County Councils (1991, Section B). Much of the debate amongst the associations surrounded the 'costs of services' adjustment noted above, and this may well have been central to securing the increases in the south east.

Although there are some large swings at the district level, the results in Table 13.2 show a smaller regional effect resulting from changes in needs assessments than that brought about by the switch from domestic rates to the community charge. The results are nevertheless striking and informative because they represent the outcome of careful analysis and scrutiny by government and local authority representatives. The redistribution in tax bills arising from the poll tax reforms could not be altered to any significant extent once the broad principles of the reforms had been determined. In contrast, the needs assessment reforms were amenable to substantial fine tuning. Many alternative SSA systems were tested, and the chosen system therefore indicates the government's preferred pattern of redistribution. At any other time, a policy change which resulted in such marked shifts between regions would have attracted widespread debate. However, the controversy surrounding the poll tax tended to overshadow the implications of needs assessment procedures. Moreover, although the changes were to the unambiguous advantage of the south east, the political analysis indicates that they were not clearly to the advantage of either of the main political parties. Indeed, the principal losers from the needs assessment reforms appear to have been the intermediate areas, under third party control, or with no majority control. This finding is an indication that the government failed to nurture support for its policies in marginal parliamentary constituencies.

The proposals for a council tax

In April 1991 the proposals were announced to replace the community charge by a domestic property tax to be known as a council tax (DoE, 1991a). Under these proposals, every domestic property would be allocated to one of seven bands on the basis of its capital value. The tax liability associated with a property would then depend on the band in which it was placed and the spending level of the local authority. The ratio of tax bills levied on properties in different bands would be specified by central government, and would remain fixed in all areas and at all spending levels. A discount of 25 per cent is proposed for one person households. As under the community charge, government grant would be set so that national standard tax bills would obtain if spending is at assessed needs. Grant and business rates would remain lump sum, so the entire burden of extra expenditure would continue to be borne by the domestic sector, this time in the form of the council tax.

In algebraic terms, the resource base RB of local authority i would become

$$RB_i = \sum_{j=1}^{7} w_j \, (1 - 0.25) \, h_{ij} \, H_{ij} \qquad (3)$$

where w_j is the national weight attached to band j ($w_4 = 1$), H_{ij} is the number of households in band j, and h_{ij} is the proportion of those households containing only one adult. Then, as under the community charge, local domestic taxation LDT is set using the relation:

$$LDT_i = EXP_i - SSA_i + h\,RB_i \qquad (4)$$

where h is the national standard rate of taxation for band D households with two or more adults. Thus all households in the same band pay the same tax rate if spending is at SSA. However, as spending moves away from SSA, the rate of change of tax rate depends on the proportions of households in the various bands. For example, the rate of increase of the band D tax bill is highest in areas which have predominantly low valued property and lowest in areas with most property in the higher bands.

Table 13.3
Change in local taxation
resulting from switch from community charge to council tax
(1989–90 base)

Local tax per adult

	Under poll tax	Under council tax	Increase
	(£)	(£)	(%)
North	288.11	256.01	−11.14
Yorkshire & Humberside	284.96	260.97	−8.42
North west	276.72	250.52	−9.47
East midlands	253.30	239.41	−5.48
East Anglia	214.93	206.62	−3.87
West midlands	228.61	206.64	−9.61
South east	227.14	251.36	10.66
South west	233.14	240.45	3.14
Greater London	359.51	399.93	11.24
Inner London boroughs	510.99	584.49	14.38
Outer London boroughs	268.88	291.62	8.46
Metropolitan districts	282.37	253.72	−10.15
Shire districts	236.85	238.21	0.58
Conservative	230.93	246.10	6.57
Labour	309.07	295.18	−4.49
Other	242.44	242.22	−0.09
England	265.17	265.17	0.00

Using property valuation data provided by the Department of the Environment, Table 13.3 illustrates the change in average domestic tax bills implied by the new proposals. The base is the long run community charge figures shown in Table 13.1, and it is assumed that all factors other than the finance system remain unchanged. That is, local authority expenditure, aggregate government grant, aggregate business taxation and individual needs assessments are assumed to be those obtaining in 1989–90. This implies a national standard rate of taxation of £452 for households with two or more adults living in properties in the middle band (band D) if spending is at assessed needs (which for the purposes of these calculations are assumed to be the 1989–90 GREA).

Scrutiny of Table 13.3 suggests that, in most areas, the new tax would succeed in abating many of the largest changes in tax liability indicated in Table 13.1. For example, the council tax will restore roughly 50 per cent of the losses borne by the northern and Yorkshire and Humberside regions on the introduction of the community charge. Note however that the high property values in inner London result in a decrease in central government grant, and therefore a substantial further increase in local domestic taxation to add to that incurred under the community charge. Again it should be emphasized that these figures only reflect average changes in tax bills, and do not consider the gains and losses accruing to individual households. There will be considerable changes in liability between households, determined by the same sort of considerations that influenced the swings in fortune on the introduction of the community charge: namely, the number of adults in the property, the capital value of the property, and the entitlement to welfare benefits.

Conclusions

This chapter has described various reforms of local government finance, both implemented and proposed. Crude estimates of the magnitude of gains and losses have been presented in terms of changes to average domestic tax bills. In preparing these estimates it has been assumed that total government grant, total business taxation and – most importantly – the spending of individual local authorities remains unchanged. Of course this latter assumption is rather artificial, as a principal aim of the 1990 reforms was indeed to put downward pressure on spending levels. Barnett, Levaggi and Smith (1991a) show how it is possible to predict the long term expenditure changes brought about by the reforms, and to measure the consequent welfare gain (or loss) in terms of the economists' concept of compensating variation.

The objective of this chapter is to isolate the impact of the changing assumptions about resource bases and needs assessments on local tax bills.

There is no suggestion that such tax bills will arise in practice. Indeed preliminary examination of expenditure responses in the first year of the poll tax suggest that, as expected, losing authorities are already starting to reduce expenditure levels relative to gaining authorities (Barnett, Levaggi and Smith, 1991b).

The results from this study indicate that the switch from domestic rates to the community charge was to the unambiguous disadvantage of northern regions and inner London. These are traditional strongholds of the Labour Party, so it is hardly surprising that, over England as a whole, areas under local Conservative control gained substantially relative to areas under local Labour control. The extent to which this feature of the reforms was their central attraction for a Conservative central government is, of course, a matter for conjecture. Nevertheless it is noteworthy that the intermediate areas – those under no overall political control, or third party control – did not enjoy especially favourable treatment. This is an indication that the 1990 reforms were not politically adroit, as the main beneficiaries were areas already under clear Conservative control. The reforms do not appear to have been aimed at the crucial marginal constituencies, and this cannot have helped Mrs Thatcher in her bid to retain the confidence of Conservative members of parliament in the November 1990 leadership battle.

The reasons for the failure of the community charge are many and complex. Undoubtedly the lump sum nature of the tax, which was unrelated to ability to pay, was perceived by many to be unfair. In addition, it introduced massive swings in the tax liability between individuals. Over the country as a whole, the number of people who considered themselves to lose as a result of the reforms far outweighed the numbers who thought they gained. And in any case the dissatisfaction of being a loser was always likely to stir stronger emotions than the pleasure at being a winner. This effect was exacerbated by the government's decision effectively to reduce (in real terms) grant support and needs assessments in the first year of the reforms. The inevitable overspending that resulted had to be borne entirely by the community charge, creating an even larger number of apparent losers. Finally, the tax was administratively disastrous. The costs of maintaining a register of charge payers, and of enforcing payment, have added at least £200 million to local government expenditure in England, and by the end of the first year of the new system, only 90 per cent of budgeted revenue had been collected (DoE, 1991b).

This chapter has shown that there were strong geographical effects caused by the reforms which might also have contributed to their failure. Politicians are particularly sensitive to such specific geographical issues because of the parliamentary constituency basis of our representative democracy. As a result, it was always likely that a policy that led to such sharp geographical variations would provoke political controversy.

The proposals to replace the community charge by a domestic property tax based on capital values – the council tax – represent a retreat from the full redistributional effects of the community charge. The principal difference between the new property tax and the rates would be the protection it would give to one person households and those living in property with a high capital value. This study has shown that, in general, the resultant average tax bills would lie somewhere between those found under the rates and those resulting from the imposition of the community charge.

Underlying all the distributional effects of these different systems of local government finance are assumptions about the relative needs of different geographical areas. Central government's assessments of needs (whether GREA or SSA) are crucial determinants of local tax bills. This has become particularly important after the institution of a national non–domestic rate because the local domestic sector has to bear the entire burden of any spending in excess of the needs assessment. Indirectly, therefore, the abolition of the local business tax has focused attention on needs assessment procedures. The measurement of spending needs has not been the central concern of this chapter. Indeed it has received scant attention in the academic literature (Mayston and Smith, 1990). Now is perhaps the time for researchers to turn their attention away from the broad principles of local government finance to the no less important area of needs assessment. Only if the burden of taxation is seen to be distributed equitably is the debate over local government finance likely to subside.

References

Association of County Councils (1989), *Rate Support Grant (England) 1989/90,* The Association, London.

Association of County Councils (1991), *Revenue Support Grant (England) 1990/91*, The Association, London.

Barnett, R.R., Levaggi, R. and Smith, P. (1991a), 'Simulating local government expenditure decisions and welfare change under a community charge (poll tax) regime', *Public Finances/Finances Publiques*, vol. 46, no. 1, pp. 24–41.

Barnett, R.R., Levaggi, R. and Smith, P. (1991b), 'Accountability and the poll tax: the impact on local authority budgets of the reform of local government finance in England', *Financial Accountability and Management*, vol. 7, no. 4, pp. 209–228.

Bramley, G. (1987), 'Less complex and more stable', Working Paper no. 64, School for Advanced Urban Studies, University of Bristol.

Chartered Institute of Public Finance and Accountancy (1989), *Finance and General Statistics 1989/90*, CIPFA, London.

DoE, (1986), *Paying for Local Government*, Cm. 9714, Department of the Environment, HMSO, London.

DoE, (1987), *The New Grant System*, Department of the Environment, HMSO, London.

DoE, (1989), *Grant Related Expenditure Assessments: How the Spending Needs of Local Authorities are Assessed*, Department of the Environment, HMSO, London.

DoE, (1991a), *A New Tax for Local Government*, Department of the Environment, HMSO, London.

DoE, (1991b), *Community Charge Collection – Fourth Quarter Results*, Press release, 29 May, Department of the Environment, London.

Derbyshire, M.E. (1987), 'Statistical rationale for grant related expenditure assessment (GREA) concerning personal social services (with discussion)', *Journal of the Royal Statistical Society A*, vol. 150, no. 4, pp. 309–33.

Gibson, J. (1990), *The Politics and Economics of the Poll Tax: Mrs Thatcher's downfall*, Emas Ltd, Warley.

Mayston, D. and Smith, P. (1990), 'Analysing the need to spend on education', *Journal of the Operational Research Society*, vol. 41, no. 2, pp. 125–31.

Smith, S. (1991), 'Distributional issues in local taxation', *Economic Journal*, vol. 101, no. 3, pp. 585–99.

Society of County Treasurers (1989), *Block Grant Indicators 1989–90*, The Society, Lincoln.

Society of County Treasurers (1990), *Standard Spending Indicators 1990–91*, The Society, Lincoln.

Taylor, S. (1989), 'Measuring need to spend on education', *Journal of the Operational Research Society*, vol. 40, no. 2, pp. 177–86.

14 Linking hospital specialities: A measure of clinical need

S.A. Ryder, W. Kirkup and R.L. Akehurst

Introduction

The National Health Service and Community Care Act 1990 introduced fundamental changes to the structure and organisation of the NHS. The most important aspect of these changes has been to separate the function of delivering and providing health care services from that of determining what has to be provided to meet the health care needs of local people. The district health authority (DHA) has now been designated as a purchasing agency, buying a mix of services to meet the health care needs of its resident population. Hospitals and community units enter into contracts and service agreements with authorities to provide specific services.

The policy objective in bringing about these changes was to achieve a more effective and efficient health service (DH, 1989). Purchasing authorities must determine the service requirements for their district and will want to obtain these at the lowest cost at a given level of quality. Provider units on the other hand will be encouraged to maximise the revenue from providing health care services. Since provider units will compete with one another for contracts it is believed that prices will be driven down and quality be driven up.

There are clearly a large number of components of quality and both purchasers and providers will have to give consideration to all elements. But in many cases it is difficult to assess quality and if changes in service agreements (or contracts) are made purchasers, providers and the local population will want to know what impact the change will have on the service delivered. The particular aspect of quality which this chapter focuses on is clinical quality. Put another way, what does a hospital *need* to have to make it function in a clinically effective way and thereby provide a good quality service?

Need and quality are never far from debates about the delivery of health care. Views originate from, among others, clinicians, nurses, managers, accountants, health economists, patients and ex–patients. In practice, however, it is very difficult to evaluate need and quality systematically, indeed the two concepts are more often than not used interchangeably. For example, a patient may feel the 'need' for a second opinion when presenting with a health related problem. This second opinion, however, can be given to enhance the quality of service rather than to meet an individual's perceived need. This paper explores a practical way of assessing the value and quality of working arrangements within hospitals. In common with other approaches (Jessome, 1988), the technique focuses on the views of professionals rather than those of health service users. This is not to say that patients have no role in defining the quality of care, but reflects the fact that patients are invariably unaware of the technical aspects of service provision and will only have limited experience related to their own care (and possibly the care of those they share a ward with).

The technique described can be used by health service managers in planning an optimal provision of health services. This technique has been used in strategic planning exercises prior to the NHS changes implemented in April 1991, but is equally relevant in the new NHS to help determine qualitative dimensions of health service provision. To this end, it may act as an aid to contract placement for acute services. The chapter will detail the historical development of the tool, describe techniques for assessment of local links between specialties, assess the consistency and homogeneity of reported links, and outline some hitherto untried uses of the approach.

Quantifying elements of clinical need

When undertaking a strategic review of hospital services it is common to encounter vociferous political and clinical views as to what constitutes the optimal configuration of services. As with any organisation, the NHS has its own mavericks and lobbyists who have often attained significant influence either for reasons of history or personality. Alongside those who 'shout loudest' are a host of less vocal clinical interests that may have been traditionally under–represented in the decision making process. In order to ascertain an optimum service configuration it is important to listen to the views of the silent majority as well as the raucous minority.

Hospital services are provided as apparently discrete entities known as specialties. However, the practices within a given specialty will often vary from one location to another. The workload undertaken in a hospital tends to reflect local historical work patterns, the special interests of local consultants, and probably the favoured practices of the medical schools where clinicians learnt their craft. With more advanced capability of data retrieval in the NHS it will be possible to determine more accurately the case mix of individual specialties. An example of observed variation in local practices was found in a study in one district where 87 per cent of orthopaedic cases were treated for musculoskeletal diseases, whereas in another district the comparative figure was only 43 per cent (YHEC, 1990). Assuming that coding practices are consistent, then clearly orthopaedic surgery in one district is very different to orthopaedic surgery in another. In the new NHS, purchasing agencies will need to be aware of such local variations in practice when contracting for health services. Providers of hospital services – whether they be NHS trusts or units directly managed by the purchasing agency – should try to optimise clinical working arrangements. One way of doing this is to ensure that patients can have access to a full range of services related to their reason for being in hospital.

In an ideal world an optimal service would be defined as one which was provided from state of the art facilities, in an amenable environment with easy access and with a desirable configuration of services. The optimal configuration of hospital services (specialties) would be determined by reference to a body of research into the effectiveness of different combinations of specialties in achieving desired outcomes for patients, coupled with knowledge of the staffing and cost implications of these configurations. In reality no such body of research exists and hospital services tend to be spread across a number of sites. In its absence, the most obvious line of enquiry is through the opinions of the clinicians themselves. However, if this is not handled in a structured way, the canvassing of clinical opinion can be very unproductive.

Clinicians will often say that it is essential that their specialty be located with all or nearly all others or that their specialty should not be split. Responses encountered range from claims that it is unthinkable that one specialty should be apart from a different but related specialty to refusals to relocate a service on a different site because of historical reasons or due to personal preference. When faced with a barrage of such comments everything appears to be essential. When everything is essential nothing is, and when everything is a priority nothing gets done.

The technique of option appraisal is often used as a means of determining the most appropriate strategic direction for NHS service providers. Option appraisal will use a set of criteria to assess a variety of options for developing local services. 'Quality of clinical service' is an important criterion to include in such exercises. Quality of clinical service is often characterised by two dimensions – the availability of appropriate facilities and the relationships between specialties and departments. The latter can be assessed by making use of an interspecialty links matrix.

In order to develop a framework for assessing the relative importance of specialties being in close proximity, a simple grid was drawn up as shown in Table 14.1. The grid lists the names of all hospital specialties both down the side (vertical) and along the top (horizontal).

Table 14.1
Interspecialty links matrix

Column key:
1. Accident and Emergency
2. Accident and Emergency (Children)
3. Intensive Therapy Unit
4. Coronary Care Unit
5. General Medicine
6. Cardiology
7. Chest Medicine
8. Gastroenterology
9. Infectious Diseases
10. Genito–Urinary Medicine
11. Elderly
12. Rheumatology
13. Haematology
14. Dermatology
15. Neurology
16. General Surgery

	1	2	3	4	5	6	7	8	9	10	11	12	13	14	15	16
Accident and Emergency		0	3	3	3	1	0	2	0	1	2	0	0	0	1	3
Accident and Emergency (Children)	0		3	0	0	1	0	0	0	1	0	0	0	0	0	0
Intensive Therapy Unit (ITU)	0	0		2	3	2	2	1	0	0	0	2	0	3	3	
Coronary Care Unit	0	0	3		3	3	2	1	0	0	0	0	0	0	0	
General Medicine	0	0	3	3		2	2	3	1	0	2	0	2	1	1	3
Cardiology	0	0	3	3	2		1	2	0	0	1	0	2	0	1	0
Chest Medicine	0	0	3	3	1	1		2	1	0	1	0	1	0	1	1
Gastroenterology	0	0	3	0	0	1	1		0	0	0	1	0	1	0	
Infectious Diseases	0	0	2	0	1	0	1	1		1	0	0	0	0	1	1
Genito–Urinary Medicine	0	0	1	0	1	0	2	1	2		0	0	1	1	1	1
Elderly	0	0	1	1	0	2	1	3	0	0		0	3	1	1	3
Rheumatology	0	0	0	0	1	0	0	1	0	0	0		0	0	0	
Haematology	0	0	3	0	1	1	2	2	0	0	0	0		0	1	3
Dermatology	0	0	1	1	2	0	0	1	0	1	0	0	1		0	1
Neurology	0	0	3	0	1	0	0	0	0	0	1	0	0	0		0
General Surgery	0	0	3	0	3	0	0	3	0	0	2	0	2	0	0	

Clinicians in each of the districts were asked to assess the importance of links between specialties in terms of possible effects on morbidity and mortality. At the highest rated end were specialties where joint management of beds was thought to be essential, through to a lesser need to have regular visits to the wards of another specialty, through to the lowest rated link between specialties which involve infrequent or non–existent consultations. A grading system from three (high rated link) to zero (low rated link) was developed to categorise each of the possible links between specialties. The choice of calibration was essentially arbitrary, but it is clear that a larger range of possible grades may lead to spurious detail being inferred from what is essentially a fairly crude technique.

One feature of the matrix is that it is directional. In a horizontal plane, specialties can be viewed as users of a service, whereas in a vertical plane those same specialties are providers of a service. Thus, for any two specialties there are two sets of relationships to describe; the reliance of one on the other and vice versa.

The directionality of the matrix is best illustrated by use of an example. As a user of a service, an accident and emergency department will depend upon general surgeons to provide a service to patients who present through casualty. This link will take the form of immediate consultation and some facility to admit to general surgery beds. On the other hand, as a provider of a service, the accident and emergency department is not required by the general surgeons (users) to assist with their day to day operations. Put another way, it would be unwise to have an accident and emergency department in a hospital without general surgery back up, yet it is easy to envisage a general surgery presence in a hospital without on–site accident and emergency facilities. It is sometimes argued that general surgeons (and consultants in other specialties) benefit from close proximity of accident and emergency in that teaching and training of staff are enhanced. For option appraisal purposes, criteria relating to these issues would be considered separately.

Callibration techniques

Links were graded from zero to three, according to the following broad categories:

0   Failure to achieve these limited links on a hospital site reflect little or no risk of adverse clinical outcomes. Consultation between the specialties is largely restricted to outpatient departments.

1   Failure to achieve these significant links may reflect occasional risks of increased morbidity.

2   Failure to achieve these important links on site may lead to life being occasionally threatened or some increases in morbidity following or during treatment.

3   Failure to achieve these very important links may frequently increase the risk of loss of life or could result in significant unnecessary morbidity.

It is worth noting that no attempt has been made to assess the cost implications associated with the links between specialties. It is, however, highly likely that *ceteris paribus* revenue costs will be less if undesirable separation of linked departments can be avoided.

The categories used to grade links are subjective and open to differences in interpretation. For this reason a core team of interviewers conducted the local consultations. This method improved consistency across specialties and the process could be clearly explained to the individuals making assessment of interdependencies. The disadvantage of the method is one of potential interviewer bias, although this can be minimised if the interviewers are consistent in their approach. A questionnaire rather than an interview based approach was attempted in one of the districts. The results in this instance were considerably different from the other exercises in that many more links were stated to be of critical importance. On balance, a questionnaire approach is not to be recommended.

Some interview based approaches were structured around a hypothetical matrix which was used as a benchmark against which local circumstances could be compared. The grades used in this matrix were drawn up using a mixture of 'impartial' medical advice and, in later exercises, results obtained from earlier work. Interviewees were asked to state whether they agreed with the grades outlined in the benchmark. In the cases where they did not they were asked to suggest alternative grades and the reasons for them. This process revealed some interesting local interpretations on the need for proximity between users and providers. The use of a benchmark matrix helped to stimulate discussion, although it was probably not essential.

Sometimes inconsistencies were registered by clinicians within a specialty, sub-specialty or clinical support department. In most cases a consensus could usually be reached between individuals representing each discipline. Two specialty views are recorded for each cell in the matrix, indicating the views of provider and user. This helps prevent overinflated claims for the importance of links and provides two clinical views which can be usefully debated, if necessary. In cases where consensus was not possible, the interviewers devised a set of rules to deal with disagreements. These rules were then consistently applied.

Variation in assessed clinical need

This technique has been employed in a number of DHAs and has generally yielded different scores for the strength of interdependency of one specialty with another. There are probably four principal sources of variation, each of which is discussed below.

Differences in definition of specialty

Specialty definitions differ, and the sub–specialties included may affect the interdependence with other specialties such that like is not being compared with like. For example, in some hospitals rheumatology is included as part of general medicine. There is then a relatively strong link between general medicine and orthopaedics, compared with those hospitals with a narrower definition of general medicine.

Historical differences in work patterns

Historical patterns of provision will inevitably colour perceptions of the necessity for close links. It is not an uncommon experience to hear a detailed description of the utter impossibility of separating one specialty from another when both are sited together, whilst in other localities the specialties are physically separated without there being any clamour to rectify the 'error'. The collation of results from several districts can begin to identify where historical artefacts occur.

Locality differences

Other sources of more minor variation include personality differences amongst respondents in different specialties and places, the variable effect of group dynamics, and even such apparent ephemera as variations in consultant dining arrangements. Some differences also occur because individuals can have different perceptions as to what constitutes a hospital. For example, in one district it was felt that two distinct hospitals were operating from virtually the same site. Indeed, the physical distance between departments across the two sites was often less then the distance between departments operating within one of the other major hospitals in the same district. In order to minimise the impact of such varying perceptions a clear set of rules has to be established as part of the local consultation process.

Differences attributable to data collection

The descriptions of strength of link may simply be interpreted differently in different places. This is particularly likely if the collection of base data for the assessment is carried out in different ways by different people.

Table 14.2

Strength of dependency of gynaecology on other specialties as separately assessed in four DHAs

Specialty	Strength of dependency			
	DHA A	DHA B	DHA C	DHA D
Accident and Emergency	1	0	0	1
Intensive Therapy Unit (ITU)	3	1	1	0
General Medicine	2	3	1	1
Elderly	1	1	0	0
Rheumatology	0	0	0	3
Dermatology	0	1	0	0
Neurology	0	0	0	0
General Surgery	2	3	2	2
Urology	2	3	1	2
Trauma and Orthopaedics	0	1	0	0
Ear, Nose and Throat	0	0	0	0
Ophthalmology	0	0	0	1
Oral Surgery	0	0	0	0
Plastic Surgery	0	1	0	0
Paediatrics	0	1	0	0
Neonatal ITU	0	0	0	0
Obstetrics	3	3	2	3
Mean score	0.82	1.06	0.41	0.76

In order to examine some of these variations, an analysis was undertaken around one specialty. Variations affecting the specialty of gynaecology were examined for the districts in which data have been collected to date; gynaecology is less prone than most specialties to the definitional problems described above. Table 14.2 shows the strengths of interdependency assessed in each DHA for the 17 other specialties common to all four DHAs.

Considerable variation is evident in one or two instances.

In order to assess the degree of agreement on scores recorded in each health authority, statistical analysis was undertaken to assess the consistency of the graded links. The graded links are ranked values and so a Friedman test was applied to the data to establish the degree of agreement.

A Friedman value of 6.83 was obtained which is not significant at the five per cent level. The observed difference is insufficient to reject the null hypothesis that there is no disagreement between the four DHAs. However, some of the variations are worthy of comment. Intensive therapy unit (ITU) and rheumatology show a very large range of graded links. In both cases this is associated with single, aberrant values. The score of three for ITU in DHA A probably reflects either an unusual case mix or particular anaesthetic arrangements; the score of three for rheumatology in DHA D appears inexplicable.

Table 14.3 shows the strength of dependency of other specialties on gynaecology. A Friedman value of 1.71 was obtained which is again insignificant at the five per cent level. Again, the districts show a high level of consistency. However, urology shows a very large range of graded links although this is associated with a single aberrant value. The score of three for urology in DHA D probably reflects the evolution of a particular style of working in this department, since there are very many gynaecology units across the country without access to specialised urology services. The spread of results for accident and emergency services probably reflects different practices for admitting emergency referrals from general practitioners, who in some cases make use of accident departments for initial assessment.

These results show a considerable degree of consistency, but there are a small number of striking exceptions, which perhaps ought to be reviewed locally. Consideration of these may begin to shed light on the reasons underlying the assessed specialty interdependencies.

Table 14.3
Strength of dependency of other specialties on gynaecology as separately assessed in four DHAs

Specialty	Strength of dependency			
	DHA A	DHA B	DHA C	DHA D
Accident and Emergency	2	3	1	0
Intensive Therapy Unit (ITU)	0	0	0	0
General Medicine	1	1	0	1
Elderly	1	1	0	0
Rheumatology	0	0	0	0
Dermatology	0	1	0	0
Neurology	0	0	0	0
General Surgery	1	1	1	1
Urology	0	0	1	3
Trauma and Orthopaedics	0	0	0	0
Ear Nose and Throat	0	0	0	0
Ophthalmology	0	0	0	0
Oral Surgery	0	0	0	0
Plastic Surgery	0	0	0	1
Paediatrics	1	0	0	1
Neonatal ITU	0	0	0	0
Obstetrics	3	3	2	3
Mean score	0.53	0.59	0.29	0.59

Key elements of clinical need

It should be noted that there are often several reasons why specialties should operate in close proximity. These fall into two broad categories, namely patient management and facility sharing. The former will invariably relate to the extent to which different specialties cooperate when caring for patients. At the lowest level of 'need' this might involve specialist opinion and advice, for example, a gynaecologist may need advice from a geriatrician when caring for elderly patients. At the highest level of 'need' there may be a requirement for joint clinical management, for example, a general physician and geriatrician may jointly plan the health care of an elderly patient with a range of medical problems. Within this range of needs there will be intermediate situations where, for example, it may become necessary to transfer patient management between specialties. The frequency and urgency of these transfers will help determine the strength of the interspecialty link.

The second broad category contains aspects relating to facility sharing. This is exemplified by the assessed high interdependency between gynaecology and obstetrics: once a patient is admitted to one or the other specialty there is very little crossover involving inpatients (although longer term crossover is common). The assessed interdependency will more likely relate to shared medical staffing. In situations where the specialties are found physically separated, the consequent difficulties are of a different nature to those resulting from the needs for patient management where, for example, the separation of gynaecology from general surgery may cause problems where emergency cross–referral or joint management of individual patients may be required on occasions.

The assessments of interspecialty links have only been undertaken in four districts to date. Reported links seem to vary from one location to another. Some of this variation can be easily explained whereas some may reflect less obvious local working practices. With a large enough sample of DHAs the variation could be examined in greater detail. The potential effects of teaching status, the extent of sub–specialisation, the number of hospitals and physical distances between sites and departments within a district, would be of particular interest.

The results presented in the interspecialty links matrices have been used to assess how well individual strategic options perform against a criterion of good quality clinical organisation. They have been instrumental in helping to formulate the strategic vision of hospital services in each of the four districts. As with any tool, the interspecialty links matrix has its limitations, but it has greatly helped clinicians, managers and planners to distinguish the priorities for hospital development. Not only have the results been used to determine what the overall configuration of hospital services should look like, but they also offer an insight into which particular phasing of an option might deliver most benefits in the shortest time.

Ideally the subjective assessments of specialty relationships should be compared to clinical outcomes. This task is a highly complex one, however, and is best left for future research. Another issue for further research is an assessment of the resource implications associated with patient management and facility sharing.

Further uses of the interspecialty links matrix

Thus far, the application of the methodology has been confined to option appraisals and prioritisation of capital schemes. There has, however, been at least one attempt to use interspecialty relationships in defining the 'core services' which a hospital must provide. Holtby and Ramaiah (1990) discuss how this approach was used in South Tees Health Authority. Although the Department of Health appears, to some extent, to have retracted from the need to define 'core services', the interspecialty links matrix may have other uses relating to the new NHS.

Contractual arrangements between purchaser and provider in the new NHS require that the quality of service be monitored. In practice this may be quite an onerous task, relying on comprehensive medical audit. A quick and simple assessment of a major aspect of quality may be the number of interspecialty links that can be provided within a hospital. All other things being equal, a contract would be placed with a provider that could guarantee more interspecialty links than other competitors.

Looking further afield, the concept of grading links between suppliers and users of services might have many applications. Japanese manufacturing companies already use similar techniques to assist with total quality management; however there seems little, if any, documented evidence as to whether the technique has been applied in the public sector. There should be some potential uses in the planning of social services, universities, transport networks, and other public services.

Conclusion

The technique outlined in this paper has been applied in several district health authorities as a means of assessing service quality and establishing the need for clinical links. Whilst the method used is not based on scientifically validated results of service efficiency it has proved a useful practical tool and a stimulus to debate. Health service managers and clinicians have found the process of assessing interspecialty links to be of mutual benefit. The new arrangements for contracting for services in the NHS will bring issues of quality and need to the fore. District health authorities are being instructed to ensure that 'changes to services should be designed to improve the health of local people while obtaining value for money and increasing efficiency from provider units'. (NHS Management Executive, 1991, p1). The technique described here should contribute, albeit in a small way, to this grand design.

References

DH (1989), *Working for Patients*, Cm. 555, Department of Health, HMSO, London.

Holtby, I. and Ramaiah, R.S. (1990), 'Core services – the South Tees way forward', *International Journal of Health Care Quality Assurance*, vol. 3, no. 2, pp. 14–16.

Jessome, P. (1988), 'The application of total quality control to a hospital setting, in Johnston, R. (ed.), *The Management of Service Organisations, Proceedings of the Third Annual International Conference of the Operations Management Association (UK)*, Springer–Verlag, Berlin.

NHS Management Executive (1991), *Moving Forward – Needs, Services and Contracts, DHA Project Paper*, National Health Service Management Executive, London.

YHEC (1990), *Future Role of the District Health Authority: Assessing Needs for Services and Setting Priorities*, York Health Economics Consortium, York.

15 The social fund: Managing budgets, meeting needs?

M. Huby

Introduction

The social fund was introduced in April 1988 to provide a flexible source of financial help at the fringes of welfare benefit regulations. The single payments system which it replaced had grown rapidly. In 1987–88 there were over 50 payments for every 100 supplementary benefit claimants. One major objective of the social fund was to halt the growth in expenditure on lump sum payments by placing fixed limits on the amount of cash available to it (Bradshaw, 1987).

The limited budget however was intended to be used to channel resources towards those groups most in need. The social fund was initially seen as a way of 'concentrating help on claimants with genuine special needs not covered by income support' (DHSS, 1985a), and by 1989 this idea had been refined 'to concentrate attention and help on those applicants facing greatest difficulties in managing on their income' (DSS, 1990). The underlying ethos was one of cost effectiveness and efficiency in conjunction with increased flexibility in responding to individual need. The introduction of a budget related to individual clients was seen to represent 'an exciting culture shift' for the Regional Organisation of the Department of Social Security (DSS, 1989a).

The non–regulated part of the social fund provides assistance in the form of discretionary community care grants, or interest–free budgeting loans and crisis loans, to meet expenses which cannot sensibly be met by normal weekly payments (DHSS, 1985b). The budget for 1988–89 was allocated among Department of Social Security (DSS) local offices partly on the basis of past expenditure on single payments and partly on the size of local office caseloads adjusted according to the proportions of pensioners and unemployed people (Walker and Lawton, 1989). In 1989–90 and 1990–91, the budget allocation for each office was adjusted slightly to take account of the size and varying composition of different income support caseloads and the amount spent on the social fund in the previous year.

Each local office has a grants budget and a loans budget for the year. These budgets are managed at local level, and office managers plan predicted month by month expenditure using profiles drawn up to anticipate demand. Actual expenditure each month depends on the discretion of social fund officers in awarding grants and loans. The officers are required to make their decisions on social fund applications in the light of the needs and circumstances of individual applicants. They are bound by the law, the Directions of the Secretary of State, and are guided by advice in the Social Fund Manual. In addition, the manager in each office takes account of particular local conditions in suggesting an order of local priorities for social fund awards. In the first two years of the fund priority lists for loans usually related to items or services; and those for community care grants, to client groups. When it became necessary to curtail expenditure in order to keep within the local budget limits, awards were restricted to applications of high priority only. If spending levels were below profile, lower priority applications were more likely to lead to awards.

The Department of Social Security has acknowledged that the budgets of certain offices have come under exceptional pressure, but that 'continued monitoring of the social fund suggests that it is generally working well' (Hansard, 1989). On the other hand independent monitoring projects have presented evidence that the fund is failing to alleviate hardship among people living on very low incomes (Benefits Research Unit, 1989). In the opinion of some social services departments, welfare rights organisations and other professional agencies, the fund is working anything but well (Stewart et al., 1989; NACAB, 1990).

How is it that feedback about the operation of the same system could lead to these two contradictory conclusions? The answer lies in the interpretation of the stated aims of the fund. It was designed to target help on areas of greatest need while remaining consistent with the Government's overall objectives for the economy. This chapter examines first, the way in which

210

its success or failure in 'targeting help' depends upon definitions of greatest need, and second, how the structure of the fund ensures that it will operate within its budget.

Meeting needs

The social fund is the latest in a long series of attempts to control expenditure on payments to people who cannot manage on income support (or, before 1988, on supplementary benefit) (Walker and Lawton, 1988). The new elements include the imposition of a fixed budget for each local DSS office, the introduction of loans rather than grants for certain categories of applicant, and the re-introduction of discretion.

It is of utmost importance that a fund which operates on a fixed budget, at a level well below that of previous single payments expenditure, should effectively target the assistance which it offers. Targeting here means directing resources towards those most in need. It is the identification of these people and their needs which is the cause of current controversy about the 'success' of the system.

The Social Fund Manual offers guidance to enable officers to recognise the kinds of circumstances in which awards are intended to be made. It lists groups such as the elderly, the disabled and families under stress as being particularly likely to experience need. In addition it lists the kinds of items, such as beds and cookers, the lack of which might be regarded as constituting need. Social fund officers must use their discretion in examining each application to decide whether the circumstances surrounding it are such that a social fund award should be made. In coming to these decisions in the light of the guidance of the Social Fund Manual, officers are effectively constructing an administrative definition of need. However, the budget limits imposed on local offices are such that even when need has been recognised (in the administrative sense) it may not be possible to provide the money to meet the need. It is at this point that the concept of 'greatest need' is introduced.

Determining priorities

The idea of ranking the needs of individuals presents an interesting source of philosophical and political debate. This aside, such a ranking is an essential prerequisite for any system which seeks to allocate resources selectively when they are insufficient to meet total demand. Within local offices, the assignation of different kinds of need to particular priority levels is inevitably complex. Ordered lists are produced which rank type of client, items requested and circumstances of application, usually grouped into high, medium and low priority categories. These lists may be ordered separately or combined, more or less explicitly, in interlocking matrices. Individual applications are then mapped onto this framework and their priority rankings assessed.

In determining priorities, local office staff may interpret the guidance more or less rigidly and may place different emphases on client groups or items, but the outcome is always an ordered listing. Depending on the amount of money in the budget, social fund awards can be made for a varying proportion of application categories. If the budget is under pressure only applications which fall into categories at the top of the list will be successful. These applications are designated as 'high priority'. Applications further down the list are always of 'lower priority'. Thus, however high the refusal rate, the 'highest priority' needs can always be met. By definition, the applications which are refused are those of lower priority, even if the needs which go unmet are quite severe by other criteria. Indeed applications which are turned down in one office might be successful in another. The social fund is certainly meeting high priority needs in this administratively defined sense; highest priority needs *are* those for which payments are made.

But 'high priority' needs can also be defined as those needs which in some normative sense are agreed to be important and which should be met by a social security safety net system. It can be argued that not all needs which conform to certain normative definitions of 'high priority' are being met by the social fund. Normative definitions of high priority need are problematic in that they largely depend upon the ethical, cultural, social and political ideals of the individuals using them. Social fund officers, advisory agencies, social fund applicants and government officials may differ in their perceptions of these needs, and these tensions and contradictions produce divergent views of the effectiveness of the scheme. Given the tautology implicit in the administrative definition of high priority need and the diversity of normative definitions, any statement that the social fund is meeting high priority needs will inevitably be fraught with controversy.

Managing budgets

Demand for the social fund

During the first two years of the social fund spending levels did not exceed budget limits. At face value this appeared to result partly from reduced demand.

Demand for social fund awards is not easily estimated. The number of applications recorded in local offices excludes cases filtered out from the process before the application form stage. Potential applicants may not be aware that the fund exists, or may only know about loans and be unwilling or unable to take out a loan which must be repaid from their weekly benefit. Others may be put off from applying for a grant because they do not perceive themselves as being in need of 'community care'. Some people may be discouraged from applying by their social workers or welfare advisers. Others may be confused and daunted by the complexities of the application procedure itself. In the DSS office, the role of reception becomes crucial. It is at least plausible that some people may be put off by the lack of privacy in which they must state their need, and others, if told at reception that there is little chance of receiving an award, may decide not to go further with their applications.

When applications *are* completed, administrative methods of recording them tend, in contrast, to overestimate demand. Some applications are recorded twice, once as a grant and once as a loan. These records constitute a measure of work completed by local office staff and feed into the calculation of staff complement so there is an incentive for double recording of applications. For all of these reasons application rates do not give an accurate picture of demand for the fund.

Nor can levels of expenditure on social fund awards be used to indicate demand since budgets for the first two years were fixed. Local office budgets were underspent in 1988–89, partly because large numbers of single payments were still being made and partly because of other factors associated with the change to a new system (Huby and Walker, 1991). The DSS in allocating local office budgets for 1989–90 used the previous year's expenditure figures as an indicator of demand for the fund, which was by implication lower than it had been for single payments (DSS, 1989b).

Community care grants

Different constraints govern the extent to which local offices can adjust spending on different kinds of social fund awards. The government is currently committed to promoting care in the community. Grants are available to help both people moving out of residential care, and those for whom a financial award reduces the risk of being placed in residential care. It would be unlikely that a social fund officer would refuse an application from a person clearly in either of these categories. Indeed, in 1988–89, only nine per cent of community care grant refusals were made on grounds of low priority. But in the first year of the social fund, applications for grants were fewer than expected and local offices were under pressure to increase spending, not to reduce it. An earlier paper discusses the ways in which offices responded to this pressure (Huby and Walker, 1991). It shows how the numbers of applications ultimately limit the extent to which more awards can be made. In 1988–89 it was not possible to increase spending much by

213

giving grants to a higher percentage of applicants since most reasons given for refusal (more than 70 per cent) were based on social fund directions and not on discretion. As applications for community care grants have increased and it has become necessary to contain spending, the options open to local offices are also limited. One possibility is for social fund officers to offer more applicants loans instead of grants. In such cases applications are only occasionally recorded as grant refusals, so published figures probably underestimate the proportion of grant applications refused. By directing pressures towards the loans budget, local offices increase the available routes through which they can regulate expenditure.

Social fund loans

Local office loans cover two kinds of payments, crisis loans and budgeting loans. Crisis loans are intended to avert risk to health or safety in circumstances where no alternative help is available. Refusal rates for these awards are low; in crisis situations help is rarely refused, and less urgent cases can be filtered out of the system before a formal application is recorded. Expenditure however has shown less fluctuation than might be expected were applications related solely to unpredictable crises. In fact a high proportion of crisis loans are made to cover the living expenses of new claimants during the period in which they are waiting for income support to be paid in arrears. This also helps to explain the very low rates of refusal. It would be inappropriate to refuse more payments where the 'crises' leading to applications are precipitated by the structure of the benefits system itself. There is little flexibility therefore in expenditure associated with crisis loans.

The mechanisms through which expenditure can be regulated over periods of fluctuating demand are more varied for budgeting loans than for grants or crisis loans. Budgeting loans were envisaged largely as a means to assist people such as the unemployed and lone parents with 'the uneven expenditure associated with the purchase of major items or services' (DSS, 1989c; 1990). It may be that it is less difficult to refuse awards to these groups than to the elderly, sick and disabled people for whom community care grants were intended. The fact that some people do not apply for, or refuse loans either because they do not feel able to take on additional debt repayments or for some other reason, also means that the level of loans spending partly depends on the behaviour of claimants themselves.

For all these reasons it is easier to constrain expenditure by offering fewer awards to applicants than it is in the case of community care grants or crisis loans. Spending can also be reduced relatively easily by offering lower amounts of money. So, for example, loans might be set at a level sufficient to meet the cost of second hand rather than new items. Alternatively, social fund officers might take a strict interpretation of the guidelines relating to

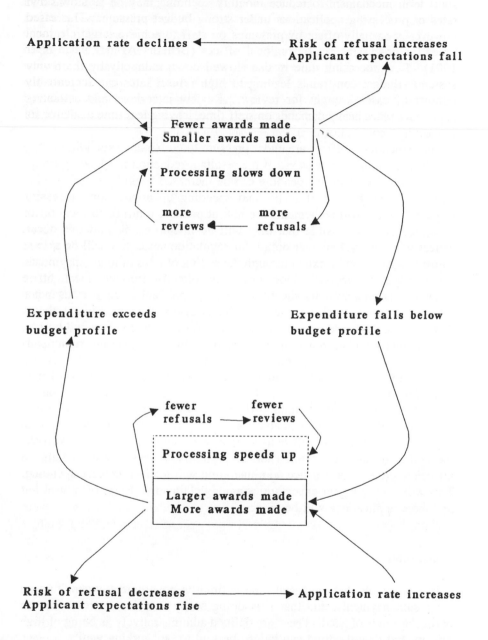

Figure 15.1: Regulating social fund expenditure

applicants' ability to repay loans within a given time or at a given rate. A short term mechanism to reduce monthly spending may be to slow down rates of processing applications under strong budget pressure. This effect however is partially offset by pressures on staff to achieve target clearance times for processing set by regional offices (Benefits Agency since April 1991). But processing time is also slowed down indirectly by the review system. Budget constraints leading to high refusal rates can increase the number of cases brought for review. Review interviews and associated paperwork place heavy demands on staff time, leaving less time available for processing new applications.

Thus, when local offices are under pressure to curb loans expenditure, they can do so in a number of ways. If the resultant reduction in spending brings the budget below profile, spending can be increased again by offering more loans, increasing sizes of loans, and speeding up application processing (Figure 15.1). Loan repayments are not, at present, returned to local office budgets, but it is possible that they will be in future. Should this occur, offices will have yet another option for regulation since they will be able to adjust budgets to some extent through the setting of rates of loan repayments.

The negative feedback loop operating directly through local office behaviour is enhanced by the behaviour of applicants. In periods when offices are cutting back on budgeting loans in the ways mentioned above, there is anecdotal evidence to suggest that expectations are lowered both in the claimant population and among social services and welfare rights staff who act as advocates for claimants applying to the social fund. If there is a high risk of refusal, applicants are less likely to apply to the fund. They may make this decision themselves or be advised to delay their applications by social workers or welfare rights officers, or DSS counter staff may inform them that little money is available for loans. The result will be a drop in application rates which will help to reduce expenditure, together with the local office behaviour described above. Similarly, when expenditure falls too far below profile, local office administration will tend to increase spending. This will lead to higher expectations among claimants. Risks of refusal fall and more applications will be made.

Conclusion

It is indisputable that the social fund is limiting government expenditure on lump sum payments, and that it is doing so by focusing its resources on particular kinds of need. These are defined administratively as being of high priority and thus the fund can indeed be said to be 'working well'.

The social fund remained within budget during the first two years of operation because it was possible to regulate expenditure by means of a wide range of mechanisms. However, on 21 February 1990 the High Court delivered judgement on applications for judicial reviews in three cases concerning the social fund. In the light of this judgement, social fund officers were advised 'that the local office budget and the level of priority that might usually be met were factors to be taken into account in reaching a decision but they were not the overriding factors' (Ministerial statement to Parliament, 26 March 1990). It then became possible for an officer to make an award if he or she considered that the need of the applicant was a more important factor than the budget. This reduced the necessity to compare one application with another and the social fund guidance was amended to reflect this change.

However, the new Social Security Act passed by parliament in July 1990 allowed the introduction of Directions 40, 41 and 42 prohibiting local offices from exceeding their annual budget allocations (Social Fund Manual).

The processes through which the fund's limited resources are targeted will continue to raise a number of complex issues. 'Targeting help on areas of greatest need' is not synonymous with simply focusing resources in particular areas. Tensions still exist between needs as defined by administrators and needs as perceived by social fund applicants. Even if these could be resolved and a socially acceptable set of 'basic needs' derived, there would remain the problem of how to choose which of these needs to meet when resources are insufficient to cover them all. The conceptual and ideological complexities in defining and ranking need make it improbable that any perfect solution to the problem can be found. However, the scheme constitutes the final safety net provided by the welfare benefits system and as such must be evaluated in a broader context. The social fund is still undergoing change and it remains essential to monitor not only the outcomes of the system but also the processes through which these outcomes are achieved.

Note

The empirical component of this research was funded by the Department of Social Security but the opinions expressed in this chapter are those of the author alone and do not necessarily reflect those of the Department.

References

Benefits Research Unit (1989), *The Bulletin of the Social Fund Project*, Issue Four, University of Nottingham, November.

217

Bradshaw, J.R. (1987), 'The social fund', in Brenton, M. and Ungerson, C. (eds), *The Year Book of Social Policy 1986/7*, Longman, London.

DHSS (1985a), *Reform of Social Security – Programme for Change*, Cm. 9518, HMSO, London.

DHSS (1985b), *The Reform of Social Security – Programme for Action*, Cm. 9691, HMSO, London.

DSS (1989a), Under Secretary, Department of Social Security, speaking at a conference 'Monitoring the Social Fund', Community Care; Social Security Research Consortium; in association with AMA, ACC and CoSLA. 13 January, Sheffield.

DSS (1989b), *Basis of Social Fund Allocation 1989/90*, Department of Social Security, London.

DSS (1989c), *Annual Report by the Secretary of State for Social Security on the Social Fund 1988/89*, Cm. 748, HMSO, London.

DSS (1990), *Annual Report by the Secretary of State for Social Security on the Social Fund 1989/90*, Cm. 1157, HMSO, London.

Hansard, (1989), 19 December, col. 174.

Huby, M. and Walker, R. (1991), 'Adapting to the Social Fund', *Social Policy and Administration*, vol. 25, no. 4, pp. 329–349.

NACAB (1990), *Hard Times for Social Fund Applicants*, National Association of Citizens Advice Bureaux, London.

Stewart, G., Stewart, J. and Walker, C. (1989), *The Social Fund: A Critical Analysis of its Introduction and First Year in Operation*, Association of County Councils Publications, London.

Walker, R. and Lawton, D. (1988), 'Social assistance and territorial justice: the example of single payments', *Journal of Social Policy*, vol. 17, no. 4, pp. 437–476.

Walker, R. and Lawton, D. (1989), 'The social fund as an exercise in resource allocation', *Public Administration*, vol. 67, no. 3, pp. 295–317.

Author index

Subject index

elderly people: and home ownership 86, 91; and need for community alarms 144–5

elliptical needs 16, 17, 18, 25

Employment and Training Act, 1973 98

ends: and efficiency 38; means to 34–5; needs and 58

equity withdrawal 85–7; uses of 87 8

ethics, and new medical technologies 125, 126

Ethiopia 50

evaluation: of means 38–9; of medical technology 126–7, 132–3

expenditure: of local government 184, 187, 192, 193; by social fund 213, 214, 216

expressed need 61

family life, changing patterns of 94 6, 102–3

Family Planning Services Act, 1967 95

felt need 61

financial services, liberalisation of 83–5

fulfilment of need 16–17, 18, 19, 23, 24, 25

fundamental needs 20–1, 22–3; see also categorical needs

funding, of communication aids 173, 176

Ghana 50, 52, 54

goals 14, 16, 17–18, 19, 26, 29

government, and access to telephones for the deaf 161

grant related expenditure assessment (GREA) 183–4, 187, 188

grants,to local authorities 181,183, 190

greed 5–6, 31, 36–7; politics and 43; in the Third World 49–54

Gross Domestic Product (GDP), and military spending 71, 72

growth rates 46, 47, 50, 52; effect of military spending on 68, 71, 72

health benefits, valuation of 126–7

health care, in the Third World 46, 197

health care costs, and medical technology 128–9

health care expenditure 8, 123–4, 125; and MTA 133–5

health care needs 59, 61–2

health promotion 134

hierarchies of wants see priorities

higher education 97–8

home equity schemes 91–2

home ownership 83, 100; growth in 80, 81, 89–90; as source of wealth 7, 85, 86–7, 88–9, 91, 92

homelessness 101, 103

Hong Kong 46

hospital specialties 10, 197–8, 200; and clinical need 198, 205–6; links between 200–4, 206; quality of 199

hospitals 196, 197

house prices, rise in 81, 83

housing: as an investment 81–91; for young people 100–1

Housing Act, 1988 101

housing authorities, provision of community alarms by 144–5

Housing (Homeless Persons) Act, 1977 101

housing tenure, change in 80, 89–90, 100–1

human nature 13; and categorical

needs 20–4, 26, 27, 28
human needs 22, 23–4, 43; in the Third World 45, 46
hypothetical needs 20–1, 24–5, 26

income, role of in alcohol consumption 108–10, 114
income elasticity 108–9
income support 101
India 45, 46; inability of state to meet needs in 47, 54
individualism 51
inequalities 44; in the Third World 47
inheritance, from housing 86–8
innovations 130–2, 133–4
instrumental needs 5, 6, 15, 16–17, 19, 24, 26; and mind dependence 27, 28
interests, and needs 13–14
interspeciality links 202–7
intervention, and community alarms 147–9
investment, effect of military spending on 72–3, 76, 78
Italy, telephones for the deaf in 161
IVF techniques 125

Jamaica 46, 52
judgements 35–6, 59, 61, 62

Latin America 46, 50
legislation, relating to the family 95
link–up service 153–4, 155–7
local government 185
local government finance 9, 181–2, 190–4; needs assessment procedures 187–90; 1990 reforms to 183–5
local taxation, changes in 185–7, 192

London, increase in local taxation in 186–7, 193

Manpower Services Commission 98
market economy, and needs–based resource allocation 4
marriage 95–6, 102, 103
Matrimonial and Family Proceedings Act, 1984 95
maximising behaviour 37
means: evaluation of 38–9; justification of 34, 36, 37
medical supply industry 123, 129, 130, 134
medical technologies 8, 125; ethical aspects of 125, 126; evaluation of see medical technology assessment; and health care costs 128–9; and innovation 130–2, 133–4
medical technology assessment (MTA) 124–5, 132–5; and economic evaluation 126–7; and incentives to innovate 130–2; and technological research and development 128–9
Mexico 46, 52
military expenditure 7; beneficial effects of 68; at cost of welfare 67, 69, 78; effect of on investment 70, 72, 73, 78
military research and development 74–7
mind dependence 27–8
monitoring, of community alarms 142
moral philosophy 39–41
morbidity 200, 201
mortgage industry 83, 84–5
motor neurone disease 164, 170

National Health Service 3, 10,

196-7, 207; effect on investment 72, 78

National Health Service and Community Care Act, 1990 196

nationalization, in the Third World 46, 51

need, and health care 197

need claims 26-7

needs 12, 33-6; assessment of 59, 61; and desires 13, 28, 57-8, 59, 61; to be efficiently met 38-9; fulfilment of 16, 17, 18, 19, 23, 24, 25; and greed 31, 42-3; and interests 13-14; language of 6; for particular ends 34-5, 58; recognition of 57-8; relativity of 28-9; in the Third World 44-54; *see* also categorical needs; instrumental needs; human needs; hypothetical need

needs assessments procedures 194; reforms to 187-90

needs equalization 183, 184

normative need 61

North Korea 53

northern England, disadvantaged by community charge 186, 188, 193

objectives *see* ends

objectivity 27

Parkinson's Disease 164

patients 197, 206

Paying for Local Government 182

peace dividend 7, 67

personal care schemes 138

personal enrichment 49-51

Philippines 52

policy values 35-6

political instability, in the Third World 47

politics, and need vs greed 43-54

poll tax *see* community charge

priorities 62, 63; for the social fund 210, 211-12

private welfare 91, 92

provider units 196, 198, 200, 207

purchasing authorities 196, 198, 207

quality of health care 196-7, 207

Quality Adjusted Life Year (QALY) 63, 126-7

rationality, and desire 13

reassurance, as aim of community alarms 139, 140

reforms: social costs of 52, 54; in the Third World 50-1

relativity of needs 28-9

relay service 153-4, 155-7

rented accommodation 89, 90, 100, 101, 103

rents 101; rebates of 100

repossession 90

resources: allocation of 4, 34; equalization of 183, 184; prioritising demand for 125; use of 38

retirement homes 91

rights, need and 43

Royal National Institute for the Deaf (RNID) 153-4, 155-7, 160

school leavers 97, 98

self-determination 147

self-interest *see* greed

sheltered housing 91, 140, 143

Sierra Leone 52-3

sign language 158-9

Singapore 46

single payments 209, 210

social acceptability, of new technologies 130, 131

social fund: demand for 212-13,